America Personified: Portraits from History
VOLUME 2

ROBERT D. MARCUS
DAVID BURNER, editors

America Personified

Portraits from History

VOLUME 2

St. Martin's Press   New York

ACKNOWLEDGMENTS

ANDREW JOHNSON AND IMPEACHMENT: "Why They Impeached Andrew Johnson," by David Donald, from *American Heritage,* December 1956. Copyright © 1956 by American Heritage Publishing Company, Inc. Reprinted by permission.

SITTING BULL AND THE INDIANS' LAST STAND: "The Indians' Story of the Custer Fight," ed. Joseph K. Dixon, from *The Vanishing Race: Little Big Horn.* First published 1913; reprinted 1973 by Rio Grande Press, Inc., Glorieta, N.M. Used by permission. "The Vision of Victory," by Stanley Vestal, from *Sitting Bull: Champion of the Sioux.* New edition copyright 1957 by the University of Oklahoma Press. Reprinted by permission. "Sitting Bull: War Chief or Swindler?" by Albert Britt, from *Great Indian Chiefs.* Copyright 1938 by McGraw-Hill, Inc. Reprinted by permission of McGraw-Hill Book Company.

JOHN D. ROCKEFELLER AND AMERICAN BUSINESS: "The Robber Barons," by Matthew Josephson, extracted from *The Robber Barons.* Copyright 1934, 1962 by Matthew Josephson. Reprinted by permission of Harcourt Brace Jovanovich, Inc. "John D. Rockefeller," by Allan Nevins, from *John D. Rockefeller,* Vol. II. Used with the permission of Charles Scribner's Sons. Copyright 1940 by Charles Scribner's Sons.

EUGENE V. DEBS AND THE LABOR MOVEMENT: "Debs and World War I," by Ray Ginger, from *The Bending Cross: A Biography of Eugene V. Debs.* Copyright 1949 by the Trustees of Rutgers College, New Jersey. Reprinted by permission.

THEODORE ROOSEVELT AND THE "BIG STICK": "Theodore Roosevelt and the Panama Canal," by Henry F. Pringle, from *Theodore Roosevelt: A Biography.* Copyright 1931, © 1956 by Henry F. Pringle. Reprinted by permission of Harcourt Brace Jovanovich, Inc.

CHARLES LINDBERGH AND THE SPIRIT OF THE 1920's: "WE," by Charles Lindbergh, from *"WE."* Copyright 1927 by Charles A. Lindbergh; renewal © 1955 by Charles A. Lindbergh. Reprinted by permission of G. P. Putnam's Sons. "New York Stages Big Celebration," from *The New York Times,* May 22, 1927, © 1927 by The New York Times Company. Reprinted by permission. "The Meaning of Lindbergh's Flight," by John William Ward, from *American Quarterly,* Vol. X, No. 1 (Spring 1958), published at the University of Pennsylvania. Copyright, 1958, Trustees of the University of Pennsylvania. Reprinted by permission of the author and the publisher.

ELEANOR ROOSEVELT AND THE CHANGING ROLE OF WOMEN: "This Is My Story," by Eleanor Roosevelt, from *This Is My Story.* Copyright 1937 by Anna Eleanor Roosevelt. Reprinted by permission of Harper & Row, Publishers, Inc. "Equal Pay for Equal Work," by Eleanor Roosevelt, from *It's Up to the Women* by Mrs. Franklin D. Roosevelt. Copyright 1933 by Anna Eleanor Roosevelt. Copyright © renewed 1961 by Mrs. Franklin D. Roosevelt. Reprinted by permission of J. B. Lippincott Company. "Eleanor's Press Conferences" and "Political Sisterhood," by Joseph P. Lash, reprinted from *Eleanor and Franklin.* Copyright © 1971 by Joseph P. Lash. Used by permission of W. W. Norton & Company, Inc. "Women During the Depression," by Tamara Hareven, from *Eleanor Roosevelt: An American Conscience,* pp. 63–68. Copyright © 1968 by Tamara K. Hareven. Reprinted by permission of Quadrangle/The New York Times Book Company.

JOSEPH R. MC CARTHY AND THE COLD WAR: "In the Witness Chair," by James A. Wechsler, from *The Age of Suspicion.* Copyright 1953 by James A. Wechsler. Reprinted by permission of Random House, Inc. Footnotes omitted. "Views of McCarthyism," by Michael Paul Rogin, from *McCarthy and the Intellectuals.* Reprinted by permission of The M.I.T. Press, Cambridge, Mass. Copyright © 1967 by The Massachusetts Institute of Technology.

MARTIN LUTHER KING, JR., AND THE CIVIL RIGHTS MOVEMENT: "The Montgomery Bus Boycott," by Martin Luther King, Jr., from "The Decisive Arrest," in *Stride*

To Charla Bolton Rutherford
and Marveen Gale Olsen

Preface

"Biography," said Thomas Carlyle, "is the only true history." Every competent biography, whether its subject be a poet or a politician, is the study not only of a life but of the politics and personalities, the manners and mores, the style and flavor of a period. As historians who have long enjoyed and valued biography, we thought that a selection of biographical readings like the one offered here would be a useful supplement to courses in American history.

Traditionally America has been rich in biographical and autobiographical material. In the colonial period the Puritans went religiously to their diaries each evening to set down their doings as visible proof of their community's progress toward the godly life. During the years of revolution and the birth of the constitutional republic, such men as John Adams observed and recorded events that were momentous both in their own lives and in the life of the nation. They were convinced that what they had to say was for the ages. In the nineteenth century the "heroic" biography was frequently used by celebrants, such as Parson Weems, of America's great personalities, and in our own age many well-known Americans seem to feel compelled to set their lives before the public.

With such a wealth of material available, our greatest difficulty has been in deciding what and whom to *ex*clude from this volume. The figures we have chosen are not included simply because they are famous; each, we thought, ought to be linked to an important theme or event in American history. Each is presented, moreover, from various points of view: after the introductory essay summarizing the person's life and significance, there are selections from his or her own works, from comments by contemporaries, and from recent evaluations by historians. In a few cases we depart from this format, but the intention in each chapter is to provide a fully rounded portrait. In many cases the selections are controversial: those on Theodore Roosevelt, for example, put the reader in the midst of the lively argument about Roosevelt's behavior in the Panama Canal affair. This kind of debate, we believe, is the best way to involve a student in the complexity and vitality of American history.

We would like to thank the many people who have helped us with this book, especially Ms. Jorj Tilson and Ms. Sandra Burner, who assisted in preparing the manuscript.

Robert D. Marcus
David Burner

Contents

America Personified: Portraits from History
VOLUME 2

ANDREW JOHNSON

&

Impeachment

In 1868 the House of Representatives voted articles of impeachment against Andrew Johnson, and the Senate came within a single vote of removing the president from office. Johnson was not charged with the least corruption, and the "high crimes and misdemeanors" with which he was charged were all technical and flimsy. His near removal from office came not from specific misdeeds but from fury built up against his Reconstruction policies.

Johnson, born in North Carolina on December 22, 1808, grew up in the direst poverty. He became a tailor and moved to Greenville, Tennessee, where he married Eliza McCardle, who taught the barely literate tailor how to read and write properly. He soon developed into a powerful if crude speaker and began a career in local politics which carried him from town government to the state legislature to the House of Representatives and, in 1857, to the United States Senate. Johnson was a peculiar sort of Jacksonian Democrat: a rhetorical champion of the working class, intensely hostile to anyone rich or well-born, advocate of a homestead law, and fiercely devoted to the sanctity of the Union.

In 1860, when the South seceded, Johnson supported the Union and condemned secession. As the only Southern senator who remained with the Union, he was an invaluable man, and he served on the Joint Committee on the Conduct of the War, the major committee overseeing the war effort. In 1862 Lincoln appointed him military governor of Tennessee, and Johnson handled the extremely difficult problems of that battlefield state with a toughness and efficiency that increased his national prominence. In 1864, looking to attract Democratic support, the

administration took him as vice-presidential candidate. Only a few
weeks after Johnson was inaugurated into that office, John Wilkes Booth's
bullet made him president.

In the White House, Johnson was the wrong man at the wrong time.
The problems of reestablishing the Union on a basis that would do
justice to all were enormous. Whatever delicate possibilities existed for a
settlement that would protect the fruits of the war for the North and
for Southern blacks and yet not be sabotaged by Southern whites
vanished under Johnson's hasty and inept policies. Johnson substantially
followed Lincoln's policy of using presidential authority to return
states to the Union as rapidly as possible. But he lacked Lincoln's careful
political touch and failed to maintain the liaison with Congress that
might have gained its acquiescence to a Reconstruction carried out from
the White House. He also lacked stability and was too easily influenced.
Radical Republicans concerned with safeguarding the rights of Southern
blacks would leave his office thinking that he was on their side. Then
he would capriciously capitulate to flattery from Southern gentlemen
and ladies: feeling inferior because of his own humble background,
he seems to have secretly admired the very group of slaveholders
whom he had denounced during the war. Northern Republicans
increasingly feared that Johnson was surrendering to the South.

The elections of 1866 in the North were a massive vote against
Johnson's Reconstruction policies. Congress took matters into its own
hands, guiding a cumbersome military Reconstruction that aimed to
secure the South for Union ideals and for the Republican party and that
gave genuine—if inadequate—benefits to black Southerners. Johnson
continued his ineffectual opposition to Congress and increasingly lost
control of his temper in public. The malady seemed to be catching since
more and more people about him lost their tempers as well. Congress
passed the Tenure of Office Act to take away the presidential prerogative
to fire Cabinet members. The legislation was simply a dare to Johnson,
and he finally took it, firing his secretary of war, Edwin M. Stanton,
who had been in the enemy camp for at least two years. Congress
responded with an impeachment trial, and when that failed it returned
to its own largely bungled effort at reconstruction.

The failure of Johnson's presidency created unendurable divisions and
precipitated congressional failure in turn. By the early 1870's
Reconstruction had collapsed; and by 1877, with the last federal troops
withdrawn from the South, a long, long night descended for black
Americans. Johnson himself suffered little. He nearly returned to the
Senate immediately after he left the White House, and six years later,
in 1875, he did reenter the body which had come within one vote of his
removal. He died a few months later on July 31, 1875.

Because Congress was unable to remove Johnson from office,
impeachment seemed doomed as a method for controlling a president

who defied the wishes of Congress and the public. For a century thereafter, impeachment was rarely mentioned as a practical suggestion in dealing with a president. Johnson's trial had not even settled the question of whether impeachment was a judicial or a political process, whether "high crimes and misdemeanors" meant offenses actionable in a court of law or whether they needed only to constitute serious damage to the body politic. Long disuse seemed to suggest that impeachment was wholly invalid as a political tool; but circumstances could alter cases. A century later, Congress again gave serious thought to the possibility of removing a president by impeachment.

"I Am Opposed to Secession" (1860)
ANDREW JOHNSON

*Johnson's rough-hewn speeches defending the Union thrilled Northerners
during the secession winter. Johnson condemned the Confederacy and
continually insisted that the slaveholders should pay for their misdeeds.
When he became president, the Northern public therefore had rather
firm expectations about what he would do. These assumptions, so
quickly proven false, added to the disappointment and anger felt by
the opponents of his Reconstruction policies.*

The following speech was delivered in the Senate on December 18, 1860.

I AM OPPOSED to secession. I believe it is no remedy for the evils complained of. Instead of acting with that division of my Southern friends
who take ground for secession, I shall take other grounds, while I try to
accomplish the same end. I think that this battle ought to be fought not
outside, but inside of the Union, and upon the battlements of the Constitution itself. I am unwilling voluntarily to walk out of the Union which
has been the result of a Constitution made by the patriots of the Revolution. They formed the Constitution; and this Union that is so much spoken
of, and which all of us are so desirous to preserve, grows out of the Constitution; and I repeat, I am not willing to walk out of a Union growing
out of the Constitution that was formed by the patriots and the soldiers
of the Revolution. So far as I am concerned, and I believe I may speak
with some degree of confidence for the people of my State, we intend to
fight that battle inside and not outside of the Union; and if anybody must
go out of the Union, it must be those who violate it. We do not intend to
go out. It is our Constitution; it is our Union, growing out of the Constitution; and we do not intend to be driven from it or out of the Union.
Those who have violated the Constitution either in the passage of what are
denominated personal-liberty bills, or by their refusal to execute the fugitive-slave law,—they having violated the instrument that binds us together,
—must go out, and not we. If we violate the Constitution by going out
ourselves, I do not think we can go before the country with the same force
of position that we shall if we stand inside of the Constitution, demanding
a compliance with its provisions and its guarantees; or if need be, as I
think it is, demanding additional securities. We should make that demand
inside of the Constitution, and in the manner and mode pointed out by

the instrument itself. Then we keep ourselves in the right; we put our adversary in the wrong; and though it may take a little longer, we take the right means to accomplish an end that is right in itself.

I know that sometimes we talk about compromises. I am not a compromiser, nor a conservative, in the usual acceptation of those terms. I have been generally considered radical, and I do not come forward to-day in any thing that I shall say or propose, asking for anything to be done upon the principle of compromise. If we ask for anything, it should be for that which is right and reasonable in itself. If it be right, those of whom we ask it, upon the great principle of right, are bound to grant it. Compromise! I know in the common acceptation of the term it is to agree upon certain propositions in which some things are conceded on one side and others conceded on the other. I shall go for enactments by Congress or for amendments to the Constitution, upon the principle that they are right, and upon no other ground. I am not for compromising right with wrong. If we have no right, we ought not to demand it. If we are in the wrong, they should not grant us what we ask. I approach this momentous subject on the great principles of right, asking for nothing and demanding nothing but what is right in itself, and what every right-minded man and a right-minded community and a right-minded people, who wish for the preservation of this Government, will be disposed to grant.

In fighting this battle, I shall do it upon the basis laid down by a portion of the people of my own State, in a large and very intelligent meeting. A committee of the most intelligent men in the country reported this resolution:—

Resolved, That we deeply sympathize with our sister Southern States, and freely admit that there is good cause of dissatisfaction and complaint on their part, on account of the recent election of sectional candidates to the Presidency and Vice-Presidency of the United States; yet we, as a portion of the people of a slaveholding community, are not for seceding or breaking up the Union of these States until every fair and honorable means has been exhausted in trying to obtain, on the part of the non-slaveholding States, a compliance with the spirit and letter of the Constitution and all its guarantees; and when this shall have been done, and the States now in open rebellion against the laws of the United States, in refusing to execute the fugitive-slave law, shall persist in their present unconstitutional course, and the Federal Government shall fail or refuse to execute the laws in good faith, it (the Government) will not have accomplished the great design of its creation, and will therefore, in fact, be a practical dissolution, and all the States, as parties, be released from the compact which formed the Union.

The people of Tennessee, irrespective of party, go on and declare further:—

That in the opinion of this meeting no State has the constitutional right to secede from the Union without the consent of the other States which ratified the compact. The compact, when ratified, formed the Union without making any provision whatever for its dissolution. It (the compact) was adopted by the States *in toto and forever, 'without reservation or condition;'* hence a secession of one or more States from the Union, without the consent of the others ratifying the compact, would be revolution, leading in the end to civil, and perhaps servile war. While we deny the right of a State, constitutionally, to secede from the Union, we admit the great and inherent right of revolution, abiding and remaining with every people, but a right which should not be exercised, except in extreme cases, and in the last resort, when grievances are without redress, and oppression has become intolerable.

They declare further:—

That in our opinion, we can more successfully resist the aggression of Black Republicanism by remaining within the Union, than we can by going out of it; and more especially so, while there is a majority of both branches in the National Legislature opposed to it, and the Supreme Court of the United States is on the side of law and the Constitution.

They go on, and declare further:—

That we are not willing to abandon our Northern friends who have stood by the Constitution of the United States, and in standing by it have vindicated our rights, and in their vindication have been struck down; and now, in their extremity, we cannot and will not desert them by seceding, or otherwise breaking up the Union.

This is the basis upon which a portion of the people of Tennessee, irrespective of party, propose to fight this battle. We believe that our true position is inside of the Union. We deny the doctrine of secession; we deny that a State has the power, of its own volition, to withdraw from the Confederacy. We are not willing to do an unconstitutional act, to induce or to coerce others to comply with the Constitution of the United States. We prefer complying with the Constitution, and fighting our battle, and making our demand inside of the Union.

Vice-Presidential Inaugural Address (1865)
ANDREW JOHNSON

This pathetic address, delivered in the United States Senate on March 4, 1865, gave Johnson the reputation of being a drunkard. He was obviously inebriated at the time, but his real problem was not heavy drinking; rather, he was unaccustomed to any large amount of alcohol. In preparation for his big day, he had taken a drink to steady his nerves and pep himself up from an illness. Nonetheless, his enemies —and he made them in profusion—never ceased making the most of this incident. Laced with uneasy references to his "plebeian origins," his inaugural speech reveals the insecurities that would make Johnson so unable to cooperate with leaders in Congress. For an ex-senator, he seemed to feel remarkably out of place in the Senate.

SENATORS: I am here to-day as the chosen Vice-President of the United States; and as such, by constitutional provision, I am made the presiding officer of this body. I therefore present myself here in obedience to the high behests of the American people, to discharge a constitutional duty, and not presumptuously to thrust myself in a position so exalted. May I at this moment—it may not be irrelevant to the occasion—advert to the workings of our institutions under the Constitution which our fathers framed and Washington approved, as exhibited by the position in which I stand before the American Senate, in the sight of the American people? Deem me not vain or arrogant; yet I should be less than man if under such circumstances I were not proud of being an American citizen, for to-day one who claims no high descent, one who comes from the ranks of the people, stands, by the choice of a free constituency, in the second place of this Government. There may be those to whom such things are not pleasing; but those who have labored for the consummation of a free Government will appreciate and cherish institutions which exclude none, however obscure his origin, from places of trust and distinction. The people, in short, are the source of all power. You, Senators, you who constitute the bench of the Supreme Court of the United States, are but the creatures of the American people; your exaltation is from them; the power of this Government consists in its nearness and approximation to the great mass of the people. You, Mr. Secretary Seward, Mr. Secretary Stanton, the Secretary of the Navy, and the others who are your associates,—you know that you have my respect and my confidence,—derive not your greatness and your power alone from President Lincoln. Humble as I am, plebeian as I may be deemed, permit me in the presence of this brilliant assemblage to enunciate the truth that courts and cabinets, the President and his advisers, derive their power and their greatness from the people. A President could not exist here forty-eight hours if he were as far removed from the people as the autocrat of Russia is separated from his subjects. Here the popular heart sustains President and cabinet officers; the popular will gives them all their strength. Such an assertion of the great principles of this Government may be considered out of place, and I will not consume the time of these intelligent and enlightened people much longer; but I could not be insensible to these great truths when I, a plebeian, elected by the people the Vice-President of the United States, am here to enter upon the discharge of my duties. For those duties I claim not the aptitude of my respected predecessor. Although I have occupied a seat in both the House of Representatives and the Senate, I am not learned in parliamentary law, and I shall be dependent on the courtesy of those Senators who have become familiar with the rules which are requisite for the good order of the body and the dispatch of its business. I have only studied how I may best advance the interests of my State and of my country, and not the technical rules of order; and if I err I shall appeal to this dignified body of representatives of States for kindness and indulgence.

Before I conclude this brief inaugural address in the presence of this audience,—and I, though a plebeian boy, am authorized by the principles of the Government under which I live to feel proudly conscious that I am a man, and grave dignitaries are but men,—before the Supreme Court, the representatives of foreign governments, Senators, and the people, I desire to proclaim that Tennessee, whose representative I have been, is free. She has bent the tyrant's rod, she has broken the yoke of slavery, and to-day she stands redeemed. She waited not for the exercise of power by Congress; it was her own act, and she is now as loyal, Mr. Attorney-General, as is the State from which you came. It is the doctrine of the Federal Constitution that no State can go out of this Union; and moreover Congress cannot reject a State from this Union. Thank God, Tennessee has never been out of the Union! It is true the operations of her government were for a time interrupted; there was an interregnum; but she is still in the Union, and I am her representative. This day she elects her Governor and her Legislature, which will be convened on the first Monday of April, and again her Senators and Representatives will soon mingle with those of her sister States; and who shall gainsay it? for the Constitution requires that to every State shall be guaranteed a republican form of government.

I now am prepared to take the oath of office, and renew my allegiance to the Constitution of the United States.

The Argument for Impeachment (1868)
CHARLES SUMNER

*Under the Constitution, the House of Representatives can vote to impeach
the president or any other officer of the United States (such as a judge);
the impeachment is tried by the Senate which acts as a court, a two-thirds
vote being necessary for removal from office.*

*The impeachment trial of Andrew Johnson was one of the great
dramas of American history, but the articles of impeachment themselves
appear about as exciting as a laundry list. Most of the articles refer to
Johnson's dismissal of Stanton; some catchall articles complain
principally about his manners and his remarks about Congress. More
illuminating than the articles of impeachment is this statement by
Charles Sumner, senator from Massachusetts and a leading opponent of
the president, which he placed in the record to explain his vote in favor
of impeachment. Sumner's explanation makes clear that the main ,
impetus for impeachment had little to do with the specific points in
the articles but came instead from Johnson's Reconstruction policy
and his abrasive personality.*

THIS [TRIAL] is one of the last great battles with slavery. Driven from these
legislative chambers, driven from the field of war, this monstrous power
has found a refuge in the Executive Mansion, where, in utter disregard
of the Constitution and laws, it seeks to exercise its ancient far-reaching
sway. . . . Andrew Johnson is the impersonation of the tyrannical slave
power. In him it lives again. He is the lineal successor of John C. Calhoun
and Jefferson Davis; and he gathers about him the same supporters. Original partisans of slavery north and south; habitual compromisers of great
principles; maligners of the Declaration of Independence; politicians without heart; lawyers, for whom a technicality is everything, and a promiscu-
ous company who at every stage of the battle have set their faces against
equal rights; these are his allies. It is the old troop of slavery, with a few
recruits, ready as of old for violence—cunning in device, and heartless in
quibble. With the President at their head, they are now entrenched in the
Executive Mansion.

Not to dislodge them is to leave the country a prey to one of the most
hateful tyrannies of history. Especially is it to surrender the Unionists of
the rebel States to violence and bloodshed. Not a month, not a week, not

a day should be lost. The safety of the Republic requires action at once. The lives of innocent men must be rescued from sacrifice.

I would not in this judgment depart from that moderation which belongs to the occasion; but God forbid that, when called to deal with so great an offender, I should affect a coldness which I cannot feel. Slavery has been our worst enemy, assailing all, murdering our children, filling our homes with mourning, and darkening the land with tragedy; and now it rears its crest anew, with Andrew Johnson as its representative. Through him it assumes once more to rule the Republic and to impose its cruel law. The enormity of his conduct is aggravated by his barefaced treachery. He once declared himself the Moses of the colored race. Behold him now the Pharaoh. With such treachery in such a cause there can be no parley. Every sentiment, every conviction, every vow against slavery must now be directed against him. Pharaoh is at the bar of the Senate for judgment. . . .

There is nothing of usurpation which he has not attempted. Beginning with an assumption of all power in the rebel States, he has shrunk from nothing in the maintenance of this unparalleled assumption. . . . Timid at first, he grew bolder and bolder. He saw too well that his attempt to substitute himself for Congress in the work of reconstruction was sheer usurpation, and therefore, by his Secretary of State, did not hesitate to announce that "it must be distinctly understood that the restoration will be *subject to the decision of Congress."* On two separate occasions, in July and September, 1865, he confessed the power of Congress over the subject; but when Congress came together in December, this confessor of congressional power found that he alone had this great prerogative. According to his new-fangled theory, Congress had nothing to do but admit the States with the governments which had been instituted through his will alone. It is difficult to measure the vastness of this usurpation, involving as it did a general nullification. [The Earl of] Strafford was not bolder, when, speaking for Charles I., he boasted that "the little finger of prerogative was heavier than the loins of the law;" but these words helped the proud minister to the scaffold. No monarch, no despot, no Sultan, could claim more than an American President; for he claimed all. By his edict alone governments were organized, taxes were levied, and even the franchises of the citizens were determined.

Had this assumption of power been incidental, for the exigency of the moment, as under the pressure of war, and especially to serve the cause of human rights, to which before his elevation the President had professed such vociferous devotion, it might have been pardoned. It would have passed into the chapter of unauthorized acts which a patriot people had condoned. But it was the opposite in every particular. Beginning and continuing in usurpation, it was hateful beyond pardon, because it sacrificed the rights of Unionists, white and black, and was in the interest of the rebellion and of those very rebels who had been in arms against their country.

More than one person was appointed provisional governor who could not take the oath of office required by act of Congress. Other persons in the same predicament were appointed in the revenue service. The effect of these appointments was disastrous. They were in the nature of notice to rebels everywhere, that participation in the rebellion was no bar to office. If one of their number could be appointed governor, if another could be appointed to a confidential position in the Treasury Department, then there was nobody on the long list of blood who might not look for preferment. And thus all offices from governor to constable were handed over to a disloyal scramble. Rebels crawled forth from their retreats. Men who had hardly ventured to expect their lives were now candidates for office, and the rebellion became strong again. The change was felt in all the gradations of government, whether in States, counties, towns, or villages. Rebels found themselves in places of trust, while the true-hearted Unionists, who had watched for the coming of our flag and ought to have enjoyed its protecting power, were driven into hiding-places. All this was under the auspices of Andrew Johnson. It was he who animated the wicked crew. He was at the head of the work. Loyalty everywhere was persecuted. White and black, whose only offence was that they had been true to their country, were insulted, abused, murdered. There was no safety for the loyal man except within the flash of our bayonets. The story is as authentic as hideous. More than two thousand murders have been reported in Texas alone since the surrender of Kirby Smith [who was the last Confederate commander to surrender]. In other States there was a similar carnival. Property, person, life, were all in jeopardy. Acts were done "to make a holiday in hell." At New Orleans there was a fearful massacre, which, considering the age and the place, was worse than that of St. Bartholomew, which darkens a century of France, or that of Glencoe, which has printed an ineffaceable stain upon one of the greatest reigns of English history. All this is directly traced to Andrew Johnson. The words of bitterness uttered at another time are justified, while Fire, Famine, and Slaughter shriek forth—

> He let me loose, and cried Halloo!
> To him alone the praise is due.

. . . The Freedmen's Bureau, that sacred charity of the Republic, was despoiled of its possessions for the sake of rebels, to whom their forfeited estates were given back after they had been vested by law in the United States. The proceeds of captured and abandoned property, lodged under the law in the national treasury, were ravished from their place of deposit and sacrificed. Rebels were allowed to fill the ante-chambers of the Executive Mansion and to enter his counsels. The pardoning power was prostituted, and pardons were issued in lots to suit rebels, thus grossly abusing that trust whose discreet exercise is so essential to the administration of justice. The powers of the senate over appointments were trifled with and disregarded by reappointing persons who had been already rejected, and by refusing to communicate the names of others appointed by him during the recess. The veto power conferred by the Constitution as a remedy for ill-considered legislation, was turned by him into a weapon of offence against Congress and into an instrument to beat down the just opposition which his usurpation had aroused. The power of removal, which patriot Presidents had exercised so sparingly, was seized as an engine of tyranny and openly employed to maintain his wicked purposes by the sacrifice of good citizens who would not consent to be his tools. Incompetent and dishonest creatures, whose only recommendation was that they echoed his voice, were appointed to office, especially in the collection of the internal revenue, through whom a new organization, known as the "Whiskey Ring," has been able to prevail over the government and to rob the treasury of millions at the cost of tax-paying citizens, whose burdens are thus increased. Laws enacted by Congress for the benefit of the colored race, including that great statute for the establishment of the Freedmen's Bureau, and that other great statute for the establishment of Civil Rights were first attacked by his veto, and when finally passed by the requisite majority over his veto, were treated by him as little better than dead letters, while he boldly attempted to prevent the adoption of a constitutional amendment, by which the right of citizens and the national debt were placed under the guarantee of irrepealable law. During these successive assumptions, usurpations, and tyrannies, utterly without precedent in our history, this deeply guilty man ventured upon public speeches, each an offence to good morals, where, lost to all shame, he appealed in coarse words to the coarse passions of the coarsest people, scattering firebrands of sedition, inflaming anew the rebel spirit, insulting good citizens and with regard to office-holders, announcing in his own characteristic phrase that he would "kick them out"—the whole succession of speeches being from their brutalities and indecencies, in the nature of a "criminal exposure of his person," indictable at common law, for which no judgment can be too severe. But even this revolting transgression is aggravated, when it is considered that through these utterances the cause of justice was imperiled and the accursed demon of civil feud was lashed again into vengeful fury. All these things from beginning to end are plain facts, already recorded in history and known to all. And it is further recorded in history and known to all, that, through these enormities, any one of which is enough for condemnation, while all together present an aggregation of crime, untold calamities have been brought upon our country; disturbing business and finance; diminishing the national revenues; postponing specie payments; dishonoring the Declaration of Independence in its grandest truths; arresting the restoration of the rebel States; reviving the dying rebellion, and instead of that peace and reconciliation so much longed for, sowing strife and wrong, whose natural fruit is violence and blood.

Why They Impeached Andrew Johnson (1956)
DAVID DONALD

David Donald, a distinguished modern historian who has written a two-volume biography of Charles Sumner, offers the following explanation of why Andrew Johnson was impeached. Compare Donald's scholarly account of Johnson with Sumner's polemical one. Do you think that any of Sumner's view of Johnson has rubbed off on his biographer?

RECONSTRUCTION after the Civil War posed some of the most discouraging problems that have ever faced American statesmen. The South was prostrate. Its defeated soldiers straggled homeward through a countryside desolated by war. Southern soil was untilled and exhausted; southern factories and railroads were worn out. The four billion dollars of southern capital invested in Negro slaves was wiped out by advancing Union armies, "the most stupendous act of sequestration in the history of Anglo-American jurisprudence." The white inhabitants of eleven states had somehow to be reclaimed from rebellion and restored to a firm loyalty to the United States. Their four million former slaves had simultaneously to be guided into a proper use of their new-found freedom.

For the victorious Union government there was no time for reflection. Immediate decisions had to be made. Thousands of destitute whites and Negroes had to be fed before long-range plans of rebuilding the southern economy could be drafted. Some kind of government had to be established in these former Confederate states, to preserve order and to direct the work of restoration.

A score of intricate questions must be answered: Should the defeated southerners be punished or pardoned? How should genuinely loyal southern Unionists be rewarded? What was to be the social, economic, and political status of the now free Negroes? What civil rights did they have? Ought they to have the ballot? Should they be given a freehold of property? Was Reconstruction to be controlled by the national government, or should the southern states work out their own salvation? If the federal government supervised the process, should the President or the Congress be in control?

Intricate as were the problems, in early April, 1865, they did not seem insuperable. President Abraham Lincoln was winning the peace as he had already won the war. He was careful to keep every detail of Reconstruction in his own hands; unwilling to be committed to any "exclusive, and inflexible plan," he was working out a pragmatic program of restoration not, perhaps, entirely satisfactory to any group, but reasonably acceptable to all sections. With his enormous prestige as commander of the victorious North and as victor in the 1864 election, he was able to promise freedom to the Negro, charity to the southern white, security to the North.

The blighting of these auspicious beginnings is one of the saddest stories in American history. The reconciliation of the sections, which seemed so imminent in 1865, was delayed for more than ten years. Northern magnanimity toward a fallen foe curdled into bitter distrust. Southern whites rejected moderate leaders, and inveterate racists spoke for the new South. The Negro, after serving as a political pawn for a decade, was regulated to a second-class citizenship, from which he is yet struggling to emerge. Rarely has democratic government so completely failed as during the Reconstruction decade.

The responsibility for this collapse of American statesmanship is, of course, complex. History is not a tale of deep-dyed villains or pure-as-snow heroes. Part of the blame must fall upon ex-Confederates who refused to recognize that the war was over: part upon freedmen who confused liberty with license and the ballot box with the lunch pail; part upon northern antislavery extremists who identified patriotism with loyalty to the Republican party; part upon the land speculators, treasury grafters, and railroad promoters who were unwilling to have a genuine peace lest it end their looting of the public till.

Yet these divisive forces were not bound to triumph. Their success was due to the failure of constructive statesmanship that could channel the magnanimous feelings shared by most Americans into a positive program of reconstruction. President Andrew Johnson was called upon for positive leadership, and he did not meet the challenge.

Andrew Johnson's greatest weakness was his insensitivity to public opinion. In contrast to Lincoln, who said, "Public opinion in this country is everything," Johnson made a career of battling the popular will. A poor white, a runaway tailor's apprentice, a self-educated Tennessee politician, Johnson was a living defiance to the dominant southern belief that leadership belonged to the plantation aristocracy.

As senator from Tennessee, he defied the sentiment of his section in 1861 and refused to join the secessionist movement. When Lincoln later appointed him military governor of occupied Tennessee, Johnson found Nashville "a furnace of treason," but he braved social ostracism and threats of assassination and discharged his duties with boldness and efficiency.

Such a man was temperamentally unable to understand the northern mood in 1865, much less to yield to it. For four years the northern people had been whipped into wartime frenzy by propaganda tales of Confederate atrocities. The assassination of Lincoln by a southern sympathizer confirmed their belief in southern brutality and heartlessness. Few northerners felt vindictive toward the South, but most felt that the rebellion they had crushed must never rise again. Johnson ignored this postwar psychosis gripping the North and plunged ahead with his program of rapidly restoring the southern states to the Union. In May, 1865, without any previous preparation of public opinion, he issued a proclamation of amnesty, granting forgiveness to nearly all the millions of former rebels and welcoming them back into peaceful fraternity. Some few Confederate leaders were excluded from his general amnesty, but even they could secure pardon by special petition. For weeks the White House corridors thronged with ex-Confederate statesmen and former southern generals who daily received presidential forgiveness.

Ignoring public opinion by pardoning the former Confederates, Johnson actually entrusted the formation of new governments in the South to them. The provisional governments established by the President proceeded, with a good deal of reluctance, to rescind their secession ordinances, to abolish slavery, and to repudiate the Confederate debt. Then, with far more enthusiasm, they turned to electing governors, representatives, and senators. By December, 1865, the southern states had their delegations in Washington waiting for admission by Congress. Alexander H. Stephens, once vice president of the Confederacy, was chosen senator from Georgia; not one of the North Carolina delegation could take a loyalty oath; and all of South Carolina's congressmen had "either held office under the Confederate States, or been in the army, or countenanced in some way the Rebellion."

Johnson himself was appalled, "There seems in many of the elections something like defiance, which is all out of place at this time." Yet on December 5, he strongly urged the Congress to seat these southern representatives "and thereby complete the work of reconstruction." But the southern states were omitted from the roll call.

Such open defiance of northern opinion was dangerous under the best of circumstances, but in Johnson's case it was little more than suicidal. The President seemed not to realize the weakness of his position. He was the representative of no major interest and had no genuine political following. He had been considered for the vice presidency in 1864 because, as a southerner and a former slaveholder, he could lend plausibility to the Republican pretension that the old parties were dead and that Lincoln was the nominee of a new, nonsectional National Union party.

A political accident, the new Vice President did little to endear himself to his countrymen. At Lincoln's second inauguration Johnson appeared before the Senate in an obviously inebriated state and made a long, intemperate harangue about his plebeian origins and his hard-won success. President, Cabinet, and senators were humiliated by the shameful display, and Charles Summer felt that "the Senate should call upon him to resign." Historians now know that Andrew Johnson was not a heavy drinker. At the time of his inaugural display, he was just recovering from a severe attack of typhoid fever. Feeling ill just before he entered the Senate chamber, he asked for some liquor to steady his nerves, and either his weakened condition or abnormal sensitivity to alcohol betrayed him.

Lincoln reassured Republicans who were worried over the affair: "I have known Andy for many years; he made a bad slip the other day, but you need not be scared. Andy ain't a drunkard." Never again was Andrew Johnson seen under the influence of alcohol, but his reformation came too late. His performance on March 4, 1865, seriously undermined his political usefulness and permitted his opponents to discredit him as a pothouse politician. Johnson was catapulted into the presidency by John Wilkes Booth's bullet. From the outset his position was weak, but it was not necessarily untenable. The President's chronic lack of discretion made it so. Where common sense dictated that a chief executive in so disadvantageous a position should act with great caution, Johnson proceeded to imitate Old Hickory, Andrew Jackson, his political idol. If Congress crossed his will, he did not hesitate to defy it. Was he not "the Tribune of the People"?

Sure of his rectitude, Johnson was indifferent to prudence. He never learned that the president of the United States cannot afford to be a quarreler. Apprenticed in the rough-and-tumble politics of frontier Tennessee, where orators exchanged violent personalities, crude humor, and bitter denunciations, Johnson continued to make stump speeches from the White House. All too often he spoke extemporaneously, and he permitted hecklers in his audience to draw from him angry charges against his critics.

On Washington's birthday in 1866, against the advice of his more sober advisers, the President made an impromptu address to justify his Reconstruction policy. "I fought traitors and treason in the South," he told the crowd; "now when I turn around, and at the other end of the line find men —I care not by what name you call them—who will stand opposed to the restoration of the Union of these States, I am free to say to you that I am still in the field."

During the "great applause" which followed, a nameless voice shouted, "Give us the names at the other end. . . . Who are they?"

"You ask me who they are," Johnson retorted. "I say [Congressman] Thaddeus Stevens of Pennsylvania is one; I say Mr. Sumner is another; and Wendell Phillips [the erstwhile abolitionist] is another." Applause urged him to continue. "Are those who want to destroy our institutions . . . not satisfied with the blood that has been shed? . . . Does not the blood of Lincoln appease the vengeance and wrath of the opponents of this government?"

The President's remarks were as untrue as they were impolitic. Not only was it manifestly false to assert that the leading Republican in the House [Stevens] and the most conspicuous Republican in the Senate [Sumner] were opposed to "the fundamental principles of this government" or that they had been responsible for Lincoln's assassination; it was incredible political folly to impute such actions to men with whom the President had to work daily. But Andrew Johnson never learned that the President of the United States must function as a party leader.

There was a temperamental coldness about this plain-featured, grave man that kept him from easy, intimate relations with even his political supporters. His massive head, dark, luxuriant hair, deep-set and piercing eyes, and cleft square chin seemed to Charles Dickens to indicate "courage, watchfulness, and certainly strength of purpose," but his was a grim face, with "no genial sunlight in it." The coldness and reserve that marked Johnson's public associations doubtless stemmed from a deep-seated feeling of insecurity; this self-educated tailor whose wife had taught him how to write could never expose himself by letting down his guard and relaxing.

Johnson knew none of the arts of managing men, and he seemed unaware that face-saving is important for a politician. When he became President, Johnson was besieged by advisers of all political complexions. To each he listened gravely and non-committally, raising no questions and by his silence seeming to give consent. With Radical Senator Sumner, already intent upon giving the freedmen both homesteads and the ballot, he had repeated interviews during the first month of his presidency. "His manner has been excellent, & even sympathetic," Sumner reported triumphantly. With Chief Justice Salmon P. Chase, Sumner urged Johnson to support immediate Negro suffrage and found the President was "well-disposed, & sees the rights & necessities of the case." In the middle of May, 1865, Sumner reassured a Republican caucus that the President was a true Radical; he had listened repeatedly to the Senator and had told him "there is no difference between us." Before the end of the month the rug was pulled from under Sumner's feet. Johnson issued his proclamation for the reconstruction of North Carolina, making no provisions for Negro suffrage. Sumner first learned about it through the newspapers.

While he was making up his mind, Johnson appeared silently receptive to all ideas; when he had made a decision, his mind was immovably closed, and he defended his course with all the obstinacy of a weak man. In December, alarmed by Johnson's Reconstruction proclamations, Sumner again sought an interview with the President. "No longer sympathetic, or even kindly," Sumner found, "he was harsh, petulant, and unreasonable." The Senator was depressed by Johnson's "prejudice, ignorance, and perversity" on the Negro suffrage issue. Far from listening amiably to Sumner's argument that the South was still torn by violence and not yet ready for readmission, Johnson attacked him with cheap analogies. "Are there no murders in Massachusetts?" the President asked.

"Unhappily yes," Sumner replied, "sometimes."

"Are there no assaults in Boston? Do not men there sometimes knock each other down, so that the police is obliged to interfere?"

"Unhappily yes."

"Would you consent that Massachusetts, on this account, should be excluded from Congress?" Johnson triumphantly queried. In the excitement the President unconsciously used Sumner's hat, which the Senator had placed on the floor beside his chair, as a spittoon!

Had Johnson been as resolute in action as he was in argument, he might conceivably have carried much of his party with him on his Reconstruction program. Promptness, publicity, and persuasion could have created a presidential following. Instead Johnson boggled. Though he talked boastfully of "kicking out" officers who failed to support his plan, he was slow to act. His own Cabinet, from the very beginning, contained members who disagreed with him, and his secretary of war, Edwin M. Stanton, was openly in league with the Republican elements most hostile to the President. For more than two years he impotently hoped that Stanton would resign; then in 1867, after Congress had passed the Tenure of Office Act, he tried to oust the Secretary. This belated firmness, against the letter of the law, led directly to Johnson's impeachment trial.

Instead of working with his party leaders and building up political support among Republicans, Johnson in 1866 undertook to organize his friends into a new party. In August a convention of white southerners, northern Democrats, moderate Republicans, and presidential appointees assembled in Philadelphia to endorse Johnson's policy. Union General Darius Couch of Massachusetts marched arm in arm down the convention aisle with Governor James L. Orr of South Carolina, to symbolize the states reunited under Johnson's rule. The convention produced fervid oratory, a dignified statement of principles—but not much else. Like most third-party reformist movements it lacked local support and grass-roots organization.

Johnson himself was unable to breathe life into his stillborn third party. Deciding to take his case to the people, he accepted an invitation to speak at a great Chicago memorial honoring Stephen A. Douglas. When his special train left Washington on August 28 for a "swing around the circle," the President was accompanied by a few Cabinet members who shared his views and by the war heroes Grant and Farragut.

At first all went well. There were some calculated political snubs to the President, but he managed at Philadelphia, New York, and Albany to present his ideas soberly and cogently to the people. But Johnson's friends were worried lest his tongue again get out of control. "In all frankness," a senator wrote him, do not "allow the excitement of the moment to draw from you any *extemporaneous speeches.*"

At St. Louis, when a Radical voice shouted that Johnson was a "Judas," the President flamed up in rage. "There was a Judas and he was one of the twelve apostles," he retorted. ". . . The twelve apostles had a Christ. . . . If I have played the Judas, who has been my Christ that I have played the Judas with? Was it Thad Stevens? Was it Wendell Phillips? Was it Charles Sumner?" Over mingled hisses and applause, he shouted. "These are the men that stop and compare themselves with the Saviour; and everybody that differs with them . . . is to be denounced as a Judas."

Johnson had played into his enemies' hands. His Radical foes denounced him as a "trickster," a "culprit," a man "touched with insanity, corrupted with lust, stimulated with drink." More serious in consequence was the reaction of northern moderates, such as James Russell Lowell, who wrote, "What an anti-Johnson lecturer we have in Johnson! Sumner has been right about the *cuss* from the first. . . ." The fall elections were an over-whelming repudiation of the President and his Reconstruction policy.

Johnson's want of political sagacity strengthened the very elements in the Republican party which he most feared. In 1865 the Republicans had no clearly defined attitude toward Reconstruction. Moderates like Gideon Welles and Orville Browning wanted to see the southern states restored with a minimum of restrictions; Radicals like Sumner and Stevens de-manded that the entire southern social system be revolutionized. Some Republicans were passionately concerned with the plight of the freedmen; others were more interested in maintaining the high tariff and land grant legislation enacted during the war. Many thought mostly of keeping them-selves in office, and many genuinely believed, with Sumner, that "the Republican party, in its objects, is identical with country and with man-kind." These diverse elements came slowly to adopt the idea of harsh Reconstruction, but Johnson's stubborn persistency in his policy left them no alternative. Every step the President took seemed to provide "a new encouragement to (1) the rebels at the South, (2) the Democrats at the North and (3) the discontented elements everywhere." Not many Re-publicans would agree with Sumner that Johnson's program was "a defiance to God and Truth," but there was genuine concern that the victory won by the war was being frittered away.

The provisional governments established by the President in the South seemed to be dubiously loyal. They were reluctant to rescind their secession ordinances and to repudiate the Confederate debt, and they chose high-ranking ex-Confederates to represent them in Congress. Northerners were even more alarmed when these southern governments began to legislate upon the Negro's civil rights. Some laws were necessary—in order to give former slaves the right to marry, to hold property, to sue and be sued, and the like—but Johnson legislatures went far beyond these immediate needs. South Carolina, for example, enacted that no Negro could pursue the trade "of an artisan, mechanic, or shopkeeper, or any other trade or em-ployment besides that of husbandry" without a special license. Alabama provided that "any stubborn or refractory servants" or "servants who loiter away their time" should be fined $50 and, if they could not pay, be hired out for six months' labor. Mississippi ordered that every Negro under eighteen years of age who was an orphan or not supported by his parents must be apprenticed to some white person, preferably the former owner of the slave. Such southern laws indicated a determination to keep the Negro in a state of peonage.

It was impossible to expect a newly emancipated race to be content with such a limping freedom. The thousands of Negroes who had served in the Union armies and had helped conquer their former Confederate masters were not willing to abandon their new-found liberty. In rural areas southern whites kept these Negroes under control through the Ku Klux Klan. But in southern cities white hegemony was less secure, and racial friction erupted in mob violence. In May, 1866, a quarrel between a Memphis Negro and a white teamster led to a riot in which the city police and the poor whites raided the Negro quarters and burned and killed promiscuously. Far more serious was the disturbance in New Orleans two months later. The Republican party in Louisiana was split into pro-Johnson conservatives and Negro suffrage advocates. The latter group determined to hold a constitutional convention, of dubious legality, in New Orleans, in order to secure the ballot for the freedmen and the offices for themselves. Through imbecility in the War Department, the Federal troops occupying the city were left without orders, and the mayor of New Orleans, strongly opposed to Negro equality, had the responsibility for preserving order. There were acts of provocation on both sides, and finally, on July 30, a procession of Negroes marching toward the convention hall was attacked.

"A shot was fired . . . by a policeman, or some colored man in the procession," General Philip Sheridan reported. "This led to other shots, and a rush after the procession. On arrival at the front of the Institute [where the convention met], there was some throwing of brick-bats by both sides. The police . . . were vigorously marched to the scene of disorder. The procession entered the Institute with the flag, about six or eight remaining outside. A row occurred between a policeman and one of these colored men, and a shot was again fired by one of the parties, which led to an indiscriminate firing on the building, through the windows, by the policemen.

"This had been going on for a short time, when a white flag was displayed from the windows of the Institute, whereupon the firing ceased and the police rushed into the building. . . . The policemen opened an indiscriminate fire upon the audience until they had emptied their revolvers, when they retired, and those inside barricaded the doors. The door was broken in, and the firing again commenced when many of the colored and white people either escaped out of the door, or were passed out by the policemen inside, but as they came out, the policemen who formed the circle nearest the building fired upon them, and they were again fired upon by the citizens that formed the outer circle."

Thirty-seven Negroes and three of their white friends were killed; 119 Negroes and seventeen of their white sympathizers were wounded. Of their assailants, ten were wounded and but one killed. President Johnson was, of course, horrified by these outbreaks, but the Memphis and New Orleans riots, together with the Black Codes, afforded a devastating illustration of how the President's policy actually operated. The southern states, it was clear, were not going to protect the Negroes' basic rights. They were only grudgingly going to accept the results of the war. Yet, with Johnson's blessing, these same states were expecting a stronger voice in Congress than ever. Before 1860, southern representation in Congress had been based upon the white population plus three fifths of the slaves; now the Negroes, though not permitted to vote, were to be counted like all other citizens, and southern states would be entitled to at least nine additional congressmen. Joining with the northern Copperheads, the southerners could easily regain at the next presidential election all that had been lost on the Civil War battlefield.

It was this political exigency, not misguided sentimentality nor vindictiveness, which united Republicans in opposition to the President.

Johnson's defenders have pictured Radical Reconstruction as the work of a fanatical minority, led by Sumner and Stevens, who drove their reluctant colleagues into adopting coercive measures against the South. In fact, every major piece of Radical legislation was adopted by the nearly unanimous vote of the entire Republican membership of Congress. Andrew Johnson had left them no other choice. Because he insisted upon rushing Confederate-dominated states back into the Union, Republicans moved to disqualify Confederate leaders under the Fourteenth Amendment. When, through Johnson's urging, the southern states rejected that amendment, the Republicans in Congress unwillingly came to see Negro suffrage as the only counterweight against Democratic majorities in the South. With the Reconstruction Acts of 1867 the way was open for a true Radical program toward the South, harsh and thorough.

Andrew Johnson became a cipher in the White House, futilely disapproving bills which were promptly passed over his veto. Through his failure to reckon with public opinion, his unwillingness to recognize his weak position, his inability to function as a party leader, he had sacrificed all influence with the party which had elected him and had turned over its control to Radicals vindictively opposed to his policies. In March, 1868, Andrew Johnson was summoned before the Senate of the United States to be tried on eleven accusations of high crimes and misdemeanors. By a narrow margin the Senate failed to convict him, and historians have dismissed the charges as flimsy and false. Yet perhaps before the bar of history itself Andrew Johnson must be impeached with an even graver charge—that through political ineptitude he threw away a magnificent opportunity.

SITTING BULL

&

the Indians' Last Stand

To nineteenth-century white Americans, Sitting Bull embodied every kind of bad Indian. His role as an Indian medicine man seemed both odd and sinister. In white eyes, medicine men looked like manipulators driving braves to battle. His white critics also accused him of cowardice, because they never understood that his progression from warrior to medicine man—the latter a suitable role for an older man—was a regular pattern of tribal politics. Sitting Bull did not fit the image of the "noble savage"; devious, dishonest, and contemptuous, he lied to white men, stole their horses, and, hating them all, refused them the deference they expected. Worst of all, he had a sharp tongue and could turn his contempt into barbed wit. Not surprisingly, legend constantly claimed him to be part or even all white: he was "darned smart" for an Indian.

A Sioux chief, Sitting Bull was born around 1834 along the Grand River in South Dakota. He considered war to the death between the races inevitable and had, one assumes, no expectation that his own people could win. He became the extremist among the various leaders of the different Sioux tribes, and as pressure on the tribes grew, so too did his influence. By June 1876 he had somehow brought together so large a group of braves that they could wipe out Custer's force at the battle of Little Big Horn. But by the end of the year his band had been chased to the Canadian border. His people destitute, he surrendered in 1881 along with a following of only 187. His defense of Indian rights never ceased, and in 1890, fighting arrest by Indian police, he was shot and killed, adamant and rebellious to the end.

Sitting Bull Speaks (1891)
WILLIS F. JOHNSON

Sitting Bull, unlike the United States officers he fought, did not write memoirs; we have only accounts of his various conversations about the battle at the Little Big Horn. Often these are cryptic defenses against obscure critics. Compare this selection and the following one with the final selection, in which Albert Britt discusses the various arguments about Sitting Bull's role in the battle.

SITTING BULL said "he was not raised to be an enemy of the whites. The pale-faces had things that we needed in order to hunt. We needed ammunition. Our interests were in peace. I never sold that much land. [Here Sitting Bull picked up with his thumb and forefinger a little of the pulverized dirt in the tent, and holding it up let it fall and blow away.] I never made or sold a treaty with the United States. I came in to claim my rights and the rights of my people. I was driven in force from my land and I now come back to claim it for my people. I never made war on the United States Government. I never stood in the white man's country. I never committed any depredations in the white man's country. I never made the white man's heart bleed. The white man came on to my land and followed me. The white men made me fight for my hunting grounds. The white man made me kill him or he would kill my friends, my women, and my children."

Speaking of the Custer fight, Sitting Bull said: "There was a Great Spirit who guided and controlled that battle. I could do nothing. I was sustained by the Great Mysterious One (pointing upwards with his forefinger). I am not afraid to talk about that. It all happened—it is passed and gone. I do not lie, but do not want to talk about it. Low Dog says I can't fight until some one lends me a heart. Gall says my heart is no bigger than that (placing one forefinger at the base of the nail of another finger). We have all fought hard. We did not know Custer. When we saw him we threw up our hands, and I cried, 'Follow me and do as I do.' We whipped each other's horses, and it was all over. There was not as many Indians as the white man says. They are all warriors. There was not more than two thousand. I did not want to kill any more men. I did not like that kind of work. I only defended my camp. When we had killed enough, that was all that was necessary.

"If the Great Father gives me a reservation I do not want to be confined to any part of it. I want no restraint. I will keep on the reservation, but want to go where I please. I don't want a white man over me. I don't want an agent. I want to have the white man with me, but not to be my chief. I ask this because I want to do right by my people, and can't trust any one else to trade with them or talk to them. I want interpreters to talk to the white man for me and transact my business, but I want it to be seen and known that I have my rights. I want my people to have light wagons to work with. They did not know how to handle heavy wagons with cattle. We want light wagons and ponies. I don't want to give up game as long as there is any game. I will be half civilized till the game is gone. Then I will be all a white man.". . .

"What treaty that the whites have kept has the red man broken? Not one. What treaty that the whites ever made with us red men have they kept? Not one. When I was a boy the Sioux owned the world. The sun rose and set in their lands. They sent 10,000 horsemen to battle. Where are the warriors to-day? Who slew them? Where are our lands? Who owns them? What white man can say I ever stole his lands or a penny of his money? Yet they say I am a thief. What white woman, however lonely, was ever when a captive insulted by me? Yet they say I am a bad Indian. What white man has ever seen me drunk? Who has ever come to me hungry and gone unfed? Who has ever seen me beat my wives or abuse my children? What law have I broken? Is it wrong for me to love my own? Is it wicked in me because my skin is red; because I am a Sioux; because I was born where my fathers lived; because I would die for my people and my country?"

Sitting Bull's Trance (1907)
FRED M. HANS

SITTING BULL WENT OUT one day, far from his lodge, in the hope of being . . . enabled to communicate with the "Great Spirit." On the second night he was seized with a strange feeling, and near morning he met the "Great Spirit," clad in a beautiful robe. His hair flowed upon his shoulders and reached almost to his feet. When Sitting Bull beheld this wonderful apparition, he fainted and lay there he knew not how long, and had a strange dream. He related his story of the trance to the author, as well as to the Indians thus:

"The Great Spirit appeared to me with a formidable band of Sioux, who have long since been dead, and they danced, inviting me to join them. Presently I was restored to my senses, and the Great Spirit talked with me. He asked me if the Indians would not be glad to see their dead ancestors and the buffalo restored to them, and to life. I assured him that they would be deeply gratified. Then the Great Spirit told me that he once came to save the white race, but that they had persecuted him; and now he had come to save and rescue the defenseless and long-persecuted Indian race. All day the Great Spirit gave me evidence of his power and instructed me.

"He said that the white men would come to take me, but as they approached the soil would become quicksand, and the men and horses would sink. He showed me how to make medicine to put on war-shirts to turn aside the bullets of the white man. He told me the Indians had suffered long enough, and that he was now coming for their deliverance. We are to occupy the earth again, which has been taken from us. Great herds of buffalo will wander about as they did long ago, and the Indian who now sleeps in death will rise again, and forever wander over the earth. There will be no reservation; no messenger from the government to say to the Indians, come back here, stay here, starve here on this spot of ground.

"The Great Spirit said that the Indians must keep dancing; that the earth was theirs at his command, and for all this privilege, they must dance the dances which are pleasing to him. He said that all the Indians who would not listen to his words, or refuse to join in the ceremonies which are pleasing to him, will be destroyed with the white race."

The Indians' Story of the Custer Fight (1913)
JOSEPH K. DIXON, EDITOR

The Indian wars rarely pitted simply white against Indian; rather, whites allied with Indians and attacked other tribes. Custer's Last Stand was no exception. Both the Indians who scouted for Custer and the Sioux chiefs who fought him gave accounts of the battle. The ones below, collected years afterward, are by Sioux chiefs Runs-the-Enemy and Red Cloud. These accounts of the cause of the battle and of Sitting Bull's role in rallying the Sioux force should be read with the caution that all such first-hand accounts require.

The Story of Chief Runs-the-Enemy

. . . I went over with the others and peeped over the hills and saw the soldiers advancing. As I looked along the line of the ridge they seemed to fill the whole hill. It looked as if there were thousands of them, and I thought we would surely be beaten. As I returned I saw hundreds of Sioux. I looked into their eyes and they looked different—they were filled with fear. I then called my own band together, and I took off the ribbons from my hair, also my shirt and pants, and threw them away, saving nothing but my belt of cartridges and gun. I thought most of the Sioux will fall to-day: I will fall with them. Just at that time Sitting-Bull made his appearance. He said, just as though I could hear him at this moment: "A bird, when it is on its nest, spreads its wings to cover the nest and eggs and protect them. It cannot use its wings for defense, but it can cackle and try to drive away the enemy. We are here to protect our wives and children, and we must not let the soldiers get them." He was on a buckskin horse, and he rode from one end of the line to the other, calling out: "Make a brave fight!" We were all hidden along the range of hills. . . .

. . . After we had killed Custer and all his men I did not think very much about it. The soldiers fired into us first and we returned the fire. Sitting-Bull had talked to us and all the tribes to make a brave fight and we made it. When we had killed all the soldiers we felt that we had done our duty, and felt that it was a great battle and not a massacre. With reference to the real reason for this fight I might say that the talk among the Indians was that they were going to compel us to stay on the reservation and take away from us our country. Our purpose was to move north and go as far north as possible away from the tribes. Our object was not to fight the Crows or any other tribe, but we learned that the soldiers were getting after us to try to compel us to go back on the reservation, and we were trying to get away from them. During the Custer fight our tents were not attacked, but after the battle the women gathered up their dead husbands and brothers, and laid them out nicely in the tepee, and left them. I understand that after we had left the tepees standing, holding our dead, the soldiers came and burned the tepees. According to my estimate there were about two thousand able-bodied warriors engaged in this fight; they were all in good fighting order. The guns and ammunition that we gathered from the dead soldiers of Custer's command put us in better fighting condition than ever before, but the sentiment ran around among the Indians that we had killed enough, and we did not want to fight any more. There has been a good deal of dispute about the number of Indians killed. About the closest estimate that we can make is that fifty Sioux were killed in the fight, and others died a short time afterward from their wounds.

The Story of Chief Red Cloud

. . . Regarding the cause of the Custer fight . . . we were pursued by the soldiers, we were on the warpath, and we were on the warpath with the Crows and other tribes. We were trying to drive them back from the hunting grounds, and the soldiers came upon us and we had to defend ourselves. We were driven out of the Black Hills by the men seeking gold, and our game was driven off, and we started on our journey in search of game. Our children were starving, and we had to have something to eat. There was buffalo in that region and we were moving, simply camping here and there and fighting our Indian enemies as we advanced, in order to get the game that was in this country. We fought this battle from daylight up until three o'clock in the afternoon, and all of the white men were killed. I think that Custer was a very brave man to fight all these Indians with his few men from daylight until the sun was almost going down.

The Vision of Victory (1957)
STANLEY VESTAL

Beginning in the late nineteenth century, writers, some of them officers who fought the Sioux in 1876, charged Sitting Bull with cowardice. This charge probably was an expression of their hostility toward the role of the medicine man, who often incited braves to battle. Sitting Bull's role in the fight against Custer remains uncertain, but this selection makes it plain that being a medicine man was no work for a coward.

SITTING BULL did not spend all his time at councils of war. Horses and guns were needed, of course. But he soon went about something far more vital to his success. One day he loosened the braids of his long hair, removed the feathers from his head, washed off the red paint he habitually wore on his face, and filled his long pipe with tobacco. Then he bound silver sprays of wild aromatic sage—a sacred plant—about the pipestem. When he was all ready to start, he called his nephew White Bull, his adopted brother Jumping Bull, and the son of his close friend and fellow chief Black Moon. He asked them to go with him to the top of a butte some distance south of the old camp site, downriver. The four reached the hill-top about noon.

There Sitting Bull renewed his vow before witnesses. He stood facing the Sun, holding the pipestem upward and wailing for mercy. When he had wailed for a while, he made his prayer: "My God, save me and give me all my wild game animals. Bring them near me, so that my people have plenty to eat this winter. Let good men on earth have more power, so that all nations may be strong and successful. Let them be of good heart, so that all Sioux people may get along well and be happy. If you do this for me, I will perform the sun-gazing dance two days, two nights, and give you a whole buffalo."

Then all four smoked the pipe in communion, and after Sitting Bull had wiped his face with the sage, set out for camp.

Sitting Bull immediately went hunting. He shot three buffalo. Of these he chose the fattest. Then, with the help of his nephew, he rolled the cow upon her belly, and together they stretched out the legs in four directions to prop it so. The head was stretched out also. Then Sitting Bull stood with raised hands and wailed for pity. Afterward, he prayed: "Wakan' Tanka, this is the one I offered you awhile back. Here it is." In this manner he offered the buffalo to God, and made his vow good.

Within a few days, the Sun Dance was begun. Black Moon conducted it, holding the office of Intercessor. Sitting Bull, having vowed the dance, was Chief of the Dancers.

That was a big Sun Dance, well remembered by the Sioux and Chey-ennes, scores of whom now living were present. Because of the wonderful prophecy that Sitting Bull made there, and because he vowed the ceremony, it has ever since been known as "Sitting Bull's Sun Dance."

All the people—both Sioux and Cheyennes—went into camp in one big circle for the ceremony. The camp was on the bank of the Rosebud, not far from the carved rocks, where the prehistoric pictures are. There the ceremony began. The virgin cut the sacred tree, the chiefs carried it into the camp circle on poles, as if it had been the body of an enemy. It was dedicated and decorated with its symbols and its offerings. A square "bed" of ground was smoothed for the altar, a buffalo skull placed thereon, and a pipe set up against the little scaffold before the skull. All the elaborate ritual of the Sun Dance was gone through with. It was all familiar to Sitting Bull: he had danced the Sun Dance many times, and his breast and back bore the scars of the torture. At last it came time for him to fulfill his vow made last autumn—to give his flesh to Wakan' Tanka. Naked to the waist, he went forward to the sacred pole.

This time he had decided to give one hundred pieces of flesh—that is to say, skin—from his arms. Jumping Bull had agreed to do the cutting.

Jumping Bull came forward, bringing a sharp steel awl, and a knife ground down to a thin, narrow blade, very sharp. He knelt beside Sitting Bull, who sat leaning back against the sacred pole, his legs straight out on the ground in front of him, and his relaxed arms resting on his thighs. Jumping Bull began at the bottom—near the wrist—of the right arm and worked upwards. He stuck the awl into the skin of the arm, lifted the skin clear of the flesh, and then used the knife. Each time he would cut out a small bit of skin, about the size of the head of a match. Then he would let the skin fall again, withdraw the awl, and begin again just above. Sitting Bull's arm was soon covered with blood.

All the time Jumping Bull was slowly and carefully cutting away on him, Sitting Bull remained perfectly still. He was wailing all the time—not because of the pain—but for mercy to Wakan' Tanka, the Great Mysterious. When Jumping Bull had worked up to the top of the right arm and cut out fifty pieces of skin, he then got up and went over to the left side. There he cut in the same manner, beginning at the wrist and working toward the shoulder, Sitting Bull sat there, wailing, never wincing, while that endless piercing, endless cutting went on, cruel and sharp, over and over. Jumping Bull was careful, his hand was sure, he worked as rapidly as he could. But it was a painful ordeal for the half-hour it lasted. White Bull stood looking on. One Bull was dancing. Sitting White Buffalo was pierced at this dance, also. Everybody in camp was looking on.

Having paid his ounce of flesh, it now remained for Sitting Bull to dance the sun-gazing dance. He took his place, and, facing the Sun while the blood ran down his fingers and slowly congealed and closed his wounds, began to bob up and down, staring up toward the Sun. All that day he danced, and that night, and the next day about noon, the crowd noticed that he appeared faint and hardly able to stand.

Black Moon and others took Sitting Bull and laid him down. He was almost unconscious. They threw cold water on him to revive him. His eyes cleared, and he spoke in a low voice to Black Moon. He had had a vision: his offering had been accepted, his prayers were heard.

Black Moon walked out into the middle of the Sun Dance enclosure and called out in a loud voice: "Sitting Bull wishes to announce that he just heard a voice from above saying, 'I give you these because they have no ears.' He looked up and saw soldiers and some Indians on horseback coming down like grasshoppers, with their heads down and their hats falling off. They were falling right into our camp."

Then the people rejoiced. They knew what that meant. Those white men, who would not listen, who made war without just cause, were coming to their camp. Since they were coming upside down, the Indians knew the soldiers would be killed there. The people had what they wanted: Wakan' Tanka would care for His own. The Sun Dance was swiftly brought to an end. It was June 14, 1876.

Afterward, Sitting Bull warned the people: "These dead soldiers who are coming are the gifts of God. Kill them, but do not take their guns or horses. Do not touch the spoils. If you set your hearts upon the goods of the white man, it will prove a curse to this nation." Twelve lesser chiefs heard this warning, but said nothing. All the people heard of this, but some of them had no ears.

The prophecy, so soon to be fulfilled, fired the Sioux and Cheyennes with martial spirit. Ice and Two Moon, Crazy Horse and Gall, all of them had faith in Sitting Bull, believed in him. They had heard him prophesy before, and nearly always his prophecies came true. Others also divined the future at this camp, and when Custer's troops reached it, ten days later, his Ree scouts found traces of ceremonies that made them tell him, "The Sioux are sure of winning."

Sitting Bull: War Chief or Swindler? (1938)
ALBERT BRITT

Although we do not usually think of him that way, Sitting Bull became one of the most famous Americans during the twenty-five years after the Civil War. Yet he remains a man of mystery, his life story shrouded with legends and his unhappy death surrounded with ambiguity. A twentieth-century scholar probes the many questions.

WAS SITTING BULL a great leader or a clever, devious schemer? Was he an able, undaunted war chief, striving to lead his people toward the realization of an impossible but heroic dream, or was he merely another plotting medicine-man, stimulating other Indians to deeds of which he was incapable? Was he a hero or a coward?

These are a few of the questions that have been argued over in connection with the famous—or infamous—Sioux leader who was—or was not—at the head of the horde of warriors who wiped out Custer and his troops on the Little Big Horn, the afternoon of June 26, 1876. More has been written about Sitting Bull than about any other famous Indian, perhaps more than about all the others put together. This is part of the difficulty in seeing him. The evidence in the case of any Indian is always obscure and contradictory, the standards by which we judge them so alien and usually inapplicable that the task of discovering the individual is hard enough under the best of circumstances. The white student sincerely seeking the truth must derive the personality by indirection and inference. This is doubly true in the case of Sitting Bull. The old equation by which character equals conduct and from which either can be deduced from the other is difficult to prove, even in the case of men of our own race.

Consider some of the statements of people who saw Sitting Bull, talked with him, at least had the chance to know him, if he could be known.

Lieutenant Ahern saw him at Fort Randall in 1882, six years after the Custer fight, and said of him: "He stood before me square-shouldered, deep-chested, fine head, and the manner of man who knew his ground. He looked squarely into your eyes and spoke deliberately and forcefully."

This agrees in general with General Miles's report in his *Personal Recollections and Observations:* "He was a strong, hardy, sturdy-looking man of about 5 ft. 11 inches in height, well built, with strongly marked features, high cheek bones, prominent nose, straight, thin lips, and strong underjaw, indicating determination and force. He had a wide, large, well developed head and low forehead. He was a man of few words and cautious in his expressions, evidently thinking twice before speaking. He was very deliberate in his movements and somewhat reserved in his manner. At first he was courteous, but evidently void of any genuine respect for the white race." The last statement in the general's characterization is one about which there need be no quarrel. Even Sitting Bull's warmest friends among the whites admit that he had neither respect for the whites nor confidence in them.

Miss Collins, a teacher in the Indian school at the Standing Rock agency, was impressed by his ability as a reader of weather signs and his standing among the Indians as a prophet of mild and hard winters, always important questions with the northern Indians. As an individual she found him "always so tender, gracious, and invariably sweet." That was because he stopped smoking in her house when he discovered that she objected to it. . . .

Sitting Bull's courage, like the courage of Pat Garrett when he put an end to Billy the Kid at Fort Sumner, has been the subject of debate in post canteens, in officers' quarters, corner grocery forums, and even Pullman smokers and club lounges. Was he brave? Yes! No! And here, too, the evidence of opinion is confused and contradictory. The Rev. A. G. McBeede, an Episcopal missionary near Bismarck, North Dakota, for a number of years, thought him temperamentally timid, but capable of personal courage of a high order on occasions. "Some Indians face death with admirable bravery, some even with temerity, but Sitting Bull faced it with painful timidity."

E. H. Allison, an old soldier and scout, married to a Brulé Sioux wife and familiar with Indian ways, as well as with Indian speech, says that Sitting Bull was "constitutionally a coward," and then admits that "Time and again he had met them [the whites] in battle, and had always been the victor." If that is true, why bother about his courage?

John F. Finerty, a correspondent for the *Chicago Tribune* and the author of the lyrical tribute quoted above, who saw Sitting Bull in Canada in the autumn after the Little Big Horn fight, concluded that his judgment was superior to his courage, and his cunning superior to both. He was not a coward, says Mr. Finerty, merely prudent. The dispassionate reader might conclude from this that Sitting Bull was a highly intelligent person and that many white generals would have been the better for so admirable a balance of personal qualities.

James McLaughlin, an Indian agent of long experience, the man who sent the Indian police to arrest Sitting Bull in 1890, always insisted that Sitting Bull was a coward, but that he was, nevertheless, the dominating figure among the hostile Sioux in 1876, and remained so for some time after, in spite of Chief Gall's enmity to him and the standing of the latter as one of the bravest of the war chiefs of the Sioux.

The most sweeping claims of all in behalf of Sitting Bull are made by Stanley Vestal in his recent biography of the old leader, *Sitting Bull, Champion of the Sioux*. According to Mr. Vestal, he was not only leader, prophet, and warrior, but he was head chief of all the Sioux, duly installed at a ceremony held, apparently, on the Yellowstone in 1868. The evidence is from the statements of old Indians who claimed to have been present, as boys. In general, students of the Sioux have denied the existence of such a single headship, although white negotiators sought to bring about the choice of such a leader or spokesman.

Mr. Vestal sums up his hero: "His strong, positive qualities, his world-wide fame; his early achievements as soldier, diplomat, organizer of the most unstable elements; his later roles of patriot, statesman, and prophet; the crushing defeats inflicted by his warriors upon hostile Indian nations and the armies of the United States—all these afford ample scope to any lover of heroics. And the stubborn persistence of the man, in the face of conquest, exile, starvation, treason, and death, cannot fail to win the hearts of all who care for lost causes and forsaken beliefs and impossible loyalties."

Was this, then, the real Sitting Bull? W. H. H. Murray called him "the George Washington of the Sioux nation. Too intelligent to be hoodwinked, too honest to be corrupted by the influences that have been at work among the unlettered wards of our government, he stood firmly for the rights of his people." Or was he something else? Perhaps the man whom Senator Sanders of Montana, an "old-timer" in the Sioux country, called "a newspaper Indian!" The army verdict on the old man, after the fighting was all over, is summed up by F. B. Fiske in the *Life and Death of Sitting Bull,* in the characteristically curt army phrase, "a darned smart Indian.". . .

The basic facts of the life of Sitting Bull are easily found, and, when found, are comparatively meaningless. Sometime in the thirties of the last century, he was born somewhere in what is now South Dakota—some authorities say on Willow Creek, a branch of the Bad River, which flows into the Missouri at Pierre, South Dakota; some say on the Grand River. Sitting Bull told Allison his birthplace was on Willow Creek. Dates range from 1831 to 1837. Indian chronology is vague, as is Indian geography, unless one is Indian enough to think Indian fashion, and few white men have ever been able to do that. His boyhood name was "Slow," "Jumping Badger," or "Sacred Standshot." There are proponents for all three versions. He killed his first buffalo at the age of ten and counted his first coup on the body of an enemy at fourteen. This precocity was not unusual among the more warlike and active of the western tribes for whom buffalo was the chief source of food and to whom the warpath was the road that must be traveled as soon and as often as possible. Most of his life, he walked with a slight limp, the result of a wound received in a fight with another Indian, and he was bowlegged, as was becoming to a man who lived mostly on horseback. . . .

Many wild tales of his origin and blood floated about after the Little Big Horn fight. That remarkable tragedy evidently required an explanation outside the realm of ordinary happenings. How else could half of a regiment under the command of seasoned officers have been blotted out with the suddenness and completeness of the breaking of a dam? White men were slow to realize it was exactly as though with the irresistible force and volume of the waters released by a bursting dam that the Sioux swept over the soldiers that day on the Little Big Horn. Meanwhile, they sought explanations, and since the occasion seemed to call for unusual power and preparation on the part of some leader among the Indians, critics sought it in the background of Sitting Bull. Some said that he was really a half-breed named Charlie Jacobs, born in Canada near old Fort Garry (Winnipeg), and educated at St. John's College. He was described as a devout Roman Catholic: a convert of the devoted Father de Smet, said some. Because the leader of the Sioux must have been a military genius of the first order, he was given a fluent command of French, which had resulted, of course, in his being a close student and admirer of Napoleon. One rumor capped the climax by making him a cadet at West Point; another had him conspiring with Louis Riel to establish an independent Indian state in Canada.

These tales and others like them are purest moonshine. Sitting Bull may have had latent military talent, but the Indians at the Little Big Horn fought in Indian fashion, and—for once—numbers, speed, and fierceness were all they needed. Sitting Bull was all Indian and all Sioux—Hunkpapa —and it is as an Indian and not an imitation white man that he must be examined and, perhaps, understood.

The early part of Sitting Bull's life is wrapped in the mists of legend. Indian narratives are vague and allusive and lacking in the precise data of name and date and place and circumstance that the white historian demands. He fought the Crows and sometimes the Blackfeet, but mostly he hunted buffalo, stole horses from the whites or Crows, as occasion offered, and loafed with the other warriors about the village, while his wives did the slight work of the tepee or prepared food against the privations of the coming winter. He took no part in the Minnesota massacres of 1862, but seems to have joined in a small skirmish with General Sibley's expedition against the western Sioux in 1863. He was probably in or near the indecisive fight with General Sully at Killdeer Mountain in 1864. He may have taken part in the random skirmishing that followed the attempt to police the Sioux, who had been thrown into turmoil by the fighting in Minnesota and the subsequent troop movements in the Dakota country.

It was not until 1868 that events began to conspire to bring Sitting Bull's peculiar talents into play. That was the year of the so-called Treaty of Laramie, negotiated at Fort Rice, which gave to the Sioux as a reservation all of Dakota Territory west of the Missouri River and south of parallel 46, about half the present state of South Dakota. Chief Gall signed the treaty for the Oglallas. Sitting Bull was not present, but always opposed the application of the terms of the treaty. Of Gall he said contemptuously: "You must not blame Gall. Everyone knows that he will do anything for a square meal." In that somewhat apocryphal statement lies the key to Sitting Bull. His comment on Gall squares with his remark to General Miles, later: "No Indian that ever lived loved the white man—and no white man that ever lived loved the Indian; God Almighty made me an Indian, but he didn't make me an agency Indian, and I don't intend to be one." Sitting Bull was all Indian and he saw no end to the conflict between the two races, except the blotting out of one or the other, at least in the territory that the Sioux wanted. The agency and the reservation were no solution for him, because they meant the subservience of the Indian to the white and he was "void of any genuine respect for the white race."

Even before the Treaty of Laramie was signed, there had been rumors of gold in the Black Hills. The Black Hills were in the southwestern part of the new reservation that had just been created for the Sioux. Here was the beginning of the trouble that caught both troops and Indians in its grip for the next ten years. The Indian did not intend to dig for gold and he had no real love for the Black Hills and the Bad Lands. In fact, the spirits that haunted them were evil and the Indian usually gave the region a wide berth, but he viewed the filtering of the prospectors into the Hills with an unfriendly eye. The thing was happening to the new treaty that had happened to all the others. The chief difference was that it was happening sooner. Four years later, Custer led a "military expedition" into the Black Hills. The results were mostly mineralogical. Surveyors for the Northern Pacific Railroad began to cross Indian territory under military escort and without the Indian consent that the treaty required.

A corollary to the Laramie treaty was permission to the Indians to hold the exclusive hunting rights in the territory west to the Big Horn Mountains. As early as 1869, General Sheridan, doubtless acting on his well-known definition of a good Indian, declared that any Indian found outside the limits of the reservation was to be regarded as hostile and dealt with accordingly. This not only violated the terms of the treaty, but made Indian observance of it a virtual impossibility, as, except for buffalo, the best hunting lay to the west. Behind Sheridan's declaration lay the determination of the army and the Indian Bureau to force the Sioux to the agencies. This sharpened the conflict and led the restless young warriors to look more to the irreconcilable Sitting Bull and less to the conciliatory urgings of Red Cloud.

Unfortunately for the whites who must deal with the turbulent tribes, other white men in Washington gave Sitting Bull abundant evidence for his charges of bad faith. Now we begin to find signs of his activity among the young men, which he expressed later in such statements as "I would have more confidence in the Grandfather at Washington if there were not so many baldheaded thieves working for him." Afterward, when he was a self-invited guest of the Canadian government at Fort Walsh, he said: "Tell them at Washington if they have one man who speaks the truth to send him to me, and I will listen to what he has to say."

The invasion of the Indian's territory by prospectors and survey parties and the severity of the army policy stirred the hell broth that Sitting Bull and his friends were only too willing to mix. From 1870 to 1876 there was sporadic fighting, chiefly in the favorite hunting ground of the Sioux along the Yellowstone in southeastern Montana. It is difficult to find any reliable evidence of Sitting Bull's presence in any of these hostilities. It was mostly of the variety in which Sioux were adept, the quick raid with the accompanying stampede of herds or attacks on small bodies of troops or isolated trappers or hunters. But white men were beginning to hear more and more of Sitting Bull, the malcontent, the agitator. He made no secret of his hatred of the whites and his belief that no white man's word was to be trusted.

There were signs, too, that his agitation and his plotting had the obvious deadly intent. In 1870, he walked into the agency store at Fort Peck and demanded ammunition. The agent refused and assured the arrogant Sitting Bull that the Great Father loved his Indian children and did not wish war. Sitting Bull made hot, scornful reply: "You are the chief of liars, and you know there does not live a white man but hates the Indian, nor an Indian who does not hate the white and it will always be so as long as the grass grows and the water runs. I did not come here to make peace, but for ammunition and I am going to have it. I and my men will fight the white men wherever and whenever we can find them."

His statement on this occasion sounds curiously like the remark attributed to him by General Miles, and the evidence in connection with Indians is generally so obscured and twisted by rumor and partisanship that it is impossible to be sure which, if either, is authentic. But the general case for Sitting Bull's sweeping distrust and hatred of the white man is so clear that he might well have made such statements on these and many other occasions.

At another time, a trader near old Fort Buford gave him a red shirt and with a rather ill-timed sense of humor suggested that he put it on when he came for war. Sitting Bull's answer was to slip the shirt over his head with the reply, "Right now would be a good time." Then, as he and his band rode away, they fired a volley into the store by way of warning that they would be coming that way again.

Sometimes, his actions took the form of sinister clowning. General Miles tells of his call at the Poplar Creek store on the Missouri. This time, it was the age-old suspicion of the trader that Sitting Bull vented. He went behind the counter, elbowing the trader aside, and pretended to be, himself, the trader. To the great delight of the other Indians, he adopted the trader lingo, criticizing the furs, beating down the Indian, burlesquing the trader's praise of the goods on the shelves. Behind the screen of horseplay, he made trades that delighted the Indians more even than his humor, because for once at least they got their money's worth. The trader finally cleared the store by threatening to drop a lighted match in an open keg of powder unless they went out quietly. Sitting Bull left, but again he had freed his mind of his opinion of the whites and their methods. As word of such exploits went round, his influence among the Sioux grew stronger.

The clouds were growing thicker and not much that was heard from or about Sitting Bull was so harmless as his horseplay in the Poplar Creek store. An Indian was killed by a drunken soldier and Sitting Bull forced General Morrow to pay many blankets for the dead man. This still further increased his popularity among his own people and every restless young brave could be sure of a welcome from Sitting Bull. Even Gall had begun to have his doubts about the permanence and value for the Indian of the treaty he had signed for the Oglallas at Fort Rice. In 1875 Sitting Bull seems to have decided that it was time to begin to assert more concrete rights. He announced a claim to the land for forty rods on both sides of the Yellowstone River, and assumed semijudicial powers in differences between individual Indians and whites. His claim to the Yellowstone meant the practical barring of the white man from any use of the river, or even from the right to cross it to reach the rich land to the north of the valley. It was time for the army to begin to take the Indian "troubles" seriously.

This was the phase of the conflict that set the stage for the battle of the Little Big Horn in which Custer and all his men died and out of which grew a discussion that made Sitting Bull one of the most talked-about men, red or white, in America. Was he the man who brought the Sioux together for their last day of victory over the whites? Was he the great chief of "all the Sioux"? Was he the war chief on that day of June 25, 1876? Was he a brave man or a coward? Was he a chief at all? Or only a scheming, skillful medicine-man?

This part of the discussion could, perhaps, best be avoided by a statement of ignorance. Nobody knows quite the correct answers to these questions. Nobody ever will know. It is my humble opinion that, as they are usually put, the answers, good or bad, are not important. Such terms as coward, brave, scheming, able, leader, agitator are question-begging words. Perhaps Sitting Bull was all that his friends and enemies have called him— and something more. Again let us turn to such of the record as we can read.

The charge that Sitting Bull was never a fighter will not hold. There is too much evidence to the contrary, even the evidence of his action on the last day of his life, when he went out into the winter dawn in the hands of the Indian policemen and shouted his sudden defiance which brought death on the instant, as he must have known it would. The only point to this part of the discussion is that it has no point at all in the attempt to discover what kind of a person Sitting Bull was. Even white men's courage comes and goes; some have more than others; all have more at one time than at another. Napoleon made the hardly astonishing discovery that four-o'clock-in-the-morning courage is the rarest kind of all. Incidentally it was early dawn in December, 1890, when the Indian police rode into Sitting Bull's camp on the Grand River to arrest him and succeeded only in killing him.

Whether he was coward or hero, the interest in Sitting Bull lies outside the scope of either word. It is not the purpose of this study to present even a condensed biography of the famous Sioux. Events of his life are important only as they are capable of interpretation. The early part of his life, as has been said, was little different from that of many other Indians. He fought, he stole, he probably gambled, he hunted, he sang, he danced. He had courage, at least, for the painful ordeal of the Sun dance. At the time of the battle with Custer, the torn muscles of his back had hardly recovered from the laceration he had endured less than two weeks before. There were tales among the Sioux of personal combats with other Indians, credible enough as evidence that he had the rating of a warrior. Cowards did not earn that among the Sioux. . . .

Naturally, the chief argument has revolved about Sitting Bull's part in the Custer fight. As has been said, the completeness of the tragedy led the white critics and chroniclers to look for the master mind, the red Napoleon, who had planned and carried through the action. After it was over, two qualities of the Indian mind worked to obscure that particular issue, if in fact it ever was an issue. The first was the tendency of the warrior to boast of his prowess on the battlefield, to count his coups over again, and to sing the songs of his own courage.

Coupled with this was the discovery which the Indian had made previously, that there were times and circumstances in which it was the part of wisdom to find out in advance what it was that the white man wanted to be told and then to tell it to him. This combined agreeably with his tendency to claim all the credit possible, as soon as he learned that such a claim carried with it no special danger. Hence, Gall's gathering to himself of the major credit, although there were others beside Sitting Bull who were entitled to mention, notably Crazy Horse, the leader in the fight with Crook on the Rosebud, two weeks earlier, and the gloomy Two Moons, who probably led the Cheyennes into battle.

Sitting Bull was vague as to his part against Custer. Three years after the battle, he made a statement to a Canadian officer, Maj. L. E. F. Crozier, in which he told of putting his wife on his best pony when the fight began and setting his own war bonnet on her head. "I now put a flag on a pole and lifted it up high and in a loud voice I shouted out so as everyone could hear me, 'I am Sitting Bull, follow me.' And I rushed up to where I thought Custer was amongst the Americans." This can be set over against Gall's later charge that Sitting Bull was a coward and absented himself from the battle on the plea that he was making victory medicine. Gall repeated his charge to Sitting Bull's face. But that was when Gall was working to secure the return of the Sioux from Canada against Sitting Bull's sullen determination to stay off the soil of the United States unless he could tread it as a free Indian. . . .

The truth is that, in the attack on Custer, there was no generalship, as the whites understand generalship; there was leadership in the Indian sense, and in that, neither Sitting Bull nor Gall had a monopoly. And there were numbers and a wild thirst for blood. The men who rode in the van among the Indians were the warriors who had the fastest ponies. The actual fight was a horse race with death for the white troopers at the end of it.

This Scotch verdict of "not proven" leaves the important question untouched! Who brought so many Indians into the camp on the Little Big Horn in June, 1876—Hunkpapas, Oglallas, Minneconjous, Sans Arcs, Cheyennes, Santees, Yanktonnais, Blackfeet, for apparently there were some Blackfeet there? In the answer to this question, if anywhere, lies Sitting Bull's title to fame in the annals of the Sioux. There is a clear case for his long hatred of the whites and his irreconcilability. Eight years before, he had flung at Gall the most bitter epithet he could conceive, that of "agency Indian," the man who would sign anything for a square meal. In the sporadic warfare that began two years after the Treaty of Laramie was signed in 1868, Sitting Bull was blamed more often than any other Indian for the isolated killings and the raids on horse herds, white or Crow. The orders of December 6, 1875, requiring all Indians to be on reservations by January 31, under penalty of being considered hostile, made specific mention of "Sitting Bull's band and all other wild and lawless bands." It was from Sitting Bull that the message was sent to General Terry, when the army started to round up these "wild and lawless bands" and herd them back on the reservation: "You need not bring any guides; you can find me easily; I will not run away." The case is clear that Sitting Bull more than any other Sioux leader or spokesman—whether war chief, "Chief of all the Sioux," or "lying medicine-man," doesn't matter—kept alive the flame of Indian hatred and finally fanned it to a devouring blaze in the last burst.

What about the final preparations for the day of battle? What part did Sitting Bull play in these? Indian preparations for battle were usually of the simplest; they consisted of warriors ready to fight, of guns and ammunition—as much as they could buy or steal—of ponies, and of fighting spirit. The last was never hard to find among the Sioux, and Sitting Bull's missionary work had guaranteed that it should be at the highest pitch. Ponies were there in quantity sufficient; as long as the Crows and the white men had ponies, the Sioux were able to keep their caballo up to reasonable needs. In this, as in other things, Sitting Bull was able to impart instruction. His pictorial autobiography, which a thieving Yanktonnais had sold at Fort Buford in 1870 for $1.50 in trade, has twelve drawings depicting his exploits as a horse thief and J. F. Dunn, Jr., said of him: "He may fairly be considered one of the ablest horse thieves the country ever produced." That, in itself, was a distinction among the Sioux.

As to the guns and ammunition, there was a different story. In spite of [Major Marcus A.] Reno's complaint that the Indian guns outranged his cavalry carbines, there is abundant evidence that probably not more than half the Sioux in the battle had guns at all, and those were mostly old Spencers, Sharps, and Ballards. Guns and cartridges were expensive and the Sioux had never been great fur traders, outside of the traffic in buffalo skins, which were then plentiful and cheap. The Indians who lacked guns fought with war clubs and axes, lances, and even bows and arrows.

The great achievement of the Sioux was in bringing together a body of warriors greater than they had ever mustered before and greater than any of the white men knew, until it was too late. Custer was not the only officer to underestimate the number of Indians on the Little Big Horn. Terry, Gibbon, and Crook all made the same mistake, but it was a tragic error only for Custer. After the battle, the living averaged up their errors by overestimates. Whatever he did on the day of the fight, Sitting Bull deserves the credit for bringing this array of fighting power together. He did it both by direct effort and by the growing recognition of him among the restless as the consistent and unflinching bearer of the banner of revolt against the whites. That was his great work and, in the light of what his horde of warriors accomplished in one short hour, it matters very little whether he led in the fight or made medicine out in the hills.

There is a paragraph in the statement which Sitting Bull made to Major Crozier which bears all the earmarks of truth. In this Sitting Bull said he had word of Custer's coming and sent out twenty scouts to watch him. Five soon came back with word that the troops were on the way. A little later, ten more came in to report; two others returned still a little later. Three stayed to watch Custer until the morning of the day of the fight. This was regular Indian practice and accords with other facts, the apparent readiness with which the Indians rushed out to meet Reno, the swift placing of the Cheyennes in the ravine to the north of the fatal ridge, while Gall drove the cavalry before him from the ford of the river so that the doomed troopers were caught between the jaws of a savage nutcracker.

The presence of so many women and children in the camp has been cited as an indication that the Indians were surprised. Under ordinary circumstances this fact would be good circumstantial evidence, but not this time. There was no place of safety to which to send them in that harried country, with troops beginning to quarter the whole region like hounds after a fox. The only recourse was to keep the noncombatants in camp until the fighting began and then rush them away from the side of danger. And this was done.

There was one final aspect of the battle for which the Sioux could thank their reputation through the length and breadth of the plains. That was the poor scouting of the Crows and the Rees, who were presumed to be the eyes of Custer's troops. They were good enough scouts under normal circumstances, but not against the Sioux when those belligerent gentry were seriously on the warpath. The scouts knew them too well and probably guessed too well the numbers that might be in the field to risk letting many miles of prairie turf intervene between the troops and their own precious selves. Timid scouts naturally do poor scouting.

Little of value in an attempted analysis of Sitting Bull appears after the battle of the Little Big Horn. That was the Indian's great day and his last. Sitting Bull, more than any other man, brought them together for the trial of strength for which he had goaded their proud spirits, since 1868 at the latest. He had rallied around one idea the western and northern tribes whom he trusted and who knew him, leaving out of the list the eastern Sioux, who had been responsible for the Minnesota massacres of 1862, and whom he distrusted because they "mingled with white men and encouraged them westward."

After the battle, the Sioux scattered in smaller bands and drifted northward, sometimes skirmishing with troops, sometimes pursued by cavalry, but always slipping away and working farther north as the pressure behind them grew. . . .

As to Sitting Bull's sincerity, I have only a guess, and a divided one at that. He may have believed what he wanted to believe, as many other men have done. But he was distinctly a man with an idea and a relentless will, quite possibly the ablest man the Sioux produced, without the organizing ability of Pontiac or the patient endurance and the quiet day-and-night courage of Chief Joseph, the Nez Percé, but still a man of marked ability. His wars are done and his wild dreams laid by, with the other hopes of other Indian leaders. Whatever he was, in his wayward, sinuous, scheming mind, he held fast to his one idea to the end and with it he drew his people to him and sent them into battle. Perhaps the army man spoke the best summary and epitaph for him: "A darned smart Indian."

JOHN D. ROCKEFELLER

&

American Business

Americans in the late nineteenth century experienced the bewilderment of large-scale industrialism, as new technologies and new institutions raised both hopes and fears. Giant industries emerged out of a murderous competition to tap the continent's riches, and "captains of industry" towered above the struggle. These industrialists—Rockefeller, Swift, Armour, Carnegie, Harriman, Morgan, Guggenheim, and many more— added a novel and controversial dimension to the American gallery of heroes. Praise and censure came all at once. Praised for stabilizing industries, improving production and distribution, reducing prices, and making the nation powerful, these men also were censured as "robber barons" who sat astride the "narrows" of trade taking their unjustified toll; they were men who crushed competition and therefore (in the long run) efficiency, eroded the ethical values built over centuries of more limited economic activity, and secretly manipulated the market that shaped the lives and opportunities of others.

For a variety of reasons, John D. Rockefeller quickly became the prime target for the attack on big business. Rockefeller, born in 1839, came from sturdy German and Scottish stock; the oldest son, John spent his early years in upstate New York living on a farm. He later went to high school in Cleveland, Ohio, and attended a commercial school there at his father's insistence. By 1859 he had formed a partnership dealing in foodstuffs, such as grain, hay, and meats, and he capitalized on the Civil War economic boom. But his eye was on the new industry of oil refining, where he saw a future.

By 1865 Rockefeller operated the largest of thirty oil refineries in Cleveland. The growth of his company into the first and most complete monopoly in the nation came from an investment in three acres of land, shrewd borrowing, and careful selection of associates. By the age of thirty-eight he controlled the piping, refining, and marketing of all petroleum in the country. His group, Standard Oil, invented the trust mechanism, the first legal device used to give uniform direction to a host of companies. Standard Oil succeeded in forcing a competitive industry into a monopolistic mold: since oil producing did not require heavy investments of capital, the industry was at first full of small operators, whom Rockefeller's men could—and did—buy, beat, or badger into subservience.

Oil, then used principally in the form of kerosene for lighting purposes, was a product found in every home. Thus Rockefeller and his monopoly touched the life of everyone. In an age when Americans liked their public men fat and jolly looking, Rockefeller's lean and sharp look seemed somehow to symbolize the practices by which untried forms of business organization replaced the comfortable and familiar ones. The monstrous power of the new organizations finally brought government action against monopolies, but the various Standard Oil companies still kept tenuous alliances. In his later life Rockefeller spent much time in philanthropical activities, founding the University of Chicago in 1889, the Rockefeller Institute in 1902, and the Rockefeller Foundation in 1913. He died at age eighty-nine in 1937.

The criticism of big business continued and rapidly flowed into fixed channels. "Muckrakers" criticized the great industrialists for their resistance to public control, their hold on competition, and their un-ethical practices. Writers like Henry Demarest Lloyd in the 1890's, Ida Tarbell and Gustavus Myers in the progressive era, Matthew Josephson in the 1930's, and Charles M. Destler in the 1940's and 1950's applied the nation's traditional moral and political standards to the great American fortunes, only occasionally mixing their attacks with some variant of Marxism. They represented an antitrust tradition that has had not only an intellectual importance but also a practical one as well. The United States remains the only industrialized country whose government still pursues (fitfully to be sure) an antitrust policy.

The Robber Barons (1934)
MATTHEW JOSEPHSON

Matthew Josephson's The Robber Barons *brought the muckraking
tradition fully into historical scholarship, and his picture of the heroes
of American business deeply influenced a generation of scholars and
publicists. Josephson added some incidental Marxism to his critique of
men like Rockefeller, expressing it all with an irony that modern readers
appreciate. His account of the Gilded Age continues to fascinate
readers despite the many piecemeal corrections historians have made
of his views in the past decades.*

JOHN ROCKEFELLER, who grew up in western New York and later near
Cleveland, as one of a struggling family of five children, recalls with
satisfaction the excellent practical training he had received and how
quickly he put it to use. His childhood seemed to have been darkened by
the misdeeds of his father, a wandering vendor of quack medicines who
rarely supported his family, and was sometimes a fugitive from the law;
yet the son invariably spoke of his parent's instructions with gratitude.
He said:

> . . . He himself trained me in practical ways. He was engaged in
> different enterprises; he used to tell me about these things . . . and he
> taught me the principles and methods of business. . . . I knew what
> a cord of good solid beech and maple wood was. My father told me to
> select only solid wood . . . and not to put any limbs in it or any
> punky wood. That was a good training for me.

But the elder Rockefeller went further than this in his sage instructions,
according to John T. Flynn [an early biographer], who attributes to him
the statement:

> I cheat my boys every chance I get, I want to make 'em sharp. I trade
> with the boys and skin 'em and I just beat 'em every time I can. I want
> to make 'em sharp.

If at times the young Rockefeller absorbed a certain shiftiness and
trading sharpness from his restless father, it was also true that his father
was absent so often and so long as to cast shame and poverty upon his
home. Thus he must have been subject far more often to the stern super-

vision of his mother, whom he has recalled in several stories. His mother would punish him, as he related, with a birch switch to "uphold the standard of the family when it showed a tendency to deteriorate." Once when she found out that she was punishing him for a misdeed at school of which he was innocent, she said, "Never mind, we have started in on this whipping and it will do for the next time." The normal outcome of such disciplinary cruelty would be deception and stealthiness in the boy, as a defense.

But his mother, who reared her children with the rigid piety of an Evangelist, also started him in his first business enterprise. When he was seven years old she encouraged him to raise turkeys, and gave him for this purpose the family's surplus milk curds. There are legends of Rockefeller as a boy stalking a turkey with the most patient stealth in order to seize her eggs.

This harshly disciplined boy, quiet, shy, reserved, serious, received but a few years' poor schooling, and worked for neighboring farmers in all his spare time. His whole youth suggests only abstinence, prudence and the growth of parsimony in his soul. The pennies he earned he would save steadily in a blue bowl that stood on a chest in his room, and accumulated until there was a small heap of gold coins. He would work, by his own account, hoeing potatoes for a neighboring farmer from morning to night for 37 cents a day. At a time when he was still very young he had fifty dollars saved, which upon invitation he one day loaned to the farmer who employed him.

"And as I was saving those little sums," he relates, "I soon learned that I could get as much interest for $50 loaned at seven per cent—then the legal rate of interest—as I could earn by digging potatoes for ten days." Thereafter, he tells us, he resolved that it was better "to let the money be my slave than to be the slave of money."

In Cleveland whither the family removed in 1854, Rockefeller went to the Central High School and studied bookkeeping for a year. This delighted him. Most of the conquering types in the coming order were to be men trained early in life in the calculations of the bookkeeper, Cooke, Huntington, Gould, Henry Frick and especially Rockefeller of whom it was said afterward: "He had the soul of a bookkeeper."

In his first position as bookkeeper to a produce merchant at the Cleveland docks, when he was sixteen, he distinguished himself by his composed orderly habits. Very carefully he examined each item on each bill before he approved it for payment. Out of a salary which began at $15 a month and advanced ultimately to $50 a month, he saved $800 in three years, the lion's share of his total earnings! This was fantastic parsimony.

He spent little money for clothing, though he was always neat; he never went to the theater, had no amusements and few friends. But he attended his Baptist Church in Cleveland as devoutly as he attended his accounts. And to the cause of the church alone, to its parish fund and mission funds, he demonstrated his only generosity by gifts that were large for him then—first of ten cents, then later of twenty-five cents at a time.

In the young Rockefeller the traits which his mother had bred in him, of piety and the economic virtue—worship of the "lean goddess of Abstinence"—were of one cloth. The pale, bony, small-eyed young Baptist served the Lord and pursued his own business unremittingly. His composed manner, which had a certain languor, hid a feverish calculation, a sleepy strength, cruel, intense, terribly alert.

As a schoolboy John Rockefeller had once announced to a companion, as they walked by a rich man's ample house along their way: "When I grow up I want to be worth $100,000. And I'm going to be too." In almost the same words, Rockefeller in Cleveland, Cooke in Philadelphia, Carnegie in Pittsburgh, or a James Hill in the Northwestern frontier could be found voicing the same hope. And Rockefeller, the bookkeeper, "not slothful in business . . . serving the Lord," as John T. Flynn describes him, watched his chances closely, learned every detail of the produce business which engaged him, until finally in 1858 he made bold to open a business of his own in partnership with a young Englishman named Clark (who was destined to be left far behind). Rockefeller's grimly accumulated savings of $800, in addition to a loan from his father at the usurious rate of 10 per cent, yielded the capital which launched him, and he was soon "gathering gear" quietly. He knew the art of using loan credit to expand his operations. His first bank loan against warehouse receipts gave him a thrill of pleasure. He now bought grain and produce of all kinds in carload lots rather than in small consignments. Prosperous, he said nothing, but began to dress his part, wearing a high silk hat, frock coat and striped trousers like other merchants of the time. His head was handsome, his eyes small, birdlike; on his pale bony cheeks were the proverbial side-whiskers, reddish in color.

At night, in his room, he read the Bible, and retiring had the queer habit of talking to his pillow about his business adventures. In his autobiography he says that "these intimate conversations with myself had a great influence upon my life." He told himself "not to get puffed up with any foolish notions" and never to be deceived about actual conditions. "Look out or you will lose your head—go steady."

He was given to secrecy; he loathed all display. When he married, a few years afterward, he lost not a day from his business. His wife, Laura Spelman, proved an excellent mate. She encouraged his furtiveness, he relates, advising him always to be silent, to say as little as possible. His composure, his self-possession was excessive. Those Clevelanders to whom Miss Ida Tarbell addressed herself in her investigations of Rockefeller, told her that he was a hard man to best in a trade, that he rarely smiled, and almost never laughed, save when he struck a good bargain. Then he might clap his hands with delight, or he might even, if the occasion warranted, throw up his hat, kick his heels and hug his informer. One time he was so overjoyed at a favorable piece of news that he burst out: "I'm bound to be rich! *Bound to be rich!*" . . .

In the life of every conquering soul there is a "turning point," a moment when a deep understanding of the self coincides with an equally deep sense of one's immediate mission in the tangible world. For Rockefeller, brooding, secretive, uneasily scenting his fortune, this moment came but a few years after his entrance into the oil trade, and at the age of thirty. He had looked upon the disorganized conditions of the Pennsylvania oil fields, the only source then known, and found them not good: the guerilla fighting of drillers, of refining firms, of rival railroad lines, the mercurial changes in supply and market value—very alarming in 1870— offended his orderly and methodical spirit. But one could see that petroleum was to be the light of the world. From the source, from the chaotic oil fields where thousands of drillers toiled, the grimy stream of the precious commodity, petroleum, flowed along many diverse channels to narrow into the hands of several hundred refineries, then to issue once more in a continuous stream to consumers throughout the world. Owner with [Henry] Flagler and [Stephen] Harkness of the largest refining company in the country, Rockefeller had a strongly entrenched position at the narrows of this stream. Now what if the Standard Oil Company should by further steps of organization possess itself wholly of the narrows? In this period of anarchic individual competition, the idea of such a movement of rationalization must have come to Rockefeller forcibly, as it had recently come to others.

Even as early as 1868 the first plan of industrial combination in the shape of the pool had been originated in the Michigan Salt Association. Desiring to correct chaotic market conditions, declaring that "in union there is strength," the salt-producers of Saginaw Bay had banded together to control the output and sale of nearly all the salt in their region, a large part of the vital national supply. Secret agreements had been executed for each year, allotting the sales and fixing the price at almost twice what it had been immediately prior to the appearance of the pool. And though the inevitable greed and self-seeking of the individual salt-producers had tended to weaken the pool, the new economic invention was launched in its infantile form. Rockefeller's partners, Flagler and Harkness, had themselves participated in the historic Michigan Salt Association.

This grand idea of industrial rationalization owed its swift, ruthless, methodical execution no doubt to the firmness of character we sense in Rockefeller, who had the temper of a great, unconscionable military captain, combining audacity with thoroughness and shrewd judgment. His plan seemed to take account of no one's feelings in the matter. Indeed there was something revolutionary in it; it seemed to fly in the face of human liberties and deep-rooted custom and common law. The notorious

"South Improvement Company," with its strange charter, ingeniously in-
strumenting the scheme of combination, was to be unraveled amid profound secrecy. By conspiring with the railroads (which also hungered for
economic order), it would be terribly armed with the power of the freight
rebate which garrotted all opposition systematically. This plan of combination, this unifying conception Rockefeller took as his ruling idea; he
breathed life into it, clung to it grimly in the face of the most menacing
attacks of legislatures, courts, rival captains, and, at moments, even of
rebellious mobs. His view of men and events justified him, and despite
many official and innocent denials, he is believed to have said once in
confidence, as Flynn relates:

> I had our plan clearly in mind. It was right. I knew it as a matter of
> conscience. It was right between me and God. If I had to do it
> tomorrow I would do it again in the same way—do it a hundred times.

The broad purpose was to control and direct the flow of crude petroleum
into the hands of a narrowed group of refiners. The refiners would be
supported by the combined railroad trunk lines which shipped the oil;
while the producers' phase of the stream would be left unorganized—*but
with power over their outlet to market* henceforth to be concentrated into
the few hands of the refiners. . . .

In John D. Rockefeller, economists and historians have often seen the
classic example of the modern monopolist of industry. It is true that he
worked with an indomitable will, and a faith in his star à la Napoleon, to
organize his industry under his own dictatorship. He was moreover a
great innovator. Though not the first to attempt the plan of the pool—
there were pools even in the time of Cicero—his South Improvement
Company was the most impressive instance in history of such an organism.
But when others had reached the stage of the pool, he was building the
solid framework of a monopoly.

Rockefeller's problems were far more difficult than those for instance of
Carnegie, who quickly won special economies through constructing a very
costly, well-integrated, technically superior plant upon a favored site.
In the oil-refining business, a small still could be thrown up in the '70's
for manufacturing kerosene or lubricating oil at a tenth the cost of the Edgar
Thompson steel works. The petroleum market was mercurial compared to
iron, steel and even coal; there were thousands of petty capitalists competing for advantage in it. Hence the tactics of Rockefeller, the bold
architecture of the industrial edifice he reared, have always aroused the
liveliest interest, and he himself appeals to us for many reasons as the
greatest of the American industrialists. In no small degree this interest is
owing to the legend of "Machiavellian" guile and relentlessness which has
always clung to this prince of oil.

After the dissolution of the South Improvement Company, Rockefeller and Flagler had come to a conference of the irate diggers of petroleum with mild proposals of peaceful cooperation, under the heading of the "Pittsburgh Plan." The two elements in the trade, those who produced the raw material from the earth and those who refined it, were to combine forces harmoniously. "You misunderstand us," Rockefeller and Flagler said. "Let us see what combination will do."

There was much suspicion. One of Titusville's independent refiners (one of those whom Standard Oil tried to erase from the scene) made a rather warlike speech against the plan, and he recalls that Rockefeller, who had been softly swinging back and forth in a rocking chair, his hands over his face, through the conference, suddenly stopped rocking, lowered his hands and looked straight at his enemy. His glance was fairly terrifying.

> You never saw such eyes. He took me all in, saw just how much fight he could expect from me, and then up went his hands and back and forth went his chair. . . .

Where a "deal" across the table could not be effected, Rockefeller might try a variety of methods of expropriation. With his measured spirit, with his organized might, he tested men and things. There were men and women of all sorts who passed under his implacable rod, and their tale, gathered together reverently by Miss Tarbell, has contributed to the legend of the "white devil" who came to rule over American industry.

A certain widow, a Mrs. Backus of Cleveland, who had inherited an oil-refinery, had appealed to Mr. Rockefeller to preserve her, "the mother of fatherless children." And he had promised "with tears in his eyes that he would stand by her." But in the end he offered her only $79,000 for a property which had cost $200,000. The whole story of the defenseless widow and her orphans, the stern command, the confiscation of two-thirds of her property, when it came out made a deep stir and moved many hearts.

In another instance a manufacturer of improved lubricating oils set himself up innocently in Cleveland, and became a client of the Standard Oil for his whole supply of residuum oils. The Rockefeller company encouraged him at first, and sold him 85 barrels a day according to a contract. He prospered for three years, then suddenly when the monopoly was well launched in 1874, his supply was cut down to 12 barrels a day, the price was increased on some pretense, and the shipping cost over the railroads similarly increased. It became impossible to supply his trade. He offered to buy of Rockefeller 5,000 barrels and store it so that he might assure himself of a future supply. This was refused.

> "I saw readily what that meant," the man Morehouse related to the Hepburn Committee in 1879. "That meant squeeze you out—Buy out your works. . . . They paid $15,000 for what cost me $41,000. He [Rockefeller] said that he had facilities for freighting and that the coal-

oil business belonged to them; and any concern that would start in that business, they had sufficient money to lay aside a fund and wipe them out—these are the words."

In the field of retail distribution, Rockefeller sought to create a great marketing machine delivering directly from the Standard Oil's tank wagons to stores in towns and villages throughout the United States. But in the laudable endeavor to wipe out wasteful wholesalers or middlemen, he would meet with resistance again, as in the producing fields. Where unexpectedly stout resistance from competing marketing agencies was met, the Standard Oil would simply apply harsher weapons. To cut off the supplies of the rebel dealer, the secret aid of the railroads and the espionage of their freight agents would be invoked again and again. A message such as the following would pass between Standard Oil officials:

> We are glad to know you are on such good terms with the railroad people that Mr. Clem [handling *independent* oil] gains nothing by marking his shipments by numbers instead of by names.

Or again:

> Wilkerson and Company received car of oil Monday 13th—70 barrels which we suspect slipped through at the usual fifth class rate—in fact we might say we knew it did—paying only $41.50 freight from here. Charges $57.40. Please turn another screw.

The process of "Turning the Screw" has been well described by Henry D. Lloyd. One example is that of a merchant in Nashville, Tennessee, who refused to come to terms and buy from Standard Oil; he first found that all his shipments were reported secretly to the enemy; then by a mysterious coincidence his freight rates on shipments of all kinds were raised 50 per cent, then doubled, even tripled, and he felt himself under fire from all parts of the field. He attempted to move his merchandise by a great roundabout route, using the Baltimore & Ohio and several other connecting roads, but was soon "tracked down," his shipments lost, spoiled. The documents show that the independent oil-dealers' clients were menaced in every way by the Standard Oil marketing agency; it threatened to open competing grocery stores, to sell oats, meat, sugar, coffee at lower prices. "If you do not buy our oil we will start a grocery store and sell goods at cost and put you out of business."

By this means, opponents in the country at large were soon "mopped up"; small refiners and small wholesalers who attempted to exploit a given district were routed at the appearance of the familiar red-and-green tank wagons, which were equal to charging drastically reduced rates for oil in one town, and twice as much in an adjacent town where the nuisance of competition no longer existed. There were, to be sure, embittered protests from the victims, but the marketing methods of Standard Oil were magnificiently efficient and centralized; waste and delay were overcome; immense savings were brought directly to the refining monopoly.

But where the Standard Oil could not carry on its expansion by peaceful means, it was ready with violence; its faithful servants knew even how to apply the modern weapon of dynamite.

In Buffalo, the Vacuum Oil Company, one of the "dummy" creatures of the Standard Oil system, became disturbed one day by the advent of a vigorous competitor who built a sizable refinery and located it favorably upon the water front. The offices of Vacuum conducted at first a furtive campaign of intimidation. Then emboldened or more desperate, they approached the chief mechanic of the enemy refinery, holding whispered conferences with him in a rowboat on Lake Erie. He was asked to "do something." He was urged to "go back to Buffalo and construct the machinery so it would bust up . . . or smash up," to fix the pipes and stills "so they cannot make a good oil. . . . And then if you would give them a little scare, they not knowing anything about the business. You know how. . . ." In return the foreman would have a life annuity which he might enjoy in another part of the country.

So in due time a small explosion took place in the independent plant, as Lloyd and Miss Tarbell tell the tale, from the records of the trial held several years later, in 1887. The mechanic, though on the payrolls of the Vacuum Oil Company, led a cursed existence, forever wandering without home or country, until in complete hysteria he returned to make a clean breast of the whole affair. The criminal suit against high officials of the Standard Oil monopoly included Henry Rogers and John Archbold, but the evil was laid by them to the "overenthusiasm" of underlings. Evidence of conspiracy was not found by the court, but heavy damages were awarded to the plaintiff, who thereafter plainly dreaded to re-enter the dangerous business. . . .

The campaigns for consolidation, once launched, permitted Rockefeller little rest, and engaged his generalship on many fronts at once. In a curious interview given while he was in Europe, cited by Flynn, he himself exclaimed:

How often I had not an unbroken night's sleep, worrying about how it was all coming out. . . . Work by day and worry by night, week in and week out, month after month. If I had foreseen the future I doubt whether I would have had the courage to go on.

With unblinking vigilance he conducted throughout his company an eternal war against waste. We have spoken of his unequaled efficiency and power of organization. There is a famous note to his barrel factory in his careful bookkeeper's hand which has been cited with amused contempt by his critics, to show how attention to small details absorbed his soul. It reads:

Last month you reported on hand, 1,119 bungs. 10,000 were sent you
beginning this month. You have used 9,527 this month. You report
1,092 on hand. What has become of the other 500?

It is not a laughing matter, this affair of 500 barrel bungs, worth at the
most a dollar or two in all. Rockefeller's hatred of waste told him that in
a large-scale industry the rescued pennies multiplied a million times or
more represented enormous potential gains. This was to be true of all
the great industrial leaders after Rockefeller's time; the spirit regarded as
parsimony is a large-visioned conception of technical efficiency in handling
big machines. Thus the feeding of horses, the making of his own glue,
hoops, barrels, all was carefully supervised and constantly reduced in cost.
Barrels were cut $1.25 apiece, saving $4,000,000 a year, cans were reduced 15 cents, saving $5,000,000 a year, and so forth. In absorbing the
services of J. J. Vandergrift, in 1872, Rockefeller had acquired as an ally
to his enterprise a combination of small pipe lines called the United Pipe
Lines. His lieutenants then constructed more pipes; and by 1876 he controlled almost half the existing pipe lines, some running 80 to 100 miles,
to the railroad terminals and shipping points. At this time the largest pipe-
line interest in competition with Standard Oil's was the Empire Transportation Company, headed by Colonel Joseph Potts, but dominated by the
officers of the Pennsylvania Railroad, which held an option over the entire
property.
    Himself an aggressive entrepreneur, Potts soon found that he must ex-
pand or suffer extinction. To the alarm of the Rockefeller organization, he
purchased several big refineries in New York and proceeded to pipe crude
oil from the oil fields and over the railroad to the seaboard. Rockefeller
vehemently petitioned the railroad to withdraw from his domain. Refused
at an interview, he promised that he would take his own measures, and
left his adversaries with expressions of sanctimonious regret, the form in
which his most deadly threats were usually offered.
    It was war, a war of rates. He moved with lightning speed. At once the
other railroads, Erie and New York Central, were ordered to stand by,
lowering their freight rates for him while he slashed the price of refined oil
in every market which Potts reached.
    But Potts, a stubborn Presbyterian, fought back harder than anyone
Rockefeller had ever encountered. He replied in kind by further price cuts;
he then began to build larger refineries at the coast ports, lined up independent oil-producers behind him, and reserves in quantities of tank cars,
in barges, ships, dock facilities. During the bitter conflict, with which, as
Flynn relates, the hills and fields of Pennsylvania resounded, both sides,
and the railroads supporting them as well, suffered heavy wounds. Yet
Rockefeller would not desist, since Standard Oil's whole system of organization was endangered.
    In the midst of this furious engagement a great blow fell upon the ene-

mies of John D. Rockefeller, as if given by the hand of the God to whom he constantly prayed. During the summer of 1877 the workers of the Baltimore & Ohio Railroad struck against wage cuts and their strike spread quickly to adjacent railroads, raging with especial violence in the Pennsylvania system. The most destructive labor war the nation had ever known was now seen in Baltimore and Pittsburgh, with militant mobs fighting armed troops and setting in flames property of great value in revenge for the many deaths they suffered. During this storm which the railroad barons had sown by cutting wages 20 per cent and doubling the length of freight trains, the Pennsylvania interests quickly came to terms with Standard Oil, so that they might be free to turn and crush the rebellious workers. The entire business of Empire Transportation was sold out to the oil combination at their own terms, while Potts was called off. In Philadelphia, Rockefeller and his partners, quietly jubilant, received the sword of the weeping Potts.

The oil industry as a whole was impressed with the victory of Standard Oil over a railroad ring which had seemed invincible in the past. In a movement of fear many other interests hastened to make terms with Rockefeller. By the end of 1878 he controlled all the existing pipe-line systems; through a new freight pool he directed traffic or quantities of supplies to the various regions or cities as he pleased.

By 1876 this industry had assumed tremendous proportions. Of the annual output of nearly 10,000,000 barrels, the Standard Oil Company controlled approximately 80 per cent, while exports of petroleum products to the value of $32,000,000 passed through their hands. But in 1877 the great Bradford oil field was opened with a wild boom, the uproarious coal-oil scenes of '59 were enacted anew, crowds rushed to the new fields, acreage values boomed, oil gushed out in an uncontrollable flood—half again as much oil as existed before came forth almost overnight. The markets grew demoralized again, just when Rockefeller seemed to have completed his conquest of the old Oil Regions.

What was he to do? In the two years that followed he directed his organization at the high tension of an ordnance department in wartime, so that piping, refining and marketing capacity might be expanded in time, and the almost untenable supply handled without faltering. With utmost energy a huge building program was carried on and further millions were staked on the hazardous business. Then, holding down the unruly producers, he imposed harsh terms through his pipe lines, refusing storage, forcing them to sell the oil they drilled "for immediate shipment" at the depressed prices of 64 to 69 cents a barrel, or have it run into the ground.

The overproduction could not be stopped. The oil men raged at the great machine which held them in bonds. Once more the independents gathered all their forces together to form a protective combination of their own. They founded the Parliament of Petroleum. They raised funds to construct an immense "free" pipe line running over the mountains to the seaboard, and ridding them at last of the railroads which hemmed them in. The new Tidewater Pipe Line would break Standard's control over railroad rates and bring crude oil to the sea.

Rockefeller's agents now lobbied in the state legislature of Pennsylvania to have the proposed pipe line banned. Failing of this his emissaries were thrown out over the state to buy up right of way in the path of the enemy's advance. But the Tidewater's engineers moved with equal speed and secrecy, eluded the defenses which Rockefeller threw in their way and by April, 1879, completed their difficult project.

From successive stations, the great pumps were to drive oil over the very top of the Alleghenies, and down to Williamsport, touching the Reading Railroad, which had joined forces with the independents. Amid picturesque celebration—while the spies of the Standard Oil looked on incredulously—the valves were opened, the oil ran over the mountain and down toward the sea! Rockefeller was checkmated—but to whom would the producers and their free pipe line sell the crude oil at the seaboard? They had no inkling, though they berated him, of the extent of his control at the outlet.

The opposition to the Rockefeller "conspiracy" now rose to its climax of enthusiasm. The hundreds of petty oil men who fought to remain "independent" and keep their sacred right to flood the market or "hold up" consumers at their own pleasure, won sympathy everywhere; and with the aid of local politicians in New York and Pennsylvania they also had their day in court. Their tumult had grown so violent that at long last the lawmakers of Pennsylvania moved to prosecute the monopolists for "conspiracy in restraint of trade." Writs were served and on April 29, 1879, a local Grand Jury indicted John D. Rockefeller, William Rockefeller, J. A. Bostwick, Henry Flagler, Daniel O'Day, J. J. Vandergrift and other chieftains of Standard Oil for criminal conspiracy, to "secure a monopoly of the oil industry, to oppress other refiners, to injure the carrying trade, to extort unreasonable railroad rates, to fraudulently control prices," etc. Simultaneously in New York State, the legislature appointed a committee of investigation of railroads, headed by the young lawyer A. Barton Hepburn. Forced to look at all the facts which were brought out by the Hepburn Committee, the nation was shocked. The railroad interests, as arch-conspirators, were at once under heavy fire. But no one understood the scope and meaning of the new phase reached in industrial life at this stage, save perhaps Mr. Chauncey Depew, who in a moment of illumination exclaimed on behalf of the railroad interests he so gallantly championed: "Every manufacturer in the state of New York existed by violence and lived by discrimination. . . . By secret rates and by deceiving their competitors as to what their rates were and by evading all laws of trade these manufacturers exist." This was God's truth and certainly true of all the other states in the Union. And of course under the prevailing circumstances there was nothing to be done, save recommend certain "regulative" laws.

With Rockefeller, there had arisen the great industrial combination in colossal and "sinister" form; he was the mighty bourgeois who was to expropriate all the petty bourgeois and his name was to be the rallying cry of parties and uprisings. The outlook for monopoly seemed dark, yet the trial, in the name of a democratic sovereignty which held "sacred" the property of the "conspirators," whatever the means by which they may have pre-empted or confiscated such property—was to be simply a comedy, and was to be enacted again and again. Before the bar of justice, Rockefeller and his brilliant lieutenants would appear, saying, "I refuse to answer on the advice of counsel." A Henry Rogers, a Flagler, would use every shift which such philosophers of the law as Joseph Choate or Samuel C. T. Dodd might counsel. They would "refuse to incriminate themselves" or evade reply on a point of technicality, or lie point-blank. Or, as in the case of the terribly cynical Archbold, they would simply jest, they would make mock of their bewildered prosecutors.

It was Rockefeller who made the most profound impression upon the public. He seemed distinguished in person; with his tall stooping figure, his long well-shaped head, his even jaw. His long, fine nose, his small birdlike eyes set wide apart, with the narrowed lids drooping a little, and the innumerable tiny wrinkles, made up a remarkable physiognomy. But his mouth was a slit, like a shark's. Rockefeller, impeccably dressed and groomed, thoroughly composed, pretendedly anxious to please, foiled his accusers with ease. Every legal subterfuge was used by him with supreme skill. Certain of his denials were legally truthful, as Flynn points out, since stock-ownership concerning which he was questioned was often entrusted temporarily (in time for such trials) to mere clerks or bookkeepers in his employ.

But the moment came when he was asked specifically about his connection with the notorious refiners' pool of 1872.

"Was there a Southern Improvement Company?"

"I have heard of such a company."

"Were you not in it?"

"I was not."

His hearers were amazed at the apparent perjury he made point-blank with even voice and an inscrutable movement of the eyes. But no! He had been only a director of the *South Improvement Company,* and not of the "Southern Improvement Company," as the prosecutor had named it by mistake.

If Rockefeller was embittered by the cruel fame he won, he never showed it. The silence he preserved toward all reproaches or questions may have been a matter of clever policy; yet it suggested at bottom a supreme contempt for his critics and accusers alike.

Some Experiences in the Oil Business (1909)
JOHN D. ROCKEFELLER

*Rockefeller's own words come second, not first in this account because
he wrote them to "shed light on matters that have been somewhat
discussed." How much of the writing was his own is hard to say, for
Rockefeller had a literary "assistant," Starr J. Murphy, and the book was
partly a concerted effort to improve Standard Oil's public relations. Yet
it is an effective work in many ways, and it communicates, for good or ill,
much of old John D.'s personality.*

THE STORY of the early history of the oil trade is too well known to bear
repeating in detail. The cleansing of crude petroleum was a simple and easy
process, and at first the profits were very large. Naturally, all sorts of people
went into it: the butcher, the baker, and the candlestick-maker began to
refine oil, and it was only a short time before more of the finished product
was put on the market than could possibly be consumed. The price went
down and down until the trade was threatened with ruin. It seemed absolutely necessary to extend the market for oil by exporting to foreign countries, which required a long and most difficult development; and also to
greatly improve the processes of refining so that oil could be made and sold
cheaply, yet with a profit, and to use as by-products all of the materials
which in the less-efficient plants were lost or thrown away.

These were the problems which confronted us almost at the outset, and
this great depression led to consultations with our neighbors and friends in
the business in the effort to bring some order out of what was rapidly
becoming a state of chaos. To accomplish all these tasks of enlarging the
market and improving the methods of manufacture in a large way was
beyond the power or ability of any concern as then constituted. It could
only be done, we reasoned, by increasing our capital and availing ourselves
of the best talent and experience.

It was with this idea that we proceeded to buy the largest and best refining concerns and centralize the administration of them with a view to securing greater economy and efficiency. The business grew faster than we had
anticipated.

This enterprise, conducted by men of application and ability working
hard together, soon built up unusual facilities in manufacture, in transportation, in finance, and in extending markets. We had our troubles and set-
backs; we suffered from some severe fires; and the supply of crude oil was
most uncertain. Our plans were constantly changed by changed conditions.

We developed great facilities in an oil centre, erected storage tanks, and connected pipe-lines; then the oil failed and our work was thrown away. At best it was a speculative trade, and I wonder that we managed to pull through so often; but we were gradually learning how to conduct a most difficult business.

Foreign Markets

Several years ago, when asked how our business grew to such large proportions, I explained that our first organization was a partnership and afterward a corporation in Ohio. That was sufficient for a local refining business. But, had we been dependent solely upon local business, we should have failed long since. We were forced to extend our markets into every part of the world. This made the seaboard cities a necessary place of business, and we soon discovered that manufacturing for export could be more economically carried on there; hence refineries were established at Brooklyn, at Bayonne, at Philadelphia, at Baltimore, and necessary corporations were organized in the different states.

We soon discovered, as the business grew, that the primary method of transporting oil in barrels could not last. The package often cost more than the contents, and the forests of the country were not sufficient to supply cheaply the necessary material for an extended time. Hence we devoted attention to other methods of transportation, adopted the pipe-line system, and found capital for pipe-line construction equal to the necessities of the business.

To operate pipe-lines required franchises from the states in which they were located—and consequently corporations in those states—just as railroads running through different states are forced to operate under separate state charters. To perfect the pipe-line system of transportation required many millions of capital. The entire oil business is dependent upon the pipe-line. Without it every well would be less valuable and every refinery at home and abroad would be more difficult to serve or retain, because of the additional cost to the consumer. The expansion of the whole industry would have been retarded without this method of transportation.

Then the pipe-line system required other improvements, such as tank-cars upon railroads, and finally the tank-steamer. Capital had to be furnished for them and corporations created to own and operate them.

Every one of the steps taken was necessary if the business was to be properly developed, and only through such successive steps and by a great aggregation of capital is America today enabled to utilize the bounty which its land pours forth, and to furnish the world with light.

The Start of the Standard Oil Company

In the year 1867 the firms of William Rockefeller & Co., Rockefeller & Andrews, Rockefeller & Co., and S. V. Harkness and H. M. Flagler united in forming the firm of Rockefeller, Andrews & Flagler.

The cause leading to the formation of this firm was the desire to unite our skill and capital in order to carry on a business of greater magnitude with economy and efficiency in place of the smaller business that each had heretofore conducted separately. As time went on and the possibilities became apparent, we found further capital to be necessary; then we interested others and organized the Standard Oil Company, with a capital of $1,000,000. Later we saw that more money could be utilized, found persons who were willing to invest with us, and increased our capital to $2,500,000, in 1872, and afterward in 1874 to $3,500,000. As the business grew, and markets were obtained at home and abroad, more persons and capital were added to the business, and new corporate agencies were obtained or organized, the object being always the same—to extend our operations by furnishing the best and cheapest products.

I ascribe the success of the Standard Oil Company to its consistent policy of making the volume of its business large through the merit and cheapness of its products. It has spared no expense in utilizing the best and most efficient method of manufacture. It has sought for the best superintendents and workmen and paid the best wages. It has not hesitated to sacrifice old machinery and old plants for new and better ones. It has placed its manufactories at the points where they could supply markets at the least expense. It has not only sought markets for its principal products, but for all possible by-products, sparing no expense in introducing them to the public in every nook and corner of the world. It has not hesitated to invest millions of dollars in methods for cheapening the gathering and distribution of oils by pipe-lines, special cars, tank-steamers, and tank-wagons. It has erected tank-stations at railroad centres in every part of the country to cheapen the storage and delivery of oil. It has had faith in American oil and has brought together vast sums of money for the purpose of making it what it is, and for holding its market against the competition of Russia and all the countries which are producers of oil and competitors against American products.

The Insurance Plans

Here is an example of one of the ways in which we achieved certain economies and gained real advantage. Fires are always to be reckoned with in oil refining and storage, as we learned by dear experience, but in having our plants distributed all over the country the unit of risk and possible loss was minimized. No one fire could ruin us, and we were able thus to establish a system of insuring ourselves. Our reserve fund which provided for this insurance could not be wiped out all at once, as might be the case with a concern having its plants together or near each other. Then we studied and perfected our organization to prevent fires, improving our appliances and plans year after year until the profit on this insurance feature became a very considerable item in the Standard earnings.

It can easily be seen that this saving in insurance and minimizing the loss by fire affected the profits, not only in refining, but touched many other associated enterprises: the manufacture of by-products, the tanks and steamers, the pumping-stations, etc.

We devoted ourselves exclusively to the oil business and its products. The company never went into outside ventures, but kept to the enormous task of perfecting its own organization. We educated our own men; we trained many of them from boyhood; we strove to keep them loyal by providing them full scope for their ability; they were given opportunities to buy stock, and the company itself helped them to finance their purchases. Not only here in America, but all over the world, our young men were given chances to advance themselves, and the sons of the old partners were welcomed to the councils and responsibilities of the administration. I may say that the company has been in all its history, and I am sure it is at present, a most happy association of busy people. . . .

A Normal Growth

Study for a moment the result of what has been a natural and absolutely normal increase in the value of the company's possessions. Many of the pipe-lines were constructed during a period when costs were about 50 per cent. of what they are now. Great fields of oil lands were purchased as virgin soil, which later yielded an immense output. Quantities of low-grade crude oil which had been bought by the company when it was believed to be of little value, but which the company hoped eventually to utilize, were greatly increased in value by inventions for refining it and for using the residues formerly considered almost worthless. Dock property was secured at low prices and made valuable by buildings and development. Large unimproved tracts of land near the important business centres were acquired. We brought our industries to these places, made the land useful, and increased the value, not only of our own property, but of the land adjacent to it to many times the original worth. Wherever we have established businesses in this and other countries we have bought largely of property. I remember a case where we paid only $1,000 or so an acre for some rough land to be used for such purposes, and, through the improvements we created, the value has gone up 40 or 50 times as much in 35 or 40 years.

Others have had similar increases in the value of their properties, but have enlarged their capitalization correspondingly. They have escaped the criticism which has been directed against us, who with our old fashioned and conservative notions have continued without such expansion of capitalization.

There is nothing strange or miraculous in all this; it was all done through this natural law of trade development. It is what the Astors and many other large landholders did.

If a man starts in business with $1,000 capital and gradually increases his property and investment by retaining in his concern much of his earn-

ings, instead of spending them, and thus accumulates values until his investment is, say, $10,000, it would be folly to base the percentage of his actual
profits only on the original $1,000 with which he started. Here, again, I
think the managers of the Standard should be praised, and not blamed.
They have set an example for upbuilding on the most conservative lines,
and in a business which has always been, to say the least, hazardous, and
to a large degree unavoidably speculative. Yet no one who has relied upon
the ownership of this stock to pay a yearly income has been disappointed,
and the stock is held by an increasing number of small holders the country
over. . . .

Character the Essential Thing

In speaking of the real beginning of the Standard Oil Company, it should
be remembered that it was not so much the consolidation of the firms in
which we had a personal interest, but the coming together of the men who
had the combined brain power to do the work, which was the actual starting-
point. Perhaps it is worth while to emphasize again the fact that it is not
merely capital and "plants" and the strictly material things which make up
a business, but the character of the men behind these things, their personalities, and their abilities; these are the essentials to be reckoned with. . . .

The Question of Rebates

Of all the subjects which seem to have attracted the attention of the public
to the affairs of the Standard Oil Company, the matter of rebates from
railroads has perhaps been uppermost. The Standard Oil Company of
Ohio, of which I was president, did receive rebates from the railroads prior
to 1880, but received no advantages for which it did not give full com-
pensation. The reason for rebates was that such was the railroads' method
of business. A public rate was made and collected by the railroad companies, but, so far as my knowledge extends, was seldom retained in full;
a portion of it was repaid to the shippers as a rebate. By this method the
real rate of freight which any shipper paid was not known by his competitors nor by other railroad companies, the amount being a matter of
bargain with the carrying company. Each shipper made the best bargain
that he could, but whether he was doing better than his competitor was
only a matter of conjecture. Much depended upon whether the shipper
had the advantage of competition of carriers.

The Standard Oil Company of Ohio, being situated at Cleveland, had
the advantage of different carrying lines, as well as of water transportation
in the summer; taking advantage of those facilities, it made the best bar-
gains possible for its freights. Other companies sought to do the same.
The Standard gave advantages to the railroads for the purpose of reducing
the cost of transportation of freight. It offered freights in large quantity,

car-loads and train-loads. It furnished loading facilities and discharging facilities at great cost. It provided regular traffic, so that a railroad could conduct its transportation to the best advantage and use its equipment to the full extent of its hauling capacity without waiting for the refiner's convenience. It exempted railroads from liability for fire and carried its own insurance. It provided at its own expense terminal facilities which permitted economies in handling. For these services it obtained contracts for special allowances on freights.

But notwithstanding these special allowances, this traffic from the Standard Oil Company was far more profitable to the railroad companies than the smaller and irregular traffic, which might have paid a higher rate.

To understand the situation which affected the giving and taking of rebates it must be remembered that the railroads were all eager to enlarge their freight traffic. They were competing with the facilities and rates offered by the boats on lake and canal and by the pipe-lines. All these means of transporting oil cut into the business of the railroads, and they were desperately anxious to successfully meet this competition. As I have stated we provided means for loading and unloading cars expeditiously, agreed to furnish a regular fixed number of carloads to transport each day, and arranged with them for all the other things that I have mentioned, the final result being to reduce the cost of transportation for both the railroads and ourselves. All this was following in the natural laws of trade.

Pipe-lines vs. Railroads

The building of the pipe-lines introduced another formidable competitor to the railroads, but as oil could be transported by pumping through pipes at a much less cost than by hauling in tank-cars in a railroad train the development of the pipe-line was inevitable. The question was simply whether the oil traffic was sufficient in volume to make the investment profitable. When pipe-lines had been built to oil fields where the wells had ceased to yield, as often happened, they were about the most useless property imaginable.

An interesting feature developed through the relations which grew up between the railroads and the pipe-lines. In many cases it was necessary to combine the facilities of both, because the pipes reached only part of the way, and from the place where they ended the railroad carried the oil to its final destination. In some instances a railroad had formerly carried the oil the entire distance upon an agreed rate, but now that this oil was partly pumped by pipe-lines and partly carried by rail, the freight payment was divided between the two. But, as a through rate had been provided, the owners of the pipe-line agreed to remit a part of its charges to the railroad, so we had cases where the Standard paid a rebate to the railroad instead of the reverse, but I do not remember having heard any complaint of this coming from the students of these complicated subjects.

The profits of the Standard Oil Company did not come from advantages given by railroads. The railroads, rather, were the ones who profited by the traffic of the Standard Oil Company, and whatever advantage it received in its constant efforts to reduce rates of freight was only one of the many elements of lessening cost to the consumer which enabled us to increase our volume of business the world over because we could reduce the selling price.

How general was the complicated bargaining for rates can hardly be imagined; everyone got the best rate that he could. After the passage of the Interstate Commerce Act, it was learned that many small companies which shipped limited quantities had received lower rates than we had been able to secure, notwithstanding the fact that we had made large investments to provide for terminal facilities, regular shipments, and other economies. I well remember a bright man from Boston who had much to say about rebates and drawbacks. He was an old and experienced merchant, and looked after his affairs with a cautious and watchful eye. He feared that some of his competitors were doing better than he in bargaining for rates, and he delivered himself of this conviction:

"I am opposed on principle to the whole system of rebates and drawbacks—unless I am in it."

John D. Rockefeller (1940)
ALLAN NEVINS

Allan Nevins, one of the most distinguished American historians of his generation, set himself deliberately athwart the muckraking tradition. Determined to do justice to the captains of industry, he gained access to personal and corporate papers to write large-scale biographies of John D. Rockefeller and Henry Ford. Nevins clearly succeeded in initiating a reassessment of the founders of the great fortunes, causing controversy among historians and changes in popular attitudes as well.

THE STORY OF ROCKEFELLER'S LIFE is one of the great romances of American history; but it is not a story which invites swift and easy judgments. For one reason, it is extremely complex; for another, it raises highly debatable economic issues. "Each great industrial trust," writes the English economist Alfred Marshall, in *Industry and Trade,* "has owed its origin to the exceptional business genius of its founders. In some cases the genius was mainly constructive; in others it was largely strategic and incidentally destructive; sometimes even dishonest." He correctly ascribes the Standard Oil Trust to a combination of exceptional constructive ability and astute destructive strategy. The pages of its history—some of them very dark, some brilliantly creditable—show the two elements inextricably mingled. They also show that, as Marshall elsewhere states, "general propositions in regard to either competition or monopoly are full of snares." While some journalists and some politicians will utter sweeping and dogmatic statements upon an industrial aggregation like the Standard Oil, and upon the work of a great business leader like Rockefeller, economists will regard these glib verdicts with distrust. Too many unsolved problems are opened up by such an industrial organization, and too many difficult issues are raised by such an individual career.

Yet on the basis of the facts recorded in these volumes, one judgment may be ventured. It is that the extremes of praise and blame heaped upon Rockefeller were both unwarranted. His enemies during his years of power treated him as one of the arch-criminals of the age. His admirers during his later years of philanthropy lauded him as one of the world's greatest benefactors. Neither estimate possessed historical truth, and neither touched Rockefeller's greatest significance to civilization.

This is not to say that much of the criticism heaped upon Rockefeller and the Standard Oil was not entirely valid. The great combination made a cruel use in its early years, and particularly in 1875-79, of railroad rate discriminations. It practised espionage. It employed bogus independent companies. It used "fighting brands" and local price-slashing to eliminate competitors. Its part in politics was sometimes reprehensible. It paid less attention than it should have done to systematic price-reduction. All this can be set off against its constructive achievements: its elimination of waste and introduction of manifold economies; its application of the Frasch process, the Burton cracking process, and the Van Dyke patents; its standardization of products on a high level of quality; its development of valuable by-products; its ready assistance to other industries, particularly in improving lubricants; its efficiency in home distribution, and its bold vigor in conquering world markets. A fairly heavy indictment can be drawn up to offset the credit items.

But it is clear that for various reasons the indictment was overdrawn. In the first place, because Rockefeller established the earliest of the great trusts a fuller and fiercer light of publicity beat upon it than upon other combinations. The constant investigations and suits placed him and the Standard under a gigantic, pitiless lens. Subsequent combinations were less severely treated. In the second place, the fact that the early investigations took place before the American public realized that combination was an irresistible tendency of the age led to a natural misconception. People thought of the trust as a conspiracy, a dark plot born in greed. Not until later did they see that the formation of trusts, pools, and cartels was a world-wide movement born of industrial conditions and in large part as natural as the upheaval of the tides. In the third place, Rockefeller was singularly unfortunate in some of his enemies, and particularly in the attacks of Henry Demarest Lloyd. Such fabrications as the Widow Backus story, and such distortions as the tale of the Buffalo "explosion," did him a gross injustice, and led to the invention of a totally false stereotype of the man. Finally, Rockefeller was open to harsher attack than most captains of industry because he touched directly the lives of the masses. Carnegie sold his steel to railroads and industries which passed on his charges to an uncomprehending public; Rockefeller sold gasolene and kerosene to every family—and most families were ready to believe the worst whenever oil went up. Altogether, it is not strange that the accusations against Rockefeller and the Standard Oil were very decidedly exaggerated.

It is plain that the place Rockefeller holds in American industrial history is that of a great innovator. He early caught a vision of combination and order in an industry bloated, lawless, and chaotic. Pursuing this vision, he devised a scheme of industrial organization which, magnificent in its symmetry and strength, world-wide in its scope, possessed a striking novelty. The opposition which he met was massive and implacable. Producers, rival manufacturers, courts, legislatures, Presidents, public opinion, fought him at every step. He and his partners marched from investigation to investigation, from suit to suit, under a growing load of opprobrium. But they moved imperturbably forward. They believed that the opposition was mistaken and irrational. In their opinion it represented a wasteful anarchy; the full victory of this competitive *laissez-faire* individualism would mean retrogression, confusion, and general loss. They kept grimly on. The day came when, with Taft in the White House, the government finally won its battle against Rockefeller and the Standard Oil. But by that time intelligent men were comprehending that the struggle against Rockefeller's movement for industrial consolidation was not a struggle against criminality; it was largely a struggle against destiny.

The dominant ideal of pioneering America was one of utter independence and self-sufficiency. Long after the new industrial era was far advanced, men clung to the old faith in a self-balancing system of private ownership, small-unit enterprise, and free competition, and to their belief that this system would give every man a reward roughly proportionate to his industry, integrity, and ability. They were slow to perceive that the industrial system was not self-balancing; that it grew less so decade by decade. They were slow to perceive that men were less and less independent, more and more interdependent. They were reluctant to admit that free competition was steadily becoming more restricted, and that its character was inexorably changing. It was ceasing to be a competition of small businesses and individual firms, and becoming a competition organized by great aggregations. They finally had to confess the truth which Donald Richberg wrote in 1940, and which might have been stated a generation earlier: "Ours is the competition of great collective organizations of capital and labor, the competition of huge corporations and large labor organizations. It is the competition of industries with other industries, the competition of overpowering advertising and propaganda." Nor was it altered merely in the scope of the units involved. It was for various reasons no longer a *free* competition in the sense in which it had been free in 1860, or 1880.

Rockefeller was a realist; one of those realists who, as Pareto teaches, have a better grasp of realities than the intellectuals who operate with theories and ideals. Partly by intuition, partly by hard thought, he divined the real nature of economic forces, and the real motives operative in American industry. He and the other leaders of the "heroic age" in American business development thus constituted the guiding elite, in a modern sense, of our industrial society. Many of the forces and elements in that society were irrational and wasteful; Rockefeller wished to impose a more rational and efficient pattern, answering to his own intuitions and deductions. Behind this desire he placed an intellectual keenness, a skill in organization, and a dynamic personal force which were not surpassed, and possibly not equalled, by those of any other industrial captain in history. He was not a product of economic determinism, for he rose superior to it; but he wished to give the economic world a form in which determinism would meet fewer obstacles. He expressed the full potentialities of a movement which shattered the old industrial order, and he naturally incurred the hostility of the masses.

Rockefeller's economic vision, and the courage shown in his fidelity to it, deserve commendation. He knew that he was carrying through a great experiment, and he believed the experiment sound and fruitful. As our national history lengthens and we gain a truer perspective, the importance of this experiment becomes clearer. It is true that some of his methods were open to criticism; but then it must be remembered that he had to use the weapons and implements of his time. Few books are more needed, in the study of our past, than a thorough examination of the development of business ethics in America. Such standards are progressive, and the steps by which they have improved from generation to generation constitute a fascinating topic. Henry Lee Higginson once told a Harvard class that when he entered the banking and brokerage business, men accepted as perfectly correct practices which the best firms a generation later sharply condemned. In 1870, when a rich customer placed a heavy order for stocks, the broker felt it proper to order a few hundred shares on his own account and thus profit from the rise. By 1900 good brokers condemned such an act. By 1940 it would have been punished by very severe penalties. In talking with Samuel Harper, Rockefeller once remarked that his trust had committed acts in the seventies and eighties which advancing business standards had later made clearly improper. When the history of our business ethics is written, it will doubtless be found that some correlation exists between boom periods and business laxity, between depression periods and an advance in morals. It will also be found that business honesty is correlated with social maturity. An old, long-settled, and fairly static community has better standards than an adolescent, fast-changing district; an old industry has higher ethics than a new industry. All this must be remembered in appraising Rockefeller's weapons and the use he made of them.

The question of motive enters into any consideration either of economic vision or of business ethics; and it is important because some writers of the muckraking school have grievously misconstrued the motives not only of Rockefeller but of a whole generation of business leaders. They sum up these motives in the word "greed," as if it were greed which led Carnegie to build steel mills, Rockefeller to organize the oil industry, Westinghouse to develop the electrical industry, and Ford to manufacture motor cars. If we wish to misuse the word greed we can apply it in many contexts. We can say that Shakespeare was greedy for fame, Lincoln greedy for political power, and Duse greedy for applause. But such a word means nothing in the analysis of motive. What these figures were really interested in was competitive achievement, self-expression, and the imposition of their wills on a given environment. And these were precisely the motives which actuated Carnegie, Westinghouse, and Rockefeller. We have quoted early in this biography a statement by Rockefeller that "achievement" was his great aim, and the statement was true. The word greed may seem apposite to industrial leaders because they accumulated large fortunes. But any careful analysis of the work of the best leaders shows that money was not the central object, but a by-product. Greedy men exist, but they seldom accumulate colossal fortunes, for greed tends to defeat itself in complex business operations. The corner grocer may be greedy, the political boss, the literary hack. But greed usually stops with the few hundred thousand dollars that purchase satiety. The men who built the really towering economic structures were not thinking primarily of dollars, or they would have halted at the first story.

And one great fact to be borne in mind when studying Rockefeller and his fellow-captains of industry is pointed out by Van Wyck Brooks in *America's Coming of Age*. It is the fact that American business has typically been a more optimistic, light-hearted venture than in other lands, and the best businessmen have been great adventurers. The giants of the "heroic age" of industry can aptly be compared with the famous Elizabethan captains—with Drake, Hawkins, Cavendish, Frobisher, Cabot (some of whom were canny businessmen too). In business, as I have pointed out, Americans of the nineteenth century found the Great Game.

They played it with zest and gusto, they enjoyed it even when it was perilous, and they took its ups and downs with equanimity. As Herbert Spencer said in 1882, for Americans it was the modern equivalent of war. If it was hard-hitting and ruthless, so is war; and even when the blows were hardest, it remained a game. "Business in America," wrote Brooks, "is not merely more engaging than elsewhere, it is even perhaps the most engaging activity in American life." Of all its leaders, none showed more boldness or swiftness than Rockefeller, and none more equanimity in accepting defeats and victories. Love of the game was one of his motives, particularly as his keen eye saw a pattern in the game that less discerning men missed.

We have said that his place in the history of business was that of a great innovator; and that is also his place in the history of philanthropy. This man who remolded one industry and offered a design for remaking others crowned his activities by the colossal grant of some $550,000,000 to various objects. But the unexampled scale of his gifts is not their most striking feature. What made his donations arresting and memorable was in larger part the skill with which he planned and organized them. From the beginning his gifts were made thoughtfully and conscientiously. The huge foundations which he, his son, and their aides set up, governed by able men working in greater and greater independence, have become models for large-scale philanthropy in this and other lands. Their aims, administrative mechanism, methods, and not least of all, their spirit, offer lessons which have been widely copied. Foundations had existed long before—but never any quite like these. His emphasis upon ameliorative work at the fountainheads of evil, upon the use of money to stimulate men to self-help, and upon the establishment of *continuing* activities, has been of the highest value.

A correct appraisal of his rôle as philanthropist will avoid the excessive praise which many have given him because of the sheer amount of his benefactions. The size of his fortune, as we have said, was a historical accident. There was obviously no true sense in which he had earned his billion dollars,* any more than Carnegie had earned his half-billion. Only the special economic, legal, and fiscal situation in the United States between 1865 and 1914 made such huge accumulations possible. Rockefeller always recognized this fact, and always regarded himself as a trustee rather than an owner. His statement at the University of Chicago that "God gave me the money" is sometimes quoted as an arrogant utterance; like Napoleon's statement in putting on the iron crown of Lombardy, "God has given it to me—let man touch it at his peril"; like George F. Baer's statement that God had given the anthracite business to a picked group of men. Actually Rockefeller made that statement in a spirit of utter humility. He devoutly believed that God had made him a trustee for these hundreds

---

* The word "billion" is here used in a general sense; Rockefeller never possessed that much at one time, though much more than that sum passed through his hands.

of millions, not to be kept but to be given wisely and carefully. And it is for the wisdom, the conscientious effort, and the vision which he and his son lent to the task of distribution—a laborious and difficult task—that gratitude is really due them. The animating generosity, too, is to be counted to his credit. For we must not forget that Rockefeller began to give as soon as he began to earn.

It is earnestly to be hoped that no such fortune will ever again pass into a single grasp. The American people have determined that such aggregations of wealth are incompatible with the best interests of the land. And yet it would be a bold critic who would say that this fortune was an unhappy accident. It passed into the hands of a man who had proved the possession of certain strong liberal impulses. As an ill-clad youth earning a few dollars a week, his own necessities poorly met, he had given a substantial part of his meager wage to charity. Few indeed are those who make such sacrifices for altruistic objects as are recorded in Ledger A. He had given from the outset without regard to religion or race, to Catholic and to Negro. He kept on giving more and more as his income grew. The fortune went to a man who had also proved a remarkable capacity for planning and organizing; who knew how to call expert and farsighted assistants to his side; and who was so devoid of egotism that, having once given funds to agents whom he trusted, he cut himself off from all further control over the money. The United States has in one form or another wasted a great many billions of its wealth. Indeed, waste is a conspicuous part of our national life. It was perhaps a happy accident that a single billion passed into the temporary control of a man who, with his son and his expert counsellors, tried to show how much of public welfare and advancement could be purchased by its careful use.

The life of Rockefeller, we can say again, is not one which invites swift and dogmatic judgments. The lessons which men draw from it will vary according to the preconceptions with which they approach the subject. Some will give a heavier weight to the debit items in the ledger than others. But it can safely be said that the prime significance of Rockefeller's career lies in the fact that he was a bold innovator in both industry and philanthropy; that he brought to the first a great unifying idea, which he insisted should be thoroughly tested, and to the second a stronger, more expert, and more enduring type of organization. It can be said also that by virtue of his organizing genius, his tenacity of purpose, his keenness of mind, and his firmness of character, he looms up as one of the most impressive figures of the century which his lifetime spanned. His fame went around the world, and it will be long before the world forgets it.

EUGENE
V. DEBS

&
the Labor
Movement

Eugene Debs remains a tantalizing as well as an appealing figure, who symbolizes as does no other person the great might-have-been of American labor history. He was a native American socialist in a land where much of socialism's strength derived from immigrants. He was self-educated, practical, and an able politician in a movement beset by theorizing, utopianism, and factions. He alone seemed capable of holding together the splintering labor movement and the intellectuals, humanitarians, and immigrants who combined into the American Socialist Party. Managing for a while to blend social idealism with the practical needs of a political party, he almost became the Theodore Roosevelt or Woodrow Wilson of socialism. His ultimate failure to achieve his goals—a result perhaps of the war, perhaps of divisions over the Russian revolution, perhaps simply of massive and successful repression— has seemed to most of those who have studied the question to have been more the product of particular circumstances and general historical trends than of shortcomings in Debs. The United States remains the only major industrialized country without a forceful socialist movement. The noon of socialism in America came under Debs, but night fell with incredible swiftness.

The greatest of America's socialists, Eugene V. Debs grew up in Terre Haute, Indiana, where he had been born in 1855, one of ten children. At fifteen he left school to work as a railroad man and later became a locomotive engineer. Although he switched to the job of clerk in a wholesale grocery house in 1874, he continued his relationships with other railroad men, actively forming a Brotherhood in Terre Haute. In 1880 Debs became editor of *The Firemen's Magazine* and national secretary and treasurer of the Brotherhood of Locomotive Firemen. Debs also tried politics. After serving as city clerk, he won election to the Indiana legislature in 1885, the year he married.

Believing in the organization of labor according to industry rather than according to craft, Debs helped form the American Railway Union in 1893 and became its first president. A strike for higher wages the following year against the Great Northern Railroad gained national attention. A similar effort by the Pullman Company employees drew sympathetic aid from Debs's union in the form of a boycott of Pullman cars. This led to a massive strike which tied up all the railroads going through Chicago until federal troops intervened. Soon thereafter Debs was indicted, tried, and convicted of acting to obstruct the mails. His six months in prison confirmed his commitment to socialism, and he wrote his first advocacy of socialism while serving his sentence.

Building on the A.R.U., the Social Democratic Party was organized in 1897, and three years later, along with a faction of the Socialist Labor Party, it nominated Debs for the presidency. He earned nearly 100,000 votes. Renamed the Socialist Party of America, the group in 1904 again supported Debs, who increased the vote to over 400,000. Debs ran in the next two presidential campaigns, earning 6 per cent of the total vote in 1912—almost a million ballots. When World War I began, Debs led American Socialists in opposing the war as a capitalist venture. Indicted for violating the Espionage Act by giving an anti-war speech, Debs was tried and sentenced to ten years' imprisonment. Appeal denied, he began to serve his term in April 1919. His party announced his nomination while he was in jail, and he again received nearly one million votes.

Debs was released from prison in 1921 by President Harding, but his activities in the following years were hampered by poor health. In 1926 Debs died, a charismatic and devoted believer in simple and pure socialism as opposed to a complex and cruel capitalist society.

Eugene Victor Debs (1946)
AUGUST CLAESSENS

*This eulogy of Debs, published by the leftist Rand School of New York
City, demonstrates the affection he generated among millions of
American workingmen. The sketch is placed first since, as a (highly
favorable) review of Debs's lifelong accomplishments, it provides a
context for the later selections.*

EUGENE VICTOR DEBS, America's most eloquent spokesman for social democracy and labor, was born on November 5, 1855, in the city of Terre
Haute, Indiana. His parents came from Colmar, Alsace, and Gene was
one of ten children, six of whom grew up with him. Little is known of his
very early life except that the family was poor. Gene's school days were
over all too soon; at fourteen he was at work in a shop.

While still a tall, slender, but well-built youth, he got a job on a local
railroad line and became a locomotive fireman. In that occupation, on and
off, for twenty-seven years, as Gene tells in one of his articles, he acquired
an intimate knowledge of the life, the joys and sorrows, the despair and
hopes of workingmen and their families.

Labor Organizer

In 1875, when Gene was twenty, he became interested in labor organization. In those early days he could not have shown much of his genius, the
unfolding and blossoming which was on its way, nevertheless, he must
have impressed his shopmates with his extraordinary qualities because
three years later he was chosen as associate editor of *The Fireman's Magazine* and in two more years as the editor and as grand secretary and
treasurer of the union. Gene must have attained much recognition and
popularity even at that early period for he was elected city clerk of Terre
Haute, serving four years, and was elected also to the legislature for one
term in 1885, representing the Democratic party.

In the nineteen years from 1875 to 1894, Gene grew to maturity, intellectually and spiritually. He completed his education from the raw facts
of life. He read wisely and deeply of the world's finest literature. He was
captivated with gems of great oratory and listened with enchantment to
such orators as Robert G. Ingersoll and Wendell Phillips, and to poets like

James Whitcomb Riley and Eugene Field. Debs' own orations written in later years show a garnering of great literature, a keen selection of the noblest in thought and sentiment, and a fine appreciation of the beauties of the English language. His education was acquired in much the same un-schooled and self-taught manner as that of his illustrious neighbor, the immortal Abraham Lincoln. John Swinton, who heard Lincoln in Cooper Union in 1860 and Debs in the same hall in 1894, said that there was a remarkable resemblance between them in appearance, style, and fervor.

Gene's greatest schooling came in the years he traveled back and forth across the country as an organizer of railway men as well as of workers in other industries. As he says "The labor agitator of the early day held no office, had no title, drew no salary, saw no footlights, heard no applause, never saw his name in print . . ." Yet they were probably joyous years for him.

Often without food or shelter, seldom with enough cash for railroad fare, riding box cars, locomotives and cabooses, getting a meal here and there, Gene worked on as one inspired. There were others like him, in those days—all pioneers, pathfinders, evangelists. In those years he became a voice in the wilderness, a messenger of a new faith. He was heard. He became known. He succeeded. He wrote somewhat later: "I believe it can be said with truth, as I am sure it can without vanity, that I personally know, and am personally known to more railroad employees than any other man in the country."

The A.R.U.

By 1893 the seeds had been sown, the harvest was near, the American Railway Union was born. It was one of the first industrial unions, an all-inclusive union of railroad workers. It grew rapidly for at its head was Gene, the man who for years had fed the fireboxes of locomotives, and who was now firing the imagination of men, arousing their faith in soli-darity, making them aware of their wrongs and inspiring them to attain their rights.

The A.R.U. was remarkably successful at first. Strikes were of short duration and victorious. Debs faced James J. Hill, powerful lord of the Great Northern Railway, and obtained a cessation of wage cuts after an eighteen-day strike. Debs became a national figure and incurred the ani-mosity of the reactionary capitalists and their press. As president of the A.R.U. he made many trips, spoke at innumerable meetings, and wrote articles, appeals and letters to the utter limit of what one man could do. He was growing in intellectual stature and effectiveness.

Then came the great turning point in his life and his mental transition from a Populist and Bryan Democrat to a brilliant Socialist. A strike was going on among the workers in the Pullman car shops near Chicago. The strikers appealed to the A.R.U. for support. It was given to them whole-heartedly. The convention of the A.R.U. then voted for a sympathy strike to aid the Pullman workers. Debs counseled against this action, but he was overruled. The strike of the railway men followed and "all hell broke loose." President Cleveland sent troops to Chicago over the protests of Governor John P. Altgeld and the Mayor. Hundreds of vicious men were sworn in as deputy marshals. Violence followed. Then came the famous injunction restraining the A.R.U. from interfering with the United States mails. Debs and three colleagues were arrested for contempt of court. They refused to give bail and spent six days in the Cook County jail. A grand jury indicted Debs and forty-six union officers. In the meantime Debs was sentenced to Woodstock jail for six months on the contempt charges. During this time the trial went on and on, postponement followed postponement and finally the case was abandoned because of a conveniently sick juror.

In Woodstock Jail

Debs came out of Woodstock a considerably changed man. Victor Berger [a prominent American socialist] visited Gene during his stay, talked with him, gave him books by Karl Marx, Karl Kautsky and others. Gene's eyes saw a new light. The whole economic struggle and political situation took on a new meaning for him. Gene emerged from Woodstock like a butterfly from its cocoon. He was aroused and vocal. A great crowd traveled some fifty miles from Chicago to greet him on his release from Woodstock. A greater crowd awaited his arrival in Chicago that night. It was a delirious evening, thousands cheering and milling around. That night, November 22, 1895, Gene delivered a speech full of fight, indignation, humor and poetry.

Presidential Candidate

The American Railway Union passed into history. Out of it came the Social Democratic Party in 1897. In the 1900 presidential campaign the standard bearers of the Social Democrats were Eugene Victor Debs and Job Harriman. Debs made an extensive tour. His ability as an orator increased and his prestige and fame widened. As presidential candidate for the Socialist Party in 1904 Debs carried the message of Socialism into every section of the country, speaking as many times a day as he had audiences. The Socialist vote rose to 402,400 and his comrades were elated. Thousands of Americans, some of them noted men and women, joined the Socialist Party and Debs became their idol, their most eloquent leader.

Gene was reaching the zenith of his remarkable powers. In persuasion and the power to convince, sway and impress he achieved great mastery. It was inevitable that he would be the standard bearer again in 1908 and 1912 and for that matter in spite of his selflessness, his sincere modesty, and his passion for service without acclaim, it appeared as if no Socialist campaign could be thought of without Debs at the head of the ticket. Again and again he spoke to audiences, huge and small, in cities, towns and hamlets; in the east, west, north and south. Between campaigns he spoke for unions in their halls, in mining camps, country fairs, farmer encampments, Chautauquas, colleges, churches, in fact, wherever human beings would gather. Invitations to speak came to him in such volume and frequency that it took all of the time of his devoted brother Theodore and Gene's beloved wife, Katharine, to handle the correspondence and the files, clippings, manuscripts, and other details of Gene's hectic career. . . .

The Man and Orator

Gene was a most fascinating personality. He was six feet two inches tall, a gaunt Lincoln-like figure, yet not awkward but rather gracefully flexible. Facing an audience he stooped forward slightly and extended one arm and with its searching finger as he appealed to his listeners, each one in the crowd felt as if he were personally solicited. Gene's face was radiantly alert, his voice soft and mellow, his delivery musical and entrancing. His diction was a mixture of lovely prose and poetry, his descriptions of wrongs and injustices moved the stoniest, and his passionate outbursts and appeals, his call for action, usually stirred audiences to wild demonstrations of approval.

He was a master of the platform and a consummate artist. He held his audience in a hypnotic spell, in an emotional trance. His speeches were filled with colorful metaphors, biting satire and gentle humor. He used quotations from the Bible and great literature, gleams of poetry and flashing epigrams and flights of fancy. Above all it was his sterling sincerity, his lack of any artificial mannerisms, his penetrating seriousness that struck sparks from the anvil of his theme. As he was enraged by brutality and injustice, so he enraged others. His vision of a better social order was transplanted into the hearts of others. His early orations can only be appreciated in relation to the brutal class struggles of his times. As Gene so wisely says:

It is the occasion that makes the orator as it is the battle that makes the veteran.

His meetings were often scenes of high emotional excitement. As he entered the hall and started for the stage, men and women would rush out of their seats and into his arms. There was often a long struggle before we could free him from the many embraces. Parents brought their children with bouquets of flowers and hastened the tots to the platform for the presentation. Gene would lift up the sometimes frightened youngster and kiss it fondly. Tears would flow freely down the cheeks of many men and women in the audience. The whole scene became suffused with a spell of love, sympathy and kindness, and Gene as he began his speech held his audience in rapt attention and understanding. They gloried in every sentence. His oration became an epic, every paragraph of it punctuated with thunderous applause. . . .

His denunciations of the evils of capitalism were bitter, his castigation of tyrants, usurpers and misleaders were vitriolic, yet he was careful not to instill hatred against any man or class. His complaint was against the economic order or disorder and the ignorance, unconcern and lack of sensitiveness on the part of the great majority. His description of socialism was warm and sensible, idealistic yet not utopian, and his lessons of the effects inevitably following basic causes, were in the manner of the best in the social sciences.

A Speech and a Ten Year Sentence

In 1917 the Socialist Party in convention at St. Louis adopted a platform declaring opposition to our country's entrance into the war. Shortly thereafter with the passing of the Espionage Act by Congress hundreds of Socialist speakers and writers were arrested, convicted and sent to jail. Debs remained unmolested for a while. However, his turn was to come. Speaking in Nimisilla Park on June 16, 1918, in Canton, Ohio, Debs delivered a passionate denunciation of war. He scorned the charge that Socialists were pro-German. Said Debs,

> Are we opposed to Prussian Militarism? Why, we have been fighting it since the day the Socialist movement was born; and we are going to fight it, day and night, until it is wiped from the face of the earth.
>
> I hate, I loathe, I despise junkers and junkerdom. I have no earthly use for the junkers of Germany, and not one particle more use for the junkers in the United States.

Debs was indicted for this speech and went on trial in the Federal Court in Cleveland, Ohio, on September 9. After a couple of days of preliminaries and the prosecution evidence, Gene's attorneys quickly rested their case and presented Gene. He addressed the jury in his own defense and for two hours he poured out his soul in a plea for the freedom of speech, for the oppressed and the miserable. He refused to take back a word of his Canton speech. He insisted:

> What you may choose to do to me will be of small consequence after all. I am not on trial here. There is an infinitely greater issue that is being tried in this court, though you may not be conscious of it. American institutions are on trial here before a court of American citizens. The future will tell.
>
> I have been accused of having obstructed the war. I admit it. Gentlemen, I abhor war. I would oppose the war if I stood alone. When I think of a cold, glittering steel bayonet being plunged in the white, quivering flesh of a human being, I recoil with horror. I have often wondered if I could ever take the life of my fellow man, even to save my own.

The jury returned a verdict of guilty. Before Debs heard his sentence he was asked if he wished to say something. Debs did. And in a short but touching speech he uttered immortal sentiments. At the very outset he told the Judge:

> Your Honor, years ago I recognized my kinship with all living beings, and I made up my mind that I was not one bit better than the meanest of earth. I said then, I say now, that while there is a lower class I am in it; while there is a criminal element, I am of it; while there is a soul in prison, I am not free.

He received a sentence of ten years in a federal penitentiary. While his attorneys were taking an appeal to the United States Supreme Court, Gene returned to Terre Haute. His movements were restricted to parts of Ohio and Indiana by order of the court and within that territory Gene answered the call from many places and spoke to great crowds eager to hear and see him. He was in no way apologetic. He was still the same rebel, the same flaming revolutionist.

Walls and Bars

The Supreme Court rejected the appeal and on April 12, 1919, a telephone call from Cleveland told him to come to prison. Calmly, smilingly and bravely he went to Cleveland. He was smuggled out by trains and trolleys to avoid demonstrations along the way and late at night he arrived at the penitentiary in Moundsville, West Virginia. Here he was kept for two months in the care of a kindly warden. Suddenly Gene was transferred to Atlanta where he remained until his release on Christmas Day, 1921.

Gene's life and experience in jail had episodes filled with drama, pathos and miracle. There is nothing in all history to compare with this remarkable story. Wardens and keepers melted before him. Hardened criminals became like children in their adoration of Gene. His attitude toward everyone, his every little gesture, his overflowing kindliness, his insistence on doing every menial task and his rejection of any attempt to favor him or set him apart from others drew men to him like a magnet draws iron. When he left Atlanta the cheers and farewells that poured out from hundreds of cells could be heard for blocks around the prison. Few have been loved by so many as was Gene Debs.

He hated brutality and injustice and fought against both. He hated warfare above all and yet he was not a pacifist. He insisted that not all wars were unjustified. He gloried in the class war. He hailed uprisings against tyranny. He was the enemy of dictatorships and a zealous, uncompromising apostle of democracy. True, in his 1919 speeches he boasted of being a Bolshevik and lauded the Russian revolution. In after years when the blood purges stained the progress of Russia he lost his enthusiasm for the Bolsheviks. Their totalitarian terror had nothing in common with his humanitarianism and love of democracy. And when the American Communists failed in their many attempts to win him to their side and then started to attack him in their press and with scurrilous leaflets distributed at his meetings they soon met the blasts of his scorn. And when Gene was angry his great command of language and choice selection of words became terrible weapons against his foes.

After he left Atlanta, a little less than five years were yet to be his. Some of this precious time was spent at home and at a sanitarium in painful illness and in an attempt to regain his health. But neither his ailing heart nor his family nor his closest friends could hold him still. Gene was soon in the field again and between 1922 and up to some months before his death he made repeated tours across the country.

The Last Chapter

He was the same Debs, the same fiery, eloquent, and lovable orator. Although he looked considerably aged he was still the Debs we always knew and loved. However, his effectiveness had weakened. The response to his message and appeals was meager. That was not Gene's fault. The sad facts were that the Socialist Party was badly shattered. The persecution of hundreds of comrades, the Palmer raids and deportations [during the Red Scare of 1919], the destruction of the party state and local organizations and the abandonment of many of our papers had caused havoc with our movement. On top of these troubles came the disastrous split engineered by the Communists and what remained of the Socialist Party was in wreck and ruin. Also, times had changed. Violent class struggles were fewer. The era of persecution and labor martyrdom was behind us. Debs was still the inspiring orator, and he was great in his last speeches, but the conditions had changed. On October 20, 1926 his breath left his worn and tired body and he took his place among the immortals in the history of our country.

But he did not labor in vain. Although the American Socialist movement declined, the heroic work of Eugene Victor Debs and his great corps of co-workers had its impress upon American economic, social and political progress. Six years after Gene's departure many of his measures, recommendations, and proposals flared up under new banners and in a little more than a decade after Gene's passing they were enacted into laws. The rights of labor gained wider recognition. Great masses were organized and their conditions vastly improved. Much of what was proposed in Socialist platforms in the list of immediate demands was no longer considered fantastic, utopian, or unrealistic. They became the laws of the land. Gene the sower of the seeds did not live to see the harvest. But many of his listeners did. . . .

Socialism (1908)
EUGENE V. DEBS

This stirring address on socialism has a common-sense appeal to many people; the very simplicity of its program seems its hallmark of truth.

THERE ARE THOSE who sneeringly class Socialism among the "isms" that appear and disappear as passing fads, and pretend to dismiss it with an impatient wave of the hand. There is just enough in this great world movement to them to excite their ridicule and provoke their contempt. At least they would have us think so and if we take them at their word their ignorance does not rise to the level of our contempt, but entitles them to our pity.

To the workingman in particular it is important to know what Socialism is and what it means.

Let us endeavor to make it so clear to him that he will readily grasp it and the moment he does he becomes a Socialist.

It is our conviction that no workingman can clearly understand what Socialism means without becoming and remaining a Socialist. It is simply impossible for him to be anything else and the only reason that all workingmen are not Socialists is that they do not know what it means.

They have heard of Socialism—and they have heard of anarchy and of other things all mixed together—and without going to any trouble about it they conclude that it is all the same thing and a good thing to let alone.

Why? Because the capitalist editor has said so; the politician has sworn to it and the preacher has said amen to it, and surely that ought to settle it.

But it doesn't. It settles but one thing and that is that the capitalist is opposed to Socialism and that the editor and politician and preacher are but the voices of the capitalist. There are some exceptions, but not enough to affect the rule.

Socialism is first of all a political movement of the working class, clearly defined and uncompromising, which aims at the overthrow of the prevailing capitalist system by securing control of the national government and by the exercise of the public powers, supplanting the existing capitalist class government with Socialist administration—that is to say, changing a republic in name into a republic in fact.

Socialism also means a coming phase of civilization, next in order to the present one, in which the collective people will own and operate the sources and means of wealth production, in which all will have equal right to work and all will co-operate together in producing wealth and all will enjoy all the fruit of their collective labor.

In the present system of society, called the capitalist system, since it is controlled by and supported in the interest of the capitalist class, we have two general classes of people; first, capitalists, and second, workers. The capitalists are few, the workers are many; the capitalists are called capitalists because they own the productive capital of the country, the lands, mines, quarries, oil and gas wells, mills, factories, shops, stores, warehouses, refineries, tanneries, elevators, docks, wharves, railroads, street cars, steamships, smelters, blast furnaces, brick and stone yards, stock pens, packing houses, telegraph wires and poles, pipe lines, and all other sources, means and tools of production, distribution and exchange. The capitalist class who own and control these things also own and control, of course, the millions of jobs that are attached to and inseparable from them.

It goes without saying that the owner of the job is the master of the fellow who depends upon the job.

Now why does the workingman depend upon the capitalist for a job? Simply because the capitalist owns the tools with which work is done, and without these the workingman is almost as helpless as if he had no arms.

Before the tool became a machine, the worker who used it also owned it; if one was lost or destroyed he got another. The tool was small; it was for individual use and what the workingman produced with it was his own. He did not have to beg some one else to allow him to use his tools—he had his own.

But a century has passed since then, and in the order of progress that simple tool has become a mammoth machine.

The old hand tool was used by a single worker—and owned by him who used it.

The machine requires a thousand or ten thousand workers to operate it, but they do not own it, and what they produce with it does not go to them, but to the capitalist who does own it.

The workers who use the machine are the slaves of the capitalist who owns it.

They can only work by his permission.

The capitalist is a capitalist solely for profit—without profit he would not be in business an instant. That is his first and only consideration.

In the capitalist system profit is prior to and more important than the life or liberty of the workingman.

The capitalist's profit first, last and always. He owns the tools and only allows the worker to use them on condition that he can extract a satisfactory profit from his labor. If he cannot do this the tools are not allowed to be used—he locks them up and waits.

The capitalist does no work himself; that is, no useful or necessary work. He spends his time watching other parasites in the capitalist game of "dog eat dog," or in idleness or dissipation. The workers who use his tools give him all the wealth they produce and he allows them a sufficient wage to keep them in working order.

The wage is to the worker what oil is to the machine.

The machine cannot run without lubricant and the worker cannot work and reproduce himself without being fed, clothed and housed; this is his lubricant and the amount he requires to keep him in running order regulates his wage. . . .

This is the capitalist system in its effect upon the working class. They have no tools, but must work to live. They throng the labor market, especially when times are hard and work is scarce, and eagerly, anxiously look for some one willing to use their labor power and bid them in at the market price.

To speak of liberty in such a system is a mockery; to surrender is a crime.

The workers of the nation and the world must be aroused.

In the capitalist system "night has drawn her sable curtain down and pinned it with a star," and the great majority grope in darkness. The pin must be removed from the curtain, even though it be a star.

But the darkness, after all, is but imaginary. The sun is marching to meridian glory and the world is flooded with light.

Charlotte Perkins Stetson, the inspired evangel of the coming civilization, says:

> We close our eyes and call it night,
> And grope and fall in seas of light,
> Would we but understand!

Not for a moment do we despair of the future. The greatest educational propaganda ever known is spreading over the earth.

The working class will both see and understand. They have the inherent power of self-development. They are but just beginning to come into consciousness of their power, and with the first glimmerings of this consciousness the capitalist system is doomed. It may hold on for a time, for even a long time, but its doom is sealed.

Even now the coming consciousness of this world-wide working class power is shaking the foundations of all governments and all civilizations.

The capitalist system has had its day and, like other systems that have gone before, it must pass away when it has fulfilled its mission and made room for another system more in harmony with the forces of progress and with the onward march of civilization.

The centralization of capital, the concentration of industry and the co-operation of workingmen mark the beginning of the end. Competition is no longer "the life of trade." Only they are clamoring for "competition" who have been worsted in the struggle and would like to have another deal.

The small class who won out in the game of competition and own the trusts want no more of it. They know what it is, and have had enough. Mr. John D. Rockefeller needs no competition to give life to his trade, and his pious son does not expatiate upon the beauties of competition in his class at Sunday school.

No successful capitalist wants competition—for himself—he only wants it for the working class, so that he can buy his labor power at the lowest competitive price in the labor market.

The simple truth is, that competition in industrial life belongs to the past, and is practically outgrown. The time is approaching when it will be no longer possible.

The improvement and enlargement of machinery, and the ever-increasing scale of production compel the concentration of capital and this makes inevitable the concentration and co-operation of the workers.

The capitalists—the successful ones, of course—co-operate on the one side; the workers—who are lucky enough to get the jobs—on the other side.

One side gets the profit, grow rich, live in palaces, ride in yachts, gamble at Monte Carlo, drink champagne, choose judges, buy editors, hire preachers, corrupt politics, build universities, endow libraries, patronize churches, get the gout, preach morals and bequeath the earth to their lineal descendants.

The other side do the work, early and late, in heat and cold; they sweat and groan and bleed and die—the steel billets they make are their corpses. They build the mills and all the machinery; they man the plant and the thing of stone and steel begins to throb. They live far away in the outskirts, in cottages, just this side of the hovels, where gaunt famine walks with despair and *Les Misérables* leer and mock at civilization. When the mills shut down, they are out of work and out of food and out of home; and when old age begins to steal away their vigor and the step is no longer agile, nor the sinew strong, nor the hand cunning; when the frame begins to bend and quiver and the eye to grow dim, and they are no longer fit as labor power to make profit for their masters, they are pushed aside into the human drift that empties into the gulf of despair and death.

The system, once adapted to human needs, has outlived its usefulness and is now an unmitigated curse. It stands in the way of progress and checks the advance of civilization.

If by its fruit we know the tree, so by the same token do we know our social system. Its corrupt fruit betrays its foul and unclean nature and condemns it to death.

The swarms of vagrants, tramps, outcasts, paupers, thieves, gamblers, pickpockets, suicides, confidence men, fallen women, consumptives, idiots, dwarfed children; the disease, poverty, insanity and crime rampant in every land under the sway of capitalism rise up and cry out against it, and hush to silence all the pleas of its *mercenaries* and strike the knell of its doom.

The ancient and middle-age civilizations had their rise, they ruled and fell, and that of our own day must follow them.

Evolution is the order of nature, and society, like the units that compose it, is subject to its inexorable law.

The day of individual effort, of small tools, free competition, hand labor, long hours and meagre results is gone never to return. The civilization reared upon this old foundation is crumbling.

The economic basis of society is being transformed.

The working class are being knit together in the bonds of co-operation, they are becoming conscious of their interests as a class, and marshalling the workers for the class struggle and collective ownership.

With the triumph of the workers the mode of production and distribution will be completely revolutionized.

Private ownership and production for profit will be supplanted by social ownership and production for use.

The economic interests of the workers will be mutual. They will work together in harmony instead of being arrayed against each other in competitive warfare.

The collective workers will own the machinery of production, and there will be work for all and all will receive their socially due share of the product of their co-operative labor.

It is for this great work that the workers and their sympathizers must organize and educate and agitate.

The Socialist movement is of the working class itself; it is from the injustice perpetrated upon, and the misery suffered by this class that the movement sprang, and it is to this class it makes its appeal. It is the voice of awakened labor arousing itself to action.

As we look abroad and see things as they are, the capitalists intrenched and fortified and the workers impoverished, ignorant and in bondage, we are apt to be overawed by the magnitude of the task that lies before the Socialist movement, but as we become grounded in the Socialist philosophy, as we understand the process of economic determinism and grasp the principles of industrial and social evolution the magnitude of the undertaking, far from daunting the Socialist spirit, appeals to each comrade to enlist in the struggle because of the very greatness of the conflict and the immeasurable good that lies beyond it, and as he girds himself and touches elbows with his comrades his own latent resources are developed and his blood thrills with new life as he feels himself rising to the majesty of a man.

Now he has found his true place, and though he be reviled against and ostracized, traduced and denounced, though he be reduced to rags, and tormented with hunger pangs, he will bear it all and more, for he is battling for a principle, he has been consecrated to a cause and he cannot turn back.

To reach the workers that are still in darkness and to open their eyes, that is the task, and to this we must give ourselves with all the strength we have, with patience that never fails and an abiding faith in the ultimate victory.

The moment a worker sees himself in his true light he severs his relations with the capitalist parties, for he realizes at once that he no more belongs there than Rockefeller belongs in the Socialist Party.

What is the actual status of the workingman in the capitalist society of today?

Is he in any true sense a citizen?

Has he any basis for the claim that he is a free man?

First of all, he cannot work unless some capitalist finds it to his interest to employ him. . . .

But admitting that he finds employment, during working hours he is virtually the property of his master.

The bell or the whistle claims him on the stroke of the hour. He is subject to the master's shop regulations and these, of course, are established solely to conserve his master's interests. He works, first of all, for his master, who extracts the surplus value from his labor, but for which he would not be allowed to work at all. He has little or no voice in determining any of the conditions of his employment.

Suddenly, without warning, the shop closes down, or he is discharged and his wage, small at best, is cut off. He has to live, the rent must be paid, the wife and children must have clothing and food, fuel must be provided, and yet he has no job, no wages and no prospect of getting any.

Is a worker in that position free?

Is he a citizen?

A man?

No! He is simply a wage-slave, a job-holder, while it lasts, here today and gone tomorrow.

For the great body of wage-workers there is no escape; they cannot rise above the level of their class. The few who do are the exceptions that prove the rule.

And yet there are those who have the effrontery to warn these wage-slaves that if they turn to Socialism they will lose all incentive to work, and their individuality will fade away.

Incentive and individuality forsooth! Where are they now?

Translated into plain terms, this warning means that a slave who is robbed of all he produces, except enough to keep him in producing condition, as in the present system, has great incentive to work and is highly individualized, but if he breaks his fetters and frees himself and becomes his own master and gets all his labor produces, as he will in Socialism, then all incentive to work vanishes, and his individuality, so used to chains and dungeons, unable to stand the air of freedom, withers away and is lost forever.

The capitalists and their emissaries who resort to such crude attempts at deception and imposture betray the low estimate they place on the intelligence of their wage-workers and also show that they fully understand to what depths of ignorance and credulity these slaves have sunk in the wage-system.

In the light of existing conditions there can be no reform that will be of any great or permanent benefit to the working class.

The present system of private ownership must be abolished and the workers themselves made the owners of the tools with which they work, and to accomplish this they must organize their class for political action and this work is already well under way in the Socialist Party, which is composed of the working class and stands for the working class on a revolutionary platform, which declares in favor of the collective ownership of the means of production and the democratic management of industry in the interest of the whole people.

What intelligent workingman can hold out against the irresistible claim the Socialist movement has upon him? What reason has he to give? What excuse can he offer?

None! Not one! . . .

Consider for a moment the beastly debasement to which womanhood is subjected in capitalist society. She is simply the property of man to be governed by him as may suit his convenience. She does not vote, she has no voice and must bear silent witness to her legally ordained inferiority.

She has to compete with man in the factories and workshops and stores, and her inferiority is taken advantage of to make her work at still lower wages than the male slave gets who works at her side.

As an economic dependent, she is compelled to sacrifice the innate refinement, the inherent purity and nobility of her sex, and for a pallet of straw she marries the man she does not love.

The debauching effect of the capitalist system upon womanhood is accurately registered in the divorce court and the house of shame.

In Socialism, woman would stand forth the equal of man—all the avenues would be open to her and she would naturally find her fitting place and rise from the low plane of menial servility to the dignity of ideal womanhood.

Breathing the air of economic freedom, amply able to provide for herself in Socialist society, we may be certain that the cruel injustice that is now perpetrated upon her sex and the degradation that results from it will disappear forever.

Consider again the barren prospect of the average boy who faces the world today. If he is the son of a workingman his father is able to do but little in the way of giving him a start.

He does not get to college, nor even to the high school, but has to be satisfied with what he can get in the lower grades, for as soon as he has physical growth enough to work he must find something to do, so that he may help support the family.

His father has no influence and he can get no preferred employment for him at the expense of some other boy, so he thankfully accepts any kind of service that he may be allowed to perform.

How hard it is to find a place for that boy of yours!

What shall we do with Johnnie? and Nellie? is the question of the anxious mother long before they are ripe for the labor market.

"The child is weak, you know," continues the nervous, loving little mother, "and can't do hard work; and I feel dreadfully worried about him."

What a picture! Yet so common that the multitude do not see it. This mother, numbered by thousands many times over, instinctively understands the capitalist system, feels its cruelty and dreads its approaching horrors which cast their shadows upon her tender, loving heart.

Nothing can be sadder than to see a mother take the boy she bore by the hand and start to town with him to peddle him off as merchandise to some one who has use for a child-slave.

To know just how that feels one must have had precisely that experience.

The mother looks down so fondly and caressingly upon her boy; and he looks up into her eyes so timidly and appealingly as she explains his good points to the business man or factory boss, who in turn inspects the lad and interrogates him to verify his mother's claims, and finally informs them that they may call again the following week, but that he does not think he can use the boy.

Well, what finally becomes of the boy? He is now grown, his mother's worry is long since ended, as the grass grows green where she sleeps— and he, the boy? Why, he's a factory hand—a *hand,* mind you, and he gets a dollar and a quarter a day when the factory is running.

That is all he will ever get.

He is an industrial life prisoner—no pardoning power for him in the capitalist system.

No sweet home, no beautiful wife, no happy children, no books, no flowers, no pictures, no comrades, no love, no joy for him.

Just a hand! A human factory hand!

Think of a hand with a soul in it!

In the capitalist system the soul has no business. It cannot produce profit by any process of capitalist calculation.

The working hand is what is needed for the capitalist's tool and so the human must be reduced to a hand.

No head, no heart, no soul—simply a hand.

A thousand hands to one brain—the hands of workingmen, the brain of a capitalist.

A thousand dumb animals, in human form—a thousand slaves in the fetters of ignorance, their heads having run to hands—all these owned and worked and fleeced by one stock-dealing, profit-mongering capitalist.

This is capitalism!

And this system is supported alternately by the Republican Party and the Democratic Party.

These two capitalist parties relieve each other in support of the capitalist system, while the capitalist system relieves the working class of what they produce.

A thousand hands to one head is the abnormal development of the capitalist system.

A thousand workingmen turned into hands to develop and gorge and decorate one capitalist paunch!

This brutal order of things must be overthrown. The human race was not born to degeneracy.

A thousand heads have grown for every thousand pairs of hands; a thousand hearts throb in testimony of the unity of heads and hands; and a thousand souls, though crushed and mangled, burn in protest and are pledged to redeem a thousand men.

Heads and hands, hearts and souls, are the heritage of all.

Full opportunity for full development is the unalienable right of all.

He who denies it is a tyrant; he who does not demand it is a coward; he who is indifferent to it is a slave; he who does not desire it is dead.

The earth for all the people! That is the demand.

The machinery of production and distribution for all the people! That is the demand.

The elimination of rent, interest and profit and the production of wealth to satisfy the wants of all the people! That is the demand.

Co-operative industry in which all shall work together in harmony as the basis of a new social order, a higher civilization, a real republic! That is the demand.

The end of class struggles and class rule, of master and slave, of ignorance and vice, of poverty and shame, of cruelty and crime—the birth of freedom, the dawn of brotherhood, the beginning of MAN! That is the demand.

This is Socialism!

Debs and World War I (1949)
RAY GINGER

Eugene Debs was prepared to make any sacrifice for the cause he believed in. When World War I came about, he denounced it as a creation of munitions makers and capitalists generally. Unlike European

*socialists who succumbed to the appeals of nationalism, Debs persuaded
many of his followers to oppose the war. On April 7, 1917—one day
after the United States entered the war—his Socialist Party met in an
emergency convention and approved the famous St. Louis Manifesto,
attributing the war to "predatory capitalists" and branding the U.S.
declaration of war "a crime against the people of the United States and
against the nations of the world."*

THE ONLY AVENUE OF EXPRESSION still open to Debs [in 1918] was the
public platform. The Socialist press had been practically wiped out. Paper
after paper had been suppressed or stripped of its second-class mailing
permit—the *American Socialist,* the New York *Call, The Masses,* finally the
International Socialist Review and Frank O'Hare's *Social Revolution.* But
Debs knew that he would have no trouble securing lecture engagements.
He deliberately framed his indictment of the war in extreme terms; such an
approach jibed with both of his objectives. He wanted to arouse resentment
and opposition to the war; he also wanted to taunt the Federal authorities
into placing him on trial. Debs had been completely serious in his statement to Kate O'Hare that, if she went to prison, he would "feel guilty to be
at large." Well, she was about to go to prison. So were hundreds of others.
Rose Pastor Stokes had re-entered the Party and publicly expressed anti-
war views, for which she had already received a ten-year sentence. Debs
was determined either to open the prison gates or to swing them shut behind himself.

But his hope was frustrated. During the first two weeks of June, he gave
his antiwar speech a dozen times in Indiana and Illinois. It was greeted
with enthusiastic approval—and the Federal government took no steps
against him. Debs became increasingly angry. After fifteen months of in-
activity he was finally free. Although he persistently baited the district attorneys and vehemently denounced the President, nothing happened. Half
of his beautiful plan was being spoiled by the callous indifference of the
law-enforcement officials. This was the final insult.

As he took the train eastward into Ohio, Debs was happier than he had
been for what seemed eternity. His own move would encourage similar
action by other Socialists. At last he had resumed his customary post, at
the head of the radical offensive. His love of a hard fight in a good cause
was being satisfied to the utmost. If only the Federal government would
take some notice of him, everything would be perfect, just perfect. And in
Ohio the fight would be even more exultant. For a decade Ohio had been
the center of the Party's left wing. It had been the only state to vote against
the "sabotage" amendment in 1912. The Socialists there had waged a
forthright struggle against every measure for the prosecution of the war.
The leading Socialists of Ohio—Alfred Wagenknecht, Charles E. Ruthen-

berg, and Charles Baker—were all serving terms at the Stark County Workhouse in Canton for their opposition to the draft act. And Eugene Debs was in Canton on June 16, 1918, to speak at the Ohio convention of the Socialist Party.

Early in the afternoon, the local reception committee picked Debs up at the Courtland Hotel to drive him to Nimisilla Park, where he was to give his speech. As the small group of Socialists passed through the hotel lobby, Debs was intercepted by Clyde R. Miller, a reporter for the Cleveland *Plain-Dealer*. Debs agreed to answer a few questions, so Miller asked if he still supported the St. Louis Manifesto. "I approved of the adoption of the platform in form and substance at the time it was created," said Debs, "but in the light of the Russian situation I think we should put forth a restatement of the aims of the Socialist Party." When asked to amplify this statement, Debs continued "that the Bolsheviki of Russia were the inspiration of the world and that he hoped their ideas would come to prevail in America." Miller also recalled that Debs "pointed out that the success of the Bolshevik movement in Russia was something on which to model and base the ideals for this country—the ideals espoused by the Socialists."

Eugene Debs did not go directly to the meeting at Nimisilla Park. He insisted that he must first stop at the Stark County Workhouse, which was almost across the street from the park. From his brief interview with the three Socialist prisoners, Debs acquired a new fury, a new determination. When the three men first were imprisoned, Wagenknecht and Ruthenberg were assigned to work in the laundry. This, they thought, was clearly discrimination against their political views, so they thanked the warden but felt compelled to refuse. For the next two days they hung by their wrists from a rafter. Charles Baker managed to smuggle this news out of the jail, and a fierce public uproar resulted in a compromise between the inmates and the warden. In spite of this experience the three men made no complaints to Debs. They felt confident that they were standing on the proper side of the battle.

A few minutes after Debs left the jail Alfred Wagenknecht, crowding up to the bars of his cell, saw him walking through the crowd in the Park. Not even the scorching heat had forced the Socialist leader to discard his tweed jacket or to unbutton his vest. As he made his way through the crowd, a Socialist on the platform opened the meeting by reading the Declaration of Independence. Then Mrs. Marguerite Prevey, Debs' hostess of preceding years, began to introduce the main speaker. Her remarks were brief, and they centered upon the widespread newspaper reports that Debs had repudiated his antiwar statements. Mrs. Prevey thought this was quite amusing, and the gales of laughter seemed to prove that the audience agreed.

Finally Eugene Debs, calm, smiling, moved to the front of the platform, a plain wooden bandstand undecorated by the American flag. That seemed strange at the public meeting on June 16, 1918. But even more strange was Debs' speech. There was not much in it that he had not said many times in the past. But that speech became a byword, a flaming document in the Socialist movement, because this was war, and men did not say the things they might say in time of peace. Thousands of Socialists warmed themselves on bleak, cold days with the memory of Eugene Debs standing on the platform at Canton, speaking his mind.

Alfred Wagenknecht, although he pressed hard against the bars of his cell, could not hear the speaker in Nimisilla Park. It was too bad, because Debs was talking about Wagenknecht and the others: "I have just returned," said Debs, "from a visit over yonder, where three of our most loyal comrades are paying the penalty for their devotion to the cause of the working class. They have come to realize, as many of us have, that it is extremely dangerous to exercise the constitutional right of free speech in a country fighting to make democracy safe in the world. I realize that, in speaking to you this afternoon, there are certain limitations placed on the right of free speech. I must be exceedingly careful, prudent, as to what I say, and even more careful and prudent as to how I say it. (Laughter) I may not be able to say all I think; (Laughter and Applause) but I am not going so say anything that I do not think. I would a thousand times rather be a free soul in jail than to be a sycophant and coward in the streets. They may put those boys in jail—and some of the rest of us in jail—but they can not put the Socialist movement in jail."

And Debs swept irresistibly onward, defying the very injunction that he had laid down in his opening words. "There is but one thing you have to be concerned about, and that is that you keep four-square with the principles of the international Socialist movement. It is only when you begin to compromise that trouble begins. So far as I am concerned, it does not matter what others may say, or think, or do, as long as I am sure that I am right with myself and the cause." Now for the first time Debs struck out at those Socialists who had deserted the Party: "They lack the fiber for the revolutionary test; they fall away; they disappear as if they had never been. On the other hand, they who are animated by the unconquerable spirit of the social revolution; they who have the moral courage to stand erect and assert their convictions; stand by them; fight for them; go to jail or to hell for them, if need be—they are writing their names, in this crucial hour— they are writing their names in fadeless letters in the history of mankind."

The crowd of twelve hundred persons was pressing forward excitedly toward the platform. They laughed, shouted, applauded, clapped their hands, and waved their hats. And all the while the Department of Justice agents and American Protective League volunteers moved through the audience, checking draft cards. Sweat ran down Debs' face as he moved back and forth across the stage, then turned to lean far over the rail and stretch his lean hands toward the men before him. "It felt," said one man, "exactly as if that forefinger was hitting you on the nose." The words, however, struck elsewhere: "They tell us that we live in a great free republic; that our institutions are democratic; that we are a free and self-governing people. (Laughter) This is too much; even for a joke. (Laughter) But it is not a subject for levity; it is an exceedingly serious matter."

The levity failed to disappear. As Debs continued his detailed indictment of American society, he often remembered that laughter is a potent weapon. The Supreme Court came in for special treatment: "Why, the other day, by a vote of five to four—a kind of craps game—come seven, come 'leven—they declared the child labor law unconstitutional . . . and this in our so-called Democracy, so that we may continue to grind the flesh and blood and bones of puny little children into profits for the junkers of Wall Street . . . The history of this country is being written in the blood of the childhood the industrial lords have murdered."

During the next two hours, Debs passionately defended the men who were being called murderers, and German agents, and hoodlums. He spoke for Tom Mooney, who had been convicted of throwing a bomb at a San Francisco preparedness parade in 1916. He spoke for Bill Haywood and the other Wobblies [members of the Industrial Workers of the World, a radical labor organization], who were even then on trial in a Chicago courtroom. He spoke for the Bolsheviks of Russia, who were being reviled and denounced in Congress, in the headlines, in the pulpits. What right had the profiteers, shouted Debs, to parade as superpatriots? The rulers of Wall Street, now vehemently denouncing the German junkers, had consorted with the junkers for years, traded with them, played golf with them, married their daughters to them. What right had Theodore Roosevelt, who had been so fond of Kaiser Wilhelm, to appear on the stage as the great enemy of German autocracy? While Theodore Roosevelt and the Kaiser were vacationing together at Potsdam in 1907, there were German socialists rotting in German prisons for their opposition to that same Kaiser. Who, in the name of truth, who was the real foe of German autocracy?

Only once in the entire speech did Debs speak about war, and even then he did not speak specifically about the World War. But his statement clearly was meant to cover the World War: "The master class has always declared the wars; the subject class has always fought the battles. The master class has had all to gain and nothing to lose, while the subject class has had nothing to gain and all to lose—especially their lives."

A government stenographer was frantically writing each word as Debs went into his stirring climax: "Yes, in good time we are going to sweep into power in this nation and throughout the world. . . . The world is changing daily before our eyes. The sun of capitalism is setting; the sun of Socialism is rising. . . . In due time the hour will strike and this great cause triumphant—the greatest in history—will proclaim the emancipation of the working class and the brotherhood of all mankind." As he walked down from the platform, roar after roar of applause and cheers broke from the audience. Each man felt surging within him a new devotion, a new strength, a strength that he had never realized in the past. Throughout the entire world socialists looked toward Eugene Debs and smiled.

But there were also frowns, and hostility, and anger. The government stenographer turned in his report of the speech, and the Federal Attorney's office in Cleveland read it carefully. The Espionage Act had just been amended to include several non-military offenses, such as uttering "profane, scurrilous and abusive language" about the government. Just thirteen days after the Canton speech, a Federal grand jury in Cleveland indicted Eugene Debs. Perhaps they thought it was "abusive" to call the Supreme Court "a kind of craps game," as he had done. They decided, at any rate, that Debs' speech at Canton had violated the new Sedition Act on ten different counts.

Debs was arrested on June 30, 1918, as he was about to enter the Bohemian Gardens in the Cleveland to address a Socialist picnic. Taken to the Federal Building in Cleveland, he rode up in the elevator with Clyde R. Miller, the *Plain-Dealer* reporter who had interviewed him two weeks earlier in Canton. Miller again asked if Debs wanted to repudiate the St. Louis Manifesto. "I do not," replied Debs, "and, if necessary, I shall die for those principles." A few minutes later in the marshal's office, Debs told the reporters about his rôle in the formation of the American Railway Union and his indictment during the Pullman boycott.

Since it was Sunday, most of the offices were closed, and the authorities refused to make arrangements for Debs to post bail. So Eugene Debs, for the first time in twenty-three years, was compelled to sleep in a cell. A jailer awakened him the next morning with the news that he had been nominated for Congress by the Socialists of Terre Haute. Mrs. Marguerite Prevey and a Cleveland comrade, A. W. Moskowitz, soon provided the ten-thousand-dollar bond, and Debs was released. . . .

When Debs began to explain [at his trial] why he was sympathetic to the Russian Bolsheviks, the Federal attorney objected that his remarks were not relevant "to the evidence in the case." But Judge Westenhaver . . . replied that he would "permit the defendant to proceed in his own way." Debs went on: "It may be that the much-despised Bolsheviks may fail at last, but let me say to you that they have written a chapter of glorious history. It will stand to their eternal credit." Lenin and Stalin and Trotzky were being denounced as "criminals and outlaws." But the vituperation against George Washington and Samuel Adams and Patrick Henry had not halted the American Revolution. The murder of Elijah Lovejoy [the "Martyr Abolitionist" killed in 1837] had merely hastened the abolition of slavery. Thus the minority of today became the majority of tomorrow, and found its vindication in universal acclaim.

Debs contended that he himself was charged with crime because he believed "as the revolutionary fathers did in their time, that a change was due in the interests of the people, that the time has come for a better form of government, an improved system, a higher social order, a nobler humanity and a grander civilization." The ruling class was helpless against "the rise of the toiling and producing masses," said Debs: "You may hasten the change; you may retard it; you can no more prevent it than you can prevent the coming of the sunrise on the morrow."

Such intensity is normally reserved for love scenes, when one person speaks to another of those visions that hold his every wish. The spectators were hushed and frozen; the jurymen were leaning forward as if to hear the next sentence before it was uttered; the Federal attorney and the judge rested in their seats of power. Gone now were the technicalities and the haggling; gone was the ludicrous tone, as men clambered above the trivial facts to reach a more concentrated atmosphere.

It was mere prattle to speak of brotherhood, Debs protested, so long as men tolerated a social system "in which we are a mass of warring units, in which millions of workers have to fight one another for jobs, and millions of business and professional men have to fight one another for trade, for practice—in which we have individual interests and each is striving to care for himself alone without reference to his fellow men." This commercial conflict led directly to armed conflict, and no amount of talk could hide the truth. American workers had been paid so little that they could not purchase the goods they produced. American businessmen, in their search for profits, had been forced to battle for foreign markets. They had been opposed by the owning classes of Germany, Austria, even of England and France. The war had resulted from exploitation in every capitalist country. Exploitation always led to militarism, as Eugene Debs had seen even in time of peace—the Pullman boycott, the bull pens at Cripple Creek, the Ludlow Massacre.

Debs asked the court for permission to present statistics on profiteering during the war, so that this point would be established beyond dispute. But Judge Westenhaver refused the permission, saying that there would be "no consensus of opinion or agreement" on the matter. Thus Debs lost the chance to say the one thing that, above all others, he truly wanted to say.

But Debs made his point in other ways. He defended his right to oppose a war that he thought was unjust: "The Mexican war was bitterly condemned by Abraham Lincoln, by Charles Sumner, by Daniel Webster and by Henry Clay." He defended all those who had exercised this right during the World War—Rose Pastor Stokes, Kate O'Hare, Big Bill Haywood, and the Wobblies. He defended the St. Louis Manifesto because "I believed then, as I believe now, that the statement correctly defined the attitude of the Socialist Party toward war. That statement, bear in mind, did not apply to the people of this country alone, but to the people of the world. It said, in effect, to the people, especially to the workers, of all countries. 'Quit going to war. Stop murdering one another for the profit and glory of the ruling classes. Cultivate the arts of peace. Humanize humanity. Civilize civilization.' That is the essential spirit and the appeal of the much-hated, condemned St. Louis platform."

Eugene Debs had been talking for nearly two hours. The shadows had completely blotted out the former streak of light across the floor. His voice became muffled: "I do not know, I cannot tell, what your verdict may be; nor does it matter much, so far as I am concerned. Gentlemen, I am the smallest part of this trial. I have lived long enough to appreciate my own personal insignificance in relation to a great issue that involves the welfare of the whole people. What you may choose to do to me will be of small consequence after all. I am not on trial here. There is an infinitely greater issue that is being tried in this court, though you may not be conscious of it. American institutions are on trial here before a court of American citizens. The future will tell."

As Debs returned slowly to his seat, Morris Wolf noticed that several of the jurymen were crying. A Department of Justice agent said to a reporter at the press table: "You've got to hand it to the old man. He came through clean."

Edwin S. Wertz, the Federal attorney, used the remainder of the afternoon to sum up for the prosecution. He reviewed all of the testimony that had been given, and attributed to Debs the willful obstruction of the draft act. Eugene Victor Debs, said the prosecutor, was "an old ewe" who was trying to lead his flock of innocent followers into prison. Debs' professions of international friendship were held up to ridicule. "I'll tell you what internationalism is," exclaimed Mr. Wertz. "Pitch all the nations into one pot with the Socialists on top and you've got internationalism." At these words the Socialists in the courtroom flushed; Judge Westenhaver looked restive; the Federal attorney seemed pleased. Hadn't Debs said that he was as guilty as Rose Stokes, and hadn't Rose Stokes been convicted by a jury in Kansas City? The conclusion was too apparent to require emphasis, but the prosecutor drew four heavy black lines under it to enlighten the jury.

Court adjourned for the day at the end of Wertz's summation. As Eugene Debs emerged from the courtroom into the corridor a young girl handed him a huge bouquet of red roses, and then fainted at his feet.

Debs spent the evening at the Gillsy House, writing letters and chatting with his friends. Max Eastman had asked him one day if the trial was an emotional strain. "No," Debs had replied, "it doesn't rest on my mind much. You see, if I'm sent to jail it can't be for a very long time, whereas if you go it may be an important part of your life. That's why my heart has been with you boys all these months."

The next morning Judge Westenhaver gave his final charge to the jury, and it was eminently fair. He instructed the jury to find the defendant Not Guilty on those counts dealing with ridicule of the Federal government. The counts remaining in the indictment charged that Debs had willfully and knowingly tried to obstruct the operation of the conscription act. Then the jurymen struggled to their feet and hobbled out of the courtroom, carrying copies of the speech and the indictment. They remained absent for six hours, while the defendant regaled his friends with dozens of anecdotes about Abraham Lincoln. . . .

Shortly before five o'clock the jurymen filed back into the courtroom. The youngest among them, Cyrus H. Stoner, aged fifty-eight years, rose to read the verdict. The inevitable words were droned out. On three separate counts: "Guilty as charged in the indictment." Judge Westenhaver fixed Saturday morning, September 14, as the time for passing sentence, and Debs left the courtroom facing a possible prison term of sixty years. Walking up the corridor, he said of the jury: "There is something pathetic about dressed up faces—smug bodies. If they had been dressed in rags it would have been all right. What a contrast to turn toward the back of the court-room and find a little group of beautiful Socialists, with stars for eyes—you can always tell them!"

Court being recessed on Friday, Debs spent the day in Akron at the home of Mrs. Marguerite Prevey. His lawyers insisted that he should take advantage of his right to make another speech before sentence was passed. Debs, tired of the whole proceeding, adamantly refused. A heated wrangle followed, and finally Debs yielded. He ventured forth on a brief errand, and then retired to a small room at the head of the stairs to write his speech. When Morris Wolf went up to see Debs a few hours later, the nature of the errand became obvious. A pint bottle of bourbon, now sorely emaciated, was on the corner of the table.

Debs was angry at the Federal attorney. Mr. Wertz, in his final summary, had referred scornfully to both Rose Pastor Stokes and Kate O'Hare. Debs was now writing a bitter attack on the prosecutor. Wolf objected that such a descent to personalities would obscure the real issues and make the entire trial a burlesque. Debs glared at Wolf: "He is a friend of yours, is he?" Wolf tried to explain that he could do more for his client if he did not alienate the Federal officials. Men like Wertz, said the attorney, were mere hired hands who had no responsibility for the proceedings, they were just trying to make a living. Debs was not convinced, and there was another long argument. Finally Wolf, close to despair, summoned Marguerite Prevey to the room. She prevailed where Wolf had met with failure and Debs agreed to delete all references to Wertz.

Then Debs had to write a new beginning for his speech. Back in January, 1913, he had crowded his entire philosophy into a single sentence that appeared in *The Masses.* He had used the same phrases, changing but a single word, on the title page of *Labor and Freedom,* a collection of his writings and speeches published in 1916. He now returned to the original version and began to write: "While there is a lower class . . ."

When court opened on Saturday, the Federal attorney moved for the imposition of sentence. The clerk asked if the defendant would like to make a final statement. Eugene Debs again rose from his chair and began talking as he moved toward the bench. There were no notes to be gathered up, no papers to guide him, but all that an honest man can learn in sixty years was contained in his opening remark: "Your Honor, years ago I recognized my kinship with all living things, and I made up my mind that I was not one bit better than the meanest of the earth. I said then, I say now, that while there is a lower class, I am in it; while there is a criminal element, I am of it; while there is a soul in prison, I am not free."

Eugene Debs had already forgotten his promise to Morris Wolf and to Marguerite Prevey: "Everything in connection with this case has been conducted upon a dignified plane, and in a respectful and decent spirit—with just one exception. Your Honor, my sainted mother inspired me with a reverence for womanhood that amounts to worship. I can think with disrespect of no woman, and I can think with respect of no man who can. I resent the manner in which the names of two noble women were bandied in this court. The levity and the wantonness in this instance was absolutely inexcusable. When I think of what was said in this connection, I feel that when I pass a woman, even though it be a sister of the street, I should take off my hat and apologize for being a man."

Debs' friends had long noticed that liquor made him even more eloquent, more sensitive, more gentle—and it was true. "In the struggle," he continued, "the unceasing struggle—between the toilers and producers and their exploiters, I have tried . . . to serve those among whom I was born, with whom I expect to share my lot until the end of my days."

"I am thinking this morning of the men in the mills and factories; I am thinking of the women who, for a paltry wage, are compelled to work out their lives; of the little children who, in this system, are robbed of their childhood, and in their early, tender years, are seized in the remorseless grasp of Mammon, and forced into the industrial dungeons, there to feed the machines while they themselves are being starved body and soul. I can see them dwarfed, diseased, stunted, their little lives broken, and their hopes blasted, because in this high noon of our twentieth century civilization money is still so much more important than human life. Gold is god and rules in the affairs of men . . ."

"I never more clearly comprehended than now the great struggle between the powers of greed on the one hand and upon the other the rising hosts of freedom. I can see the dawn of a better day of humanity. The people are awakening. In due course of time they will come into their own. . . ."

When the end came, Judge Westenhaver still sat, unshaken and severe. The judge declared that he was second to no man in his sympathy for the poor and suffering. But he was amazed by the "remarkable self-delusion and self-deception of Mr. Debs who assumes that he is serving humanity and the down-trodden." Those who violate the law must suffer the penalties. This applied with double force to those persons "within our borders who would strike the sword from the hand of this nation while she is engaged in defending herself against a foreign and brutal power." Declaring himself "a conserver of the peace and a defender of the Constitution of the United States," Judge Westenhaver imposed a sentence of ten years in prison upon the Socialist leader.

Many spectators scarcely heard the sentence. They had been transported into a cleaner, better land by the speech of Eugene Debs, which caused many a strangled gasp in the courtroom. He had appeared as a gigantic bridge, a man who stood with one foot firmly anchored in the present,

the other in the future, while the multitude walked across his shoulders.
A portion of humanity felt purified in the sacramental vision of Eugene
Debs:

> Let the people take heart and hope everywhere,
> for the cross is bending,
> the midnight is passing,
> and joy cometh with the morning.

With the exception of the Pullman boycott, no incident in Debs' career
aroused so much comment as the Canton speech and the subsequent trial.
Thousands of people who neither knew nor cared about his Socialist beliefs vaguely understood that he was sent to prison because he opposed
the World War. Some men adopted the romantic viewpoint that it was a
transmuted Eugene Debs who faced the jury in a Cleveland courtroom.
So gradually, over a number of years, the events of 1918 came to form
an important part of the Debs Legend. Typical are the comments of [the
journalist] Heywood Broun: "Debs . . . was never the brains of his party.
I never met him, but I read many of his speeches, and most of them
seemed to be second-rate utterances. But when his great moment came a
miracle occurred. Debs made a speech to the judge and jury at Columbus
after his conviction, and to me it seems one of the most beautiful and moving passages in the English language. He was for that one afternoon touched
with inspiration. If anybody told me that tongues of fire danced upon his
shoulders as he spoke, I would believe it."

This statement by Broun probably missed the main point. Debs' speech
in Cleveland was a culmination, not an explosive miracle. Given his early
convictions, given his intimate acquaintance with the workingman of America, given his two decades in the Socialist movement, he inevitably faced
his accusers in a Federal courtroom. Arrived there, he said nothing that
he had not said in the past. Even his phrases, his images, had been accumulated during countless appearances on the lecture platform. The importance of Eugene Debs derives from the road he followed to reach that
courtroom in Cleveland, not from a single afternoon when "tongues of fire
danced upon his shoulders as he spoke."

Equally popular was Broun's belief that Debs "was never the brains of
his party." This description was endorsed by most Socialist leaders, whether
radical or reformist. Although they acknowledged Debs' "spiritual" leadership, they steadfastly contended that he was no thinker or theoretician.
This too became an unquestioned segment of the Debs Legend, but it
seems just as mistaken as Broun's other concept about Debs. Certainly
Eugene Debs was untutored in both literature and science, lacked the will
for serious scholarship, was unable to reach decisions by theoretical study.
Sometimes he reacted to new conditions with astonishing tardiness. His
flirtation with the IWW badly retarded the growth of industrial unionism.

His opposition to reform parties hindered the development of a working-class political movement. He misjudged the plight of the Negro people. His failure to insist on a united Socialist movement had tragic consequences in 1917.

But in spite of these faults Eugene Debs deserves to be known as the political leader of American socialism. He clung with stubborn insistence to the basic principles of Marxian socialism. He showed an uncanny ability to foresee issues and to devise remedies. He first raised the standard against the prosecution of Bill Haywood and Fred Warren and the McNamaras; against intervention in Mexico; against participation in the World War. He played a part in hundreds of hard-fought strikes. He hurled his waning energies into the struggle for American recognition of Soviet Russia. Debs' sole purpose was to inspire a working-class revolt against the capitalist system, and his success was truly remarkable. He kindled the fires of a newer hope for millions of his fellow citizens.

And through all of these temporary battles, Debs held to the twin objectives that he had announced before 1900, industrial unionism and revolutionary politics. No other prominent radical was entitled to the same boast. The right wing of the party had become enamored with reform platforms and machine methods; the left wing had sought the illusory success of anarcho-syndicalism; Debs had stanchly opposed both trends. He had consistently been among the first to capitalize on immediate issues, and he had never forgotten his ultimate goal of socialism. Debs' career is startling, not because he made mistakes, but because he made so few of them.

The attacks on Eugene Debs were directed against his associates as well as his principles. In 1910, for instance, Ernest Untermann said of Debs: "Nearly all of his advisers in the labor movement have turned out to be crooked." Certainly the facts lend weight to the charge that Debs was both naïve and sentimental in his estimates of other people. His cordiality toward the prowar Socialists, even after they had deserted the Party, is illustrative of the value [he placed] on personal friendship and the former records of his associates.

A second explanation, however, is needed to complete the story. Eugene Debs was neither a purist nor a moralist, but a trade-union leader and a Socialist. He firmly believed that basic changes in human behavior would follow rather than precede the establishment of socialism. So he took help where he could find it, balancing the risks against the benefits. These colleagues inevitably acquired a measure of power, and some of them used it to their personal advantage. In the Socialist Party this policy led to chaos; in the American Railway Union it led to success. No criticism of Debs is involved in the splotchy records of such men as George Howard; actually it is a tribute that Debs was able to use Howard's abilities for a constructive purpose.

THEODORE ROOSEVELT

&
the "Big Stick"

Throughout most of American history, the power of the presidency has waxed and waned like the tides, but in the twentieth century it has seemed only to rise higher and higher. Theodore Roosevelt in particular grafted responsibilities onto the White House and developed the political resources of the office. In part this increase in presidential power grew out of newly formed domestic concerns—regulation of the economy, conservation, and an executive role in labor-management disputes. But more than anything else, the growing role of the United States in world affairs gave Roosevelt and the presidents who followed a continuing central position among the institutions of government.

Personally popular, Teddy, as Americans universally knew him, found the White House a "bully pulpit." He loved to preach, had a flair for the dramatic, and possessed vast reserves of humor and of self-righteousness—a most unusual combination. As a result, Roosevelt thoroughly enjoyed the office he held, relished his responsibilities, and adored exercising power. He never complained of the loneliness and anguish of high office; he made hard choices and justified them later.

Teddy was not only a president but also a military hero, a big game hunter, a rancher, and an author. His early life does not suggest the ferocious range of activity he later demonstrated. Born of an old New York City merchant family in 1858, Roosevelt was the second of four children. As a child he suffered from asthma and poor eyesight. He was tutored at home and then sent to Harvard, graduating in 1880. Law did not interest him, but history did, and he began a lifelong avocation of writing. His writings—on the West, on historical subjects, on art and cultural criticism, on his public life—all were variations on his one favorite subject: Teddy. Yet this pleased his reading public and, in turn, his political supporters.

Roosevelt's social standing helped him get elected to the New York state legislature in 1882. There he established a pattern he rarely swerved from: publicizing and loudly declaring his views on all subjects. He was always a newsworthy source for eager reporters. From 1884 to 1886, he spent time on his ranch land in the Dakota territory and rapidly wrote a series of books on ranching, politics, and history. His support of Benjamin Harrison in the 1888 presidential election earned him a civil service commissioner's job, and he zestfully invaded Washington, aiming to end corruption there.

Back in New York City in 1895, he was appointed to the board of police commissioners and again brought the attention of the press to graft in politics. But his first real chance to show his moral crusading spirit came when President McKinley reluctantly offered him the post of Assistant Secretary of the Navy. When war with Spain became likely, Teddy resigned to form his famous cavalry regiment, the Rough Riders, which enabled him to become a popular war hero and then to win election as governor of New York in 1898. Two years later, through a combination of popular appeal and private antagonisms that made associates eager to be rid of him, Roosevelt was nominated for the vice-presidential slot on McKinley's ticket. The assassination of the president pushed Roosevelt into the highest office in September 1901.

Roosevelt's trademark was perhaps his swift decisions and actions, which contrasted with the slow ways of his predecessors. He pursued foreign policy with particular relish, taking an active part in settling disputes among European and Asian powers. In 1907 Roosevelt sent an American armada, the "Great White Fleet," around the world, dramatizing the country's new international position to friends, potential foes, and the American public. He summed up his pugnacious attitude in the famous motto, "Speak softly and carry a big stick."

Rooseveltian foreign policy had its greatest effect in Latin America, where the president initiated a policy of intervening freely in the affairs of other Western Hemisphere countries to forestall European incursions to collect debts. The keystone of Roosevelt's Latin American policy was the construction of a canal across Panama to complete United States domination of Central America and to increase the mobility of the American navy. The remarkable way that he gained the Panama Canal route is perhaps the best single example of his quickness and his high-handedness. It has had energetic defenders (beginning with TR himself) and equally insistent critics. Roosevelt took high ground in defending this and similar actions. He asserted, in the Roosevelt Corollary to the Monroe Doctrine (enunciated in his annual message for 1904), that in the interests of civilization the United States had a right to intervene in the affairs of other Western Hemisphere nations. This kind of assertion eventually spread to the entire world, and it defined the issues for the debate over the limits of the United States' role in the world—the debate that has raged, in continually changing terms, from the turn of the century to the present.

The Panama Canal (1913)
THEODORE ROOSEVELT

*Roosevelt had a remarkably consistent self-image: that of the virtuous
man in the middle, understanding and moderating the extremes on all
sides of him. Applicable in domestic affairs, where he promised to bring
about a "square deal" between the rich and the poor, the powerful
and the weak, it applied as well in foreign affairs, where he saw himself
as one of the "strong and daring men who with wisdom love peace,
but who love righteousness more than peace." Is the story he tells below
one of the triumphs of righteousness over peace?*

BY FAR the most important action I took in foreign affairs during the time
I was President related to the Panama Canal. Here again there was much
accusation about my having acted in an "unconstitutional" manner—a
position which can be upheld only if Jefferson's action in acquiring Louisiana be also treated as unconstitutional; and at different stages of the affair
believers in a do-nothing policy denounced me as having "usurped authority"—which meant, that when nobody else could or would exercise
efficient authority, I exercised it.

During the nearly four hundred years that had elapsed since Balboa
crossed the Isthmus, there had been a good deal of talk about building
an Isthmus Canal, and there had been various discussions of the subject
and negotiations about it in Washington for the previous half-century. So
far it had all resulted merely in conversation; and the time had come when
unless somebody was prepared to act with decision we would have to
resign ourselves to at least half a century of further conversation. Under
the Hay-Pauncefote Treaty signed shortly after I became President, and
thanks to our negotiations with the French Panama Company, the United
States at last acquired a possession, so far as Europe was concerned, which
warranted her in immediately undertaking the task. It remained to decide
where the canal should be, whether along the line already pioneered by
the French company in Panama, or in Nicaragua. Panama belonged to
the Republic of Colombia. Nicaragua bid eagerly for the privilege of having the United States build the canal through her territory. As long as it
was doubtful which route we would decide upon, Colombia extended
every promise of friendly co-operation: at the Pan-American Congress
in Mexico her delegate joined in the unanimous vote which requested the

United States forthwith to build the canal; and at her eager request we negotiated the Hay-Herran Treaty with her, which gave us the right to build the canal across Panama. A board of experts sent to the Isthmus had reported that this route was better than the Nicaragua route, and that it would be well to build the canal over it provided we could purchase the rights of the French Company for forty million dollars; but that otherwise they would advise taking the Nicaragua route. Ever since 1846 we had had a treaty with the power then in control of the Isthmus, the Republic of New Granada, the predecessor of the Republic of Colombia and of the present Republic of Panama, by which treaty the United States was guaranteed free and open right of way across the Isthmus of Panama by any mode of communication that might be constructed, while in return our government guaranteed the perfect neutrality of the Isthmus with a view to the preservation of free transit.

For nearly fifty years we had asserted the right to prevent the closing of this highway of commerce. Secretary of State Cass in 1858 officially stated the American position as follows:

"Sovereignty has its duties as well as its rights, and none of these local governments, even if administered with more regard to the just demands of other nations than they have been, would be permitted, in a spirit of Eastern isolation, to close the gates of intercourse of the great highways of the world, and justify the act by the pretension that these avenues of trade and travel belong to them and that they choose to shut them, or, what is almost equivalent, to encumber them with such unjust relations as would prevent their general use."

We had again and again been forced to intervene to protect the transit across the Isthmus, and the intervention was frequently at the request of Colombia herself. The effort to build a canal by private capital had been made under De Lesseps and had resulted in lamentable failure. Every serious proposal to build the canal in such manner had been abandoned. The United States had repeatedly announced that we would not permit it to be built or controlled by any Old World government. Colombia was utterly impotent to build it herself. Under these circumstances it had become a matter of imperative obligation that we should build it ourselves without further delay.

I took final action in 1903. During the preceding fifty-three years the governments of New Granada and of its successor, Colombia, had been in a constant state of flux; and the state of Panama had sometimes been treated as almost independent, in a loose Federal league, and sometimes as the mere property of the government at Bogota; and there had been innumerable appeals to arms, sometimes for adequate, sometimes for inadequate, reasons. . . .

The above [a list omitted here] is only a partial list of the revolutions, rebellions, insurrections, riots, and other outbreaks that occurred during the period in question; yet they number fifty-three for the fifty-three years, and they showed a tendency to increase, rather than decrease, in numbers and intensity. One of them lasted for nearly three years before it was quelled; another for nearly a year. In short, the experience of over half a century had shown Colombia to be utterly incapable of keeping order on the Isthmus. Only the active interference of the United States had enabled her to preserve so much as a semblance of sovereignty. Had it not been for the exercise by the United States of the police power in her interest, her connection with the Isthmus would have been sundered long before it was. In 1856, in 1860, in 1873, in 1885, in 1901, and again in 1902, sailors and marines from United States war-ships were forced to land in order to patrol the Isthmus, to protect life and property, and to see that the transit across the Isthmus was kept open. In 1861, in 1862, in 1885, and in 1900, the Colombian Government asked that the United States Government would land troops to protect Colombian interests and maintain order on the Isthmus. The people of Panama during the preceding twenty years had three times sought to establish their independence by revolution or secession—in 1885, in 1895, and in 1899.

The peculiar relations of the United States toward the Isthmus, and the acquiescence by Colombia in acts which were quite incompatible with the theory of her having an absolute and unconditioned sovereignty on the Isthmus, are illustrated by the following three telegrams between two of our naval officers whose ships were at the Isthmus and the secretary of the navy on the occasion of the first outbreak that occurred on the Isthmus after I became President (a year before Panama became independent):

September 12, 1902

RANGER, PANAMA: United States guarantees perfect neutrality of Isthmus and that a free transit from sea to sea be not interrupted or embarrassed. . . . Any transportation of troops which might contravene these provisions of treaty should not be sanctioned by you, nor should use of road be permitted which might convert the line of transit into theatre of hostility.

MOODY

Colon, September 20, 1902

SECRETARY NAVY, WASHINGTON: Everything is conceded. The United States guards and guarantees traffic and the line of transit. To-day I permitted the exchange of Colombian troops from Panama to Colon, about 1,000 men each way, the troops without arms in trains guarded by American naval force in the same manner as other passengers; arms and ammunition in separate train, guarded also by naval force in the same manner as other freight.

MC LEAN

Panama, October 3, 1902

SECRETARY NAVY, WASHINGTON, D. C.: Have sent this communication to the American Consul at Panama:

"Inform Governor, while trains running under United States protection, I must decline transportation any combatants, ammunition, arms, which might cause interruption to traffic or convert line of transit into theatre hostilities."

CASEY

When the government in nominal control of the Isthmus continually besought American interference to protect the "rights" it could not itself protect, and permitted our government to transport Colombian troops un-armed, under protection of our own armed men, while the Colombian arms and ammunition came in a separate train, it is obvious that the Colombian "sovereignty" was of such a character as to warrant our in-sisting that inasmuch as it only existed because of our protection there should be in requital a sense of the obligations that the acceptance of this protection implied.

Meanwhile Colombia was under a dictatorship. In 1898 M. A. San-clamente was elected president, and J. M. Maroquin vice-president, of the Republic of Colombia. On July 31, 1900, the vice-president, Maroquin, executed a *coup d'état* by seizing the person of the president, Sanclamente, and imprisoning him at a place a few miles out of Bogota. Maroquin there-upon declared himself possessed of the executive power because of "the absence of the president"—a delightful touch of unconscious humor. He then issued a decree that public order was disturbed, and, upon that ground, assumed to himself legislative power under another provision of the constitution; that is, having himself disturbed the public order, he alleged the disturbance as a justification for seizing absolute power. Thence-forth Maroquin, without the aid of any legislative body, ruled as a dictator, combining the supreme executive, legislative, civil, and military authorities, in the so-called Republic of Colombia. The "absence" of Sanclamente from the capital became permanent by his death in prison in the year 1902. When the people of Panama declared their independence in No-vember, 1903, no congress had sat in Colombia since the year 1898, ex-cept the special congress called by Maroquin to reject the canal treaty, and which did reject it by a unanimous vote, and adjourned without legis-lating on any other subject. The constitution of 1886 had taken away from Panama the power of self-government and vested it in Colombia. The *coup d'état* of Maroquin took away from Colombia herself the power of government and vested it in an irresponsible dictator.

Consideration of the above facts ought to be enough to show any human being that we were not dealing with normal conditions on the Isthmus and in Colombia. We were dealing with the government of an irresponsible alien dictator, and with a condition of affairs on the Isthmus itself which was marked by one uninterrupted series of outbreaks and revolutions. As for the "consent-of-the-governed" theory, that absolutely justified our action; the people on the Isthmus were the "governed"; they were governed by Colombia, without their consent, and they unanimously repudiated the Colombian Government, and demanded that the United States build the canal.

I had done everything possible, personally and through Secretary Hay, to persuade the Colombian Government to keep faith. Under the Hay-Pauncefote Treaty, it was explicitly provided that the United States should build the canal, should control, police, and protect it, and keep it open to the vessels of all nations on equal terms. We had assumed the position of guarantor of the canal, including, of course, the building of the canal, and of its peaceful use by all the world. The enterprise was recognized everywhere as responding to an international need. It was a mere travesty on justice to treat the government in possession of the Isthmus as having the right—which Secretary Cass forty-five years before had so emphatically repudiated—to close the gates of intercourse on one of the great highways of the world. When we submitted to Colombia the Hay-Herran Treaty, it had been settled that the time for delay, the time for permitting any government of antisocial character, or of imperfect development, to bar the work, had passed. The United States had assumed in connection with the canal certain responsibilities not only to its own people, but to the civilized world which imperatively demanded that there should be no further delay in beginning the work. The Hay-Herran Treaty, if it erred at all, erred in being overgenerous toward Colombia. The people of Panama were delighted with the treaty, and the president of Colombia, who embodied in his own person the entire government of Colombia, had authorized the treaty to be made. But after the treaty had been made the Colombia Government thought it had the matter in its own hands; and the further thought, equally wicked and foolish, came into the heads of the people in control at Bogota that they would seize the French Company at the end of another year and take for themselves the forty million dollars which the United States had agreed to pay the Panama Canal Company.

President Maroquin, through his minister, had agreed to the Hay-Herran Treaty in January, 1903. He had the absolute power of an unconstitutional dictator to keep his promise or break it. He determined to break it. To furnish himself an excuse for breaking it he devised the plan of summoning a congress especially called to reject the canal treaty. This the congress—a congress of mere puppets—did, without a dissenting vote; and the puppets adjourned forthwith without legislating on any other subject. The fact that this was a mere sham, and that the president had entire power to confirm his own treaty and act on it if he desired, was shown as soon as the revolution took place, for on November 6 General Reyes, of Colombia, addressed the American minister at Bogota, on behalf of President Maroquin, saying that "if the government of the United States would land troops and restore the Colombian sovereignty" the Colombian president would "declare martial law; and, by virtue of vested constitutional authority, when public order is disturbed, would approve by decree the ratification of the canal treaty as signed; or, if the government of the United States prefers, would call an extra session of the congress—with new and friendly members—next May to approve the treaty." This, of course, is proof positive that the Colombian dictator had used his congress as a mere shield, and a sham shield at that, and it shows how utterly useless it would have been further to trust his good faith in the matter.

When, in August, 1903, I became convinced that Colombia intended to repudiate the treaty made the preceding January, under cover of securing its rejection by the Colombian legislature, I began carefully to consider what should be done. By my direction, Secretary Hay, personally and through the minister at Bogota, repeatedly warned Colombia that grave consequences might follow her rejection of the treaty. The possibility of ratification did not wholly pass away until the close of the session of the Colombian congress on the last day of October. There would then be two possibilities. One was that Panama would remain quiet. In that case I was prepared to recommend to Congress that we should at once occupy the Isthmus anyhow, and proceed to dig the canal; and I had drawn out a draft of my message to this effect. But from the information I received, I deemed it likely that there would be a revolution in Panama as soon as the Colombian congress adjourned without ratifying the treaty, for the entire population of Panama felt that the immediate building of the canal was of vital concern to their well-being. Correspondents of the different newspapers on the Isthmus had sent to their respective papers widely published forecasts indicating that there would be a revolution in such event.

Moreover, on October 16, at the request of Lieutenant-General Young, Captain Humphrey, and Lieutenant Murphy, two army officers who had returned from the Isthmus, saw me and told me that there would unquestionably be a revolution on the Isthmus, that the people were unanimous in their criticism of the Bogota Government and their disgust over the failure of that government to ratify the treaty; and that the revolution would probably take place immediately after the adjournment of the Colombian congress. They did not believe that it would be before October 20, but they were confident that it would certainly come at the end of October or immediately afterward, when the Colombian congress had adjourned. Accordingly I directed the Navy Department to station various ships within easy reach of the Isthmus, to be ready to act in the event of need arising.

These ships were barely in time. On November 3 the revolution occurred. Practically everybody on the Isthmus, including all the Colombian troops that were already stationed there, joined in the revolution, and there was no bloodshed. But on that same day four hundred new Colombian troops were landed at Colon. Fortunately, the gunboat *Nashville,* under Commander Hubbard, reached Colon almost immediately afterward, and when the commander of the Colombian forces threatened the lives and property of the American citizens, including women and children, in Colon, Commander Hubbard landed a few score sailors and marines to protect them. By a mixture of firmness and tact he not only prevented any assault on our citizens, but persuaded the Colombian commander to reembark his troops for Cartagena. On the Pacific side a Colombian gunboat shelled the city of Panama, with the result of killing one Chinaman—the only life lost in the whole affair.

No one connected with the American Government had any part in preparing, inciting, or encouraging the revolution, and except for the reports of our military and naval officers, which I forwarded to Congress, no one connected with the government had any previous knowledge concerning the proposed revolution, except such as was accessible to any person who read the newspapers and kept abreast of current questions and current affairs. By the unanimous action of its people, and without the firing of a shot, the state of Panama declared themselves an independent republic. The time for hesitation on our part had passed.

My belief then was, and the events that have occurred since have more than justified it, that from the standpoint of the United States it was imperative, not only for civil but for military reasons, that there should be the immediate establishment of easy and speedy communication by sea between the Atlantic and the Pacific. These reasons were not of convenience only, but of vital necessity, and did not admit of indefinite delay. The action of Colombia had shown not only that the delay would be indefinite, but that she intended to confiscate the property and rights of the French Panama Canal Company. The report of the Panama Canal Committee of the Colombian senate on October 14, 1903, on the proposed treaty with the United States, proposed that all consideration of the matter should be postponed until October 31, 1904, when the next Colombian congress would have convened, because by that time the new Congress would be in condition to determine whether through lapse of time the French Company had not forfeited its property and rights. "When that time arrives," the report significantly declared, "the Republic, without any impediment, will be able to contract and will be in more clear, more definite and more advantageous possession, both legally and materially." The naked meaning of this was that Colombia proposed to wait a year, and then enforce a forfeiture of the rights and property of the French Panama Company, so as to secure the forty million dollars our government had authorized as payment to this company. If we had sat supine, this would doubtless have meant that France would have interfered to protect the company, and we should then have had on the Isthmus, not the company, but France; and the gravest international complications might have ensued.

Every consideration of international morality and expediency, of duty to
the Panama people, and of satisfaction of our own national interests and
honor, bade us take immediate action. I recognized Panama forthwith on
behalf of the United States, and practically all the countries of the world
immediately followed suit. The State Department immediately negotiated
a canal treaty with the new republic. One of the foremost men in securing
the independence of Panama, and the treaty which authorized the United
States forthwith to build the canal, was M. Philippe Bunau-Varilla, an
eminent French engineer formerly associated with De Lesseps and then
living on the Isthmus; his services to civilization were notable, and deserve
the fullest recognition.

From the beginning to the end our course was straightforward and in
absolute accord with the highest of standards of international morality.
Criticism of it can come only from misinformation, or else from a sentimentality which represents both mental weakness and a moral twist. To
have acted otherwise than I did would have been on my part betrayal of
the interests of the United States, indifference to the interests of Panama,
and recreancy to the interests of the world at large. Colombia had forfeited every claim to consideration; indeed, this is not stating the case
strongly enough: she had so acted that yielding to her would have meant
on our part that culpable form of weakness which stands on a level with
wickedness. As for me personally, if I had hesitated to act, and had not in
advance discounted the clamor of those Americans who have made a fetich
of disloyalty to their country, I should have esteemed myself as deserving
a place in Dante's inferno beside the faint-hearted cleric who was guilty
of *il gran rifiuto*. The facts I have given above are mere bald statements
from the record. They show that from the beginning there had been acceptance of our right to insist on free transit, in whatever form was best,
across the Isthmus; and that toward the end there had been a no less universal feeling that it was our duty to the world to provide this transit in
the shape of a canal—the resolution of the Pan-American Congress was
practically a mandate to this effect. Colombia was then under a one-man
government, a dictatorship, founded on usurpation of absolute and irresponsible power. She eagerly pressed us to enter into an agreement with
her, as long as there was any chance of our going to the alternative route
through Nicaragua. When she thought we were committed, she refused to
fulfil the agreement, with the avowed hope of seizing the French company's
property for nothing and thereby holding us up. This was a bit of pure
bandit morality. It would have achieved its purpose had I possessed as
weak moral fibre as those of my critics who announced that I ought to
have confined my action to feeble scolding and temporizing until the opportunity for action passed. I did not lift my finger to incite the revolutionists. The right simile to use is totally different. I simply ceased to stamp
out the different revolutionary fuses that were already burning. When
Colombia committed flagrant wrong against us, I considered it no part of

my duty to aid and abet her in her wrong-doing at our expense, and also at the expense of Panama, of the French company, and of the world generally. There had been fifty years of continuous bloodshed and civil strife in Panama; because of my action Panama has now known ten years of such peace and prosperity as she never before saw during the four centuries of her existence—for in Panama, as in Cuba and Santo Domingo, it was the action of the American people, against the outcries of the professed apostles of peace, which alone brought peace. We gave to the people of Panama self-government, and freed them from subjection to alien oppressors. We did our best to get Colombia to let us treat her with a more than generous justice; we exercised patience to beyond the verge of proper forbearance. When we did act and recognize Panama, Colombia at once acknowledged her own guilt by promptly offering to do what we had demanded, and what she had protested it was not in her power to do. But the offer came too late. What we would gladly have done before, it had by that time become impossible for us honorably to do; for it would have necessitated our abandoning the people of Panama, our friends, and turning them over to their and our foes, who would have wreaked vengeance on them precisely because they had shown friendship to us. Colombia was solely responsible for her own humiliation; and she had not then, and has not now, one shadow of claim upon us, moral or legal; all the wrong that was done was done by her. If, as representing the American people, I had not acted precisely as I did, I would have been an unfaithful or incompetent representative; and inaction at that crisis would have meant not only indefinite delay in building the canal, but also practical admission on our part that we were not fit to play the part on the Isthmus which we had arrogated to ourselves. I acted on my own responsibility in the Panama matter. John Hay spoke of this action as follows: "The action of the President in the Panama matter is not only in the strictest accordance with the principles of justice and equity, and in line with all the best precedents of our public policy, but it was the only course he could have taken in compliance with our treaty rights and obligations."

I deeply regretted, and now deeply regret, the fact that the Colombian Government rendered it imperative for me to take the action I took; but I had no alternative, consistent with the full performance of my duty to my own people, and to the nations of mankind. (For, be it remembered, that certain other nations, Chile for example, will probably benefit even more by our action than will the United States itself.) I am well aware that the Colombian people have many fine traits; that there is among them a circle of high-bred men and women which would reflect honor on the social life of any country; and that there has been an intellectual and literary development within this small circle which partially atones for the stagnation and illiteracy of the mass of the people; and I also know that even the illiterate mass possesses many sterling qualities. But unfortunately in international matters every nation must be judged by the action of its government. The good people in Colombia apparently made no effort, certainly no successful effort, to cause the government to act with reasonable good faith toward the United States; and Colombia had to take the consequences. If Brazil, or the Argentine, or Chile, had been in possession of the Isthmus, doubtless the canal would have been built under the governmental control of the nation thus controlling the Isthmus, with the hearty acquiescence of the United States and of all other powers. But in the actual fact the canal would not have been built at all save for the action I took. If men choose to say that it would have been better not to build it, than to build it as the result of such action, their position, although foolish, is compatible with belief in their wrong-headed sincerity. But it is hypocrisy, alike odious and contemptible, for any man to say both that we ought to have built the canal and that we ought not to have acted in the way we did act. . . .

A Critique of Roosevelt's Panama Policy (1904)
THE NATION

Teddy Roosevelt's contemporaries were by no means silent while he took his giant steps in Panama. Many, thinking of the advantages the canal would offer, applauded his actions; some, more concerned about the laws and rights he seemed to be disregarding, voiced a sharp criticism. The following commentary appeared in The Nation *on January 7, 1904.*

PRESIDENT ROOSEVELT has heard from the country. He knows now, what he did not appear to dream of when he wrote his easy paragraphs about Panama in his annual message, that his course is open to serious objection. It has been challenged by men of weight in his own party, to say nothing of the independent press, on grounds of both morality and law. It is no longer possible to whistle down this opposition, or to put us off with the comfortable assurance that the President can do no wrong. Mr. Roosevelt himself has seen the need of attempting his own defence; and he makes it at great length in the message which he sent to Congress on Monday. . . .
. . . He frankly admits now that his course has been irregular. The

recognition of Panama was, he surprisingly declares, "in no way dependent for its justification upon our action in ordinary cases." Mr. Roosevelt confesses that the "general rule" is against him. This is a great advance since November and December, when he was asserting that he had but done what this Government had "always" done. He does not deny to-day that "a new state should not be recognized as independent till it has shown its ability to maintain its independence." That is, he acknowledges that the precedents and the rules are adverse to the course he has followed. Then what is his defence? Why, simply that our "national interests" and "the interests of civilization" demand that we take this extraordinary and lawless step! In other words, when we want a thing intensely, we are entitled to trample upon propriety and the law in order to get it!

Now it is unnecessary to remind an historical student like President Roosevelt that every execrated political crime, every ruthless act of conquest, every wicked oppression of the weak, has been justified by its perpetrators on precisely this ground. Has he never read Napoleon's proclamations? That giant despoiler of the nations held exactly the language of President Roosevelt—all his plundering and murdering was for the "national defence" of France and the good of humanity. It is more than a coincidence that the President cites the words of Secretary Cass. They were written at the time when the slave-holding Democracy of this country was looking everywhere for new lands to subdue and pollute, and only shortly after that infamous Ostend manifesto which the first Republican platform denounced as "the highwayman's plea." What would those founders of the party have said had they conceived it possible that a Republican President in 1904 would make that plea his own?

What we say is that, with such principles of action avowed by the President, no country is safe from his aggressions. This Government was founded as a government of law. When the Executive sets the army or navy in motion, he must be able to point to warrant in the Constitution or in the statutes. But here we have Mr. Roosevelt erecting as the true standard the "national interest"—or what *he* conceives to be the national interest. Apparently, this chivalrous President intends for the present to confine his attacks to weak nations—those which, as he says with fine magnanimity of Colombia, are "helplessly unable to enforce" their will as against us. But who shall put a check upon him? If he is to be a law unto himself and set up his notion of the national interest as his sufficient guide, where shall we stop? Nowhere short of becoming a standing threat to the peace of the world. Such wild and lawless conceptions of public policy must be put down, or the man professing them rebuked by the people, unless we wish to see this nation embark upon a career of universal aggression.

The President's message, far from being the end of debate, is only the beginning of it. He has not answered the searching questions put to him. . . . He passes over entirely his commission of an act of war against a friendly nation. This and his other violations of law and precedent are the real points at issue. They cannot be hidden by the President's cloud of irrelevances. The question before Congress and before the country is simply whether this great nation is willing to twist a treaty, to turn its back on admitted precedents, and to violate international law, all in order to win a mean and mercenary advantage. . . .

It is evident that the master-motive of both Mr. Roosevelt and Secretary Hay in all this Panama recklessness has been a thorough contempt of the Colombians because they are not altogether such as we are, and because they are weak. This crops out in the President's message. He speaks of the "anti-social spirit" and "imperfect development" of the Colombians. How could such wretched inferiors expect to have their rights respected by the flower of Christian civilization? The old conception that laws were made for the protection of the weak has no place in Mr. Roosevelt's philosophy. Whom we can afford to despise we may wrong with impunity. Now contempt is as perilous a basis of intercourse between nations as between men. From despising people you soon pass to despising their rights; from contempt of their wishes you pass to contempt of our laws. The President's latest revelation of the way in which that spirit actuates him, has been too much for some of his warmest supporters. Whatever the immediate political and public effect may be there can be no doubt what the verdict of the judicious will be upon the Panama highhandedness. Apropos of one of Palmerston's international aggressions, Lord Malmesbury wrote in his diary: "A low trick and unworthy of England." When the letters and journals of the present day come to light, how many honorable Americans will be found to have written in secret a like condemnation of John Hay and Theodore Roosevelt!

Theodore Roosevelt and the Panama Canal (1931)
HENRY F. PRINGLE

Henry F. Pringle brought careful scholarship and a sharp eye for irony to his biography of Theodore Roosevelt. No biography, of course, gives the final word on any event; but neither does any first-hand account like Roosevelt's.

WHILE [William N.] Cromwell and [Philippe] Bunau-Varilla were busy with plans for a revolution in Panama in the summer and fall of 1903, President Roosevelt was giving consideration to a solution of his own. Virtuously, he "cast aside . . . the proposition to foment the secession of Panama." The United States could not, "by such underhanded means," encourage a revolt against Colombia. The President admitted, however, in communicating these views to Dr. Albert Shaw on October 10, 1903, that he would "be delighted if Panama were an independent State." The same idea was expressed in other letters. Roosevelt told President Schurman of Cornell that "for me to announce my feelings would be taken as equivalent to an effort to incite an insurrection in Panama. . . . If I were to state what I, in the abstract, thought would be most desirable, it would . . . be deemed . . . an effort to bring that state of affairs in the concrete.

"If Congress will give me a certain amount of freedom and a certain amount of time," he added, "I believe I can do much better than by any action taken out of hand."

Three days before the United States Senate confirmed the Hay-Herran Treaty in March, 1903, Roosevelt prepared for possible trouble with Colombia. He ordered Secretary of War Root to send two or three army officers "to map out and gather information concerning the coasts of those portions of South America which would be of especial interest . . . in the event of any struggle in the Gulf of Mexico or the Caribbean Sea." Work on the canal might soon start and data on Venezuela, Colombia, and the Guianas would be valuable. The officers, he directed, should go in civilian dress.

These were merely precautionary measures. Roosevelt still counted upon ratification by Colombia. When the "foolish and homicidal corruptionists" actually rejected the too generous offer of the United States, the President was unwilling to rely on the prospect of a revolution. This might fail inasmuch as the United States could not openly assist in the plans. An alternative solution was transmitted to Roosevelt on August 15, 1903, three days after the rash action by Bogotá. Francis B. Loomis, First Assistant Secretary of State, forwarded a memorandum drafted by Professor John Bassett Moore of Columbia University and said that it contained "strong and well supported suggestions . . . which may be of very great importance." Roosevelt agreed as to their importance. Four days later, from Sagamore Hill, where he was resting from the heat of Washington, he sent the memorandum to John Hay. The "Bogotá lot of corruptionists," he wrote, should not be permitted "permanently to bar one of the future highways of civilization." It was evident that some new plan for a canal across the Panama was taking shape in Roosevelt's mind.

The memorandum from Dr. Moore vanished for some years and was a subject for speculation by historians. A copy is among the Roosevelt papers at the Library of Congress, however, and it is not difficult to understand why the President promptly sent it to his Secretary of State. Dr.

Moore, already an authority on international law, had independently evolved a theory which fitted admirably into Roosevelt's views on Colombia and the canal. The United States, he wrote, "in undertaking to build the canal, does a work not only for itself but for the world." If, as expert opinion agreed, Panama was the best route, "it is the one that we should have. . . . May Colombia be permitted to stand in the way?" Dr. Moore felt that it must not, and he offered an ingenious, but also a scholarly, argument in support of his belief. He pointed to the Treaty of 1846 with New Granada, a country which became the Republic of Colombia in 1863, and its clause that "the right of way or transit across the Isthmus of Panama . . . shall be free and open *to the Government* and citizens of the United States." This provision (Article XXXV of the Treaty of 1846) applied to "any modes of communication that now exist, or that may be hereafter constructed."

In return for this privilege, the memorandum continued, the United States guaranteed "the perfect neutrality of the . . . isthmus, with the view that free transit from one to the other sea may not be interrupted or embarrassed in any future time . . . and guarantees, in the same manner, the rights of sovereignty and property which New Granada has and possesses over the said territory." The object in assuming this burden was to secure a canal, said Dr. Moore, and "in view of the fact that the United States has for more than fifty years secured to Colombia her sovereignty . . . Colombia . . . is . . . not in a position to obstruct the building of the canal." As for technicalities or disagreement on the meaning of the treaty or international law, the memorandum said:

Once on the ground and duly installed, this Government would find no difficulty in meeting questions as they arose. It has done so under the Treaty of 1846. Colombia's guarantee of a free and open transit has not secured it to us. We have usually found, when the emergency arose, that we were dependent upon our own resources for the enjoyment of the privileges which the treaty was designed to secure to us.

The position of the United States is altogether different from that of private capitalists who, unless expressly exempted, are altogether subject to the local jurdisdiction, and who, before invoking their governments' protection, *may be required to tread the paths of ordinary litigation* and establish their rights before the tribunals of the governments against which they assert them. Under such conditions, the private capitalist *must have everything beforehand nominated in the bond*. The United States is not subject to such disabilities, and can take care of the future.

Obviously, the President was interested; a philosophy more Rooseveltian would be difficult to find. Unhampered by "the paths of ordinary litigation" or by stipulations "nominated in the bond," a great deal could be accomplished by a courageous and impatient Chief Executive. Dr. Moore was invited to Oyster Bay to discuss "matters of foreign policy." The President told Hay that if, under the Treaty of 1846, "we have a color of right to start in and build a canal, my off-hand judgment would favor such proceeding." It may have been a rather dim color of right, but to Roosevelt it was sufficient. By September, 1903, he was intimating to Hay and to Taft that action would be taken in Panama without reference to the Bogotan Government. To a warning from Senator Hanna on October 4 that patience was essential, that ultimately an agreement with Colombia would be effected, Roosevelt expressed doubt that "the only virtue we need is patience":

> This does not mean that we must necessarily go to Nicaragua. I feel we are *certainly justified in morals, and therefore justified in law,* in interfering summarily and saying that the canal is to be built and that they must not stop it.

All the while Bunau-Varilla and Cromwell were urging a policy of action. The Frenchman, hoping that his words would reach the President, wrote Dr. Moore on October 3, 1903, that Colombia sought a year's delay. This, he added craftily, would carry the situation close to Election Day in 1904 and would force Roosevelt "to come before the people without a solution of the canal problem." The administration "would be accused of having bowed to the opposition of the transcontinental railroads or of having forfeited its opportunity by waiting too long for Colombia." Cromwell, equally skillful in playing upon Roosevelt's ambitions, wrote that "this problem of the ages" had never been so near to solution. If lost, it would be lost "for centuries to come."

"Your virile and masterful policy," he said, "will prove the solution of this great problem."

The secession of Panama was to make it unnecessary to put in operation a plan based on Dr. Moore's memorandum. Roosevelt formulated it late in October in a rough draft of his message to Congress. Either Nicaragua should be substituted or "without any further parley with Colombia [we should] enter upon the completion of the canal which the French company has begun." The latter course "is the one demanded by the interest of this nation." In a private letter, Roosevelt described it more bluntly:

> . . . if they had not revolted, I should have recommended to Congress to take possession of the Isthmus by force of arms; and . . . I had actually written the first draft of my message to this effect.

Inciting the "most just and proper revolution," as Roosevelt described it, was a task that took all the skill of Bunau-Varilla, Cromwell, and the other conspirators. The faltering courage of Panamanian patriots had to be fortified by promises that the United States would, in spirit and probably actively, be behind them. Gold with which to bribe the Colombian troops had to be supplied. It was necessary to point out that the $10,000,000 to be paid by the United States would, in the event of independence, go to

Panama and not to Colombia. This $10,000,000 could be spent as the sons of liberty saw fit.

In considering the relation of the United States to the revolution, and thereby the part played by Roosevelt, it is important to recall that Bunau-Varilla and Cromwell were men who commanded the ear of John Hay, of Senator Hanna, and of the President himself. The former, because he was clever and active and well informed, could pass at will among the members of the administration. The latter, as befitted a Republican who had given $60,000 to the last campaign chest, was equally well received. So, during 1903, these two worked zealously and to great effect. Roosevelt did nothing to incite the revolution, perhaps, but he was extremely well informed regarding the plans.

The first hint regarding them came in June, 1903. Colombia had not yet acted on the Hay-Herran Treaty when a curiously prophetic item appeared in the New York *World*. A dispatch from Washington stated, without giving an authority, that President Roosevelt was determined to have the Panama route. But Washington had been informed that Colombia did not propose to ratify and had received the further information that "Panama stands ready to secede . . . and enter into a canal treaty with the United States." The dispatch concluded with the news that on that day, June 13, 1903, William Nelson Cromwell had "a long conversation with the President." Subsequently, this aroused much interest and was offered as proof that Roosevelt had fomented the revolution. It eventually became known, however, that the dispatch had been inspired by a press agent for Cromwell and its purpose had been to frighten Colombia into signing the Hay-Herran agreement. The occurrence, together with a second visit by Cromwell to the White House on October 7, 1903, is of interest principally in connection with Roosevelt's ultimate insistence that

. . . no one connected with this government had any part in preparing, inciting or *encouraging* the revolution . . . *no one had any previous knowledge . . . except such as was available to any person . . . who read the newspapers.* . . . I do not remember whether Mr. Cromwell was . . . among my callers during the months immediately preceding the revolution. But if he was, I certainly did not discuss with him anything connected with the revolution. I do not remember his ever speaking to me about the revolution until after it occurred, and my understanding was, and is, that he had nothing to do with the revolutionary movement.

Surely Roosevelt was not as naïve as all that. It is inconceivable that a President so well informed on other subjects did not know about Cromwell's activities. Such a statement places a severe strain upon my theory that Roosevelt was not consciously untruthful. He could hardly have discussed birth control with Cromwell or the French drama with Bunau-Varilla. For Roosevelt to say that his administration knew no more of the revolutionary plans than a newspaper reader was untrue. A second source

of information to which the general public had no access was Bunau-
Varilla, who had again arrived from Paris in September, 1903. In recording
with pride the means by which he brought independence to Panama,
Bunau-Varilla enumerated conferences with Loomis, with Hay, and with
the President. He saw Roosevelt on October 9 and predicted a revolution.

"A revolution?" murmured Roosevelt, thinking of his own plan to seize
Panama by force. "Would it be possible? But if it became a reality, what
would become of the plan we had thought of?"

Roosevelt not only knew, in a general way, of the conspiracy; he was
considering what action the United States would take when it came and
whether, under the Treaty of 1846, Colombia could be prevented from putting down the rebellion. He even received memoranda from the State Department to the effect that Colombian officers and soldiers had not been
paid for weeks, were close to starvation, and therefore open to bribery.
Finally, he had confidential reports from two of the army officers who had
been detailed to the South American coast and the Caribbean. Roosevelt
admitted that Capt. Thomas B. Humphrey and Lieut. Grayson M-P.
Murphy had been to Panama—"on their own initiative (and without my
knowledge)"—and had learned that a revolution would take place the
end of October or early in November. No one at Washington, he said, had
told them of the possibility that Panama would secede.

The youthful Lieutenant (later Colonel) Murphy, subsequently the head
of Grayson M-P. Murphy & Company of Wall Street, has recalled his visit
to Panama. While the two officers were in Venezuela during July, 1903,
Captain Humphrey received word from a friend in Washington that anything regarding Panama which could be learned would be of interest to
the War Department. This was quite unofficial, but on the strength of it,
Colonel Murphy remembered, they hurried to Panama, where they accumulated facts regarding the probable revolution. The prospects for Panamanian freedom looked so bright, indeed, that Humphrey and Murphy
debated the wisdom of resigning their army commissions forthwith and
assisting in its consummation. On returning to Washington in October,
they considered a visit to J. P. Morgan & Company to ask financial assistance. They were prepared to supply the revolution if Morgan would agree
to let them have $100,000 each as their share of the $10,000,000 that the
United States would turn over to Panama.

On the night of October 16, however, the officers were summoned to the
White House. President Roosevelt cautioned them to say nothing about
seeing him, and questioned them exhaustively on the data they had obtained on the isthmus. He astonished both officers by his knowledge of the
topography of the country. They gathered from the conversation that
Roosevelt intended some sort of action, but he said nothing to indicate that
the Government was taking part in the revolution. Nor did he ask them
when it would take place. After an hour, Murphy and Humphrey left,
their dream of participation gone.

"There goes our revolution," Murphy said. "I sail for the Philippines."

The plans of Cromwell and Bunau-Varilla, meanwhile, were making progress. The usefulness of the New York attorney lay partly in the fact that the Panama Railroad and Steamship Company was owned by his clients, the New Panama Canal Company. It had agents in Panama City and Colón who were to be very useful in hastening the day when, according to Roosevelt, "the people of Panama rose literally as one man" against the tyranny of Bogotá. During the summer of 1903 this rising tide of patriotism was barely discernible to the two major conspirators.

One of the patriots was Dr. Manuel Amador de Guerrero, who had shortened his name to Manuel Amador and who was, by strange coincidence, physician to Mr. Cromwell's Panama Railroad and Steamship Company. The railroad physician aspired to the status of the George Washington of the Republic of Panama, and he went to New York early in September, 1903, to determine whether funds and support were forthcoming. It was a poverty-stricken cause at that time; Dr. Amador, taking passage on the S.S. *Seguranco,* had been embarrassed for funds. Happily, however, the doctor was an excellent poker player and he managed to win enough during the voyage north to take rooms at the Hotel Endicott in New York.

But Cromwell, to whom Amador looked for aid, had grown somewhat cautious. A leak had developed and Herran, the Colombian chargé at Washington, had telegraphed his government on September 4, that the United States was undoubtedly in favor of a revolution. Amador encountered a distressing coolness when he called at the offices of Sullivan & Cromwell, and it was not until M. Bunau-Varilla arrived from France on September 23 that the prospects of assistance rose. Until then, the Frenchman had been carrying on negotiations from Paris. Now, he established himself in Room 1162 of the Waldorf-Astoria Hotel, a room, he wrote, which "deserves to be considered as the cradle of the Panama Republic." Having seen Roosevelt on October 9 and finding encouragement, although no pledge was given, in the attitude of the President, Bunau-Varilla called upon John Hay. The Secretary of State, Bunau-Varilla recalled, said that "we shall not be caught napping . . . orders have been given to naval forces in the Pacific to sail toward the isthmus." This was precisely what Bunau-Varilla wanted to hear. He returned, greatly encouraged, to Room 1162.

On October 14, Dr. Amador presented himself at the shrine in the Waldorf. He received full instructions. Bunau-Varilla would supply $100,000 for the preliminary expenses of a revolution to be staged on November 3, 1903—Election Day in the United States. He was handed a draft of Panama's new constitution, a code whereby the rebels could communicate with the cradle of their liberty, a proclamation of independence and, most important of all, a message to be sent as soon as Truth had triumphed against Passion and Panama was free. This message was an appeal to

Bunau-Varilla to become, though a citizen of France, first Panamanian minister to the United States. On this point Bunau-Varilla was firm, although Amador protested that the selection of a foreigner might offend the nationalistic pride of the yet unborn republic.

"Nothing remains but to make the model of the flag," said Bunau-Varilla as he ushered Amador out of Room 1162. "I am going tomorrow to join my family . . . I shall find . . . the agile and discreet fingers that will make a new flag."

On the following day, a Sunday, Mme. Bunau-Varilla, the Betsy Ross of Panama, secreted herself and stitched "the flag of liberation." It was, her husband felt as he gazed on its folds, a fitting emblem; very much like that of the United States, but with yellow instead of white for the background and with two suns in place of stars. He recalled with irritation that the ungrateful Panamanians ultimately changed the design.

It is lamentable that Roosevelt, whose sense of humor and love for the dramatic would have been gratified, was denied detailed knowledge of these preparations. While Bunau-Varilla waited at the Waldorf, while Cromwell left for Paris to be near his clients, lesser conspirators were busy in mosquito-infested Panama. Amador, sailing southward on the S.S. *Yucatan,* the identical vessel that had borne Roosevelt and his Rough Riders to Cuba in 1898, arrived at Colón on October 27, 1903, and was greeted at the wharf by H. G. Prescott, another employee of the Panama Railroad and Steamship Company. The patriots met that night at the home of Frederico Boyd and soon were expressing disgust at the meager assurances brought back by Amador. Why had he not obtained a secret treaty of defense signed by Hay? How were they to know that the United States would really save them from the wrath of Bogotá?

"You are an old man," protested Tomas Arias, ". . . and you don't care if you are hung. I do not like to be hung."

This reasonable sentiment was echoed by others. To make matters worse, word came that Colombian troops had been dispatched to reinforce the garrison on the isthmus. Depressed and alarmed, Amador cabled Bunau-Varilla on October 28, that the Bogotan forces would arrive at Colón on November 2 or 3. If the revolution was to have a chance of success, an American warship must be rushed to the scene. Like Mark Twain's Yankee in the Court of King Arthur, Bunau-Varilla decided to predict the movement of forces over which he had no actual control. Instead of an almanac to determine the hour of an eclipse, he had the newspapers. He had read that the U.S.S. *Dixie* had sailed from Philadelphia, ostensibly for Guantanamo. The U.S.S. *Nashville* was off Kingston, ready to steam for the isthmus. On October 29, Bunau-Varilla was again in Washington and told every one of importance whom he could reach that the revolution would take place on November 3. On the train carrying him back to New York on the following day, he indulged in some calculations. The *Nashville,* about 500 miles from the isthmus, could steam at ten knots and so would arrive within two and a half days. During the interview with Hay on October 16, he had been told that two other vessels would rush toward the isthmus from San Francisco. Bunau-Varilla felt, in view of his knowledge, that the rôle of prophet was safe. He telegraphed Amador that one warship would arrive at Colón, on the Atlantic side, within two days. Within four days, two other American vessels would drop anchor at Panama on the Pacific side.

His cable gave heart to the conspirators and they set November 4, presumably to allow the *Nashville* plenty of time, as the day on which the blow for liberty would be struck. Señorita Maria Amelia de la Ossa, a lady engaged to be married to the brother of Prescott of the railroad company, was commissioned to design a new flag. J. Gabriel Duqué, owner of the Panama *Star and Herald,* was placed in charge of 287 members of the fire brigade at Panama City and drilled them for battle. Three hundred section hands of the Panama Railroad were mustered into service at Colón.

The strategy of the revolution was not complicated. General Huertas, in command of the Colombian troops at Panama City, was to be commander in chief. His men were to be bribed for $50 a head. An arrangement was effected whereby José Domingo de Obaldia, governor of Panama, would consent to friendly arrest early on November 4; he was very close to the revolutionists and was living in Amador's house. A few more citizens would be arrested, as a gesture, and a rocket sent up by the fire brigade. To prevent the possibility that the troops bound for Colón could cross the isthmus, it was arranged that all rolling stock on the railroad would be sent to Panama City. This detail was the work of Col. J. R. Shaler, superintendent of the Panama Railroad.

Behind all this, in influence and in power, was the United States. Roosevelt insisted, probably truthfully, that he had no idea what assurances might have been given by Bunau-Varilla to the revolutionists. He was "a very able fellow, and it was his business to find out what our government would do. I have no doubt that he was able to make a very shrewd guess, and to advise his people accordingly." In other words, by November 1, 1903, the plans had progressed so far that no need existed for further encouragement. The Roosevelt Administration had concluded, and Bunau-Varilla knew it, to make the Treaty of 1846 with New Granada an excuse to assist the revolutionists. This, of course, was distinct from Dr. Moore's plan, now obsolete, for the seizure of Panama by the United States.

The decision of the conspirators to delay the revolution until November 4 was very nearly fatal to the cause of liberty. The *Nashville* arrived at Colón at 6:30 o'clock on the evening of November 2. That same day the Navy Department sent instructions to Commander John Hubbard of the *Nashville* and to the commanding officers of the other vessels steaming toward Panama. They were directed to "maintain free and uninterrupted transit" on the isthmus. If this was threatened "by armed force," they were to "occupy the line of railroad" and prevent any troops, government or insurgent, from landing "at any point within fifty miles of Panama." But Hubbard's cable had not arrived. He saw no disturbance nor any basis for action in the uncontested landing at midnight on November 2 of 500 Colombian soldiers from the gunboat *Cartagena*. On the morning of November 3 all remained quiet, and he cabled Washington to that effect.

On hearing that the Bogotan warriors had arrived, and that only the narrow isthmus stood between them and the patriotic revolutionists, Dr. Amador and his associates at Panama City were again plunged into gloom. This time Señora Maria de la Ora de Amador (de Guerrero), the leader's wife, buoyed their courage. It was too late to retreat, said the future First Lady of Panama. Their plans had been carried so far that retreat was impossible. In this crisis, Cromwell's men saved the day. Generals Tovar and Amaya were greeted at 8 o'clock that morning at Colón by Shaler, the Panama Railroad superintendent. He exuded cordiality, and he led them with appropriate flourishes to a special train with a single car attached to the locomotive. The troops would follow at 1 o'clock that day, the superintendent explained, when the Colombian generals asked why they were being shipped to Panama City by themselves. Then, as they still hesitated, Shaler pulled the bell cord, hopped off, and waved a genial farewell as the train rolled out. In due time it arrived on the other side of the isthmus, where Tovar and Amaya received a reception worthy of their high rank. Governor Obaldia, a member of the reception committee, was at the station to meet them, but he said nothing about the revolution shortly to take place.

Amador, his courage fortified by desperation, had decided to strike. Shaler telegraphed that the troops would not be transported. When Colonel Torres, the commanding officer at Colón, demanded a train, the bluff and hearty railroad superintendent said that this was impossible unless the fares of the troops were paid in advance. When Torres protested that his superior officers had all the money, $65,000 conveniently borrowed from the collectors of customs at Barranquilla and Cartagena, Shaler said that he was desolated, but what could he do? Regulations were regulations; tickets must be bought for the troops. If only Governor Obaldia were present, he could sign authorizations in lieu of cash. But the governor was at Panama City and, as Shaler was well aware but kept to himself, was hand in hand with the rebels. Thus it was Shaler, in the employ of Cromwell's clients, who saved the day. No train was supplied. Tovar and Amaya, being elaborately entertained at the Government House in Panama City, grew slightly uneasy as the afternoon wore away and the soldiers did not appear.

A highly excited Colombian colonel demanding transportation, a puzzled American naval officer wondering whether he had made a mistake, and a regiment of soldiers encamped at the railroad station, naturally attracted attention in sleepy Colón. Malmross, the American consul, felt it wise to report these unusual activities to the State Department and his descriptive cable was received at Washington at 2:35 in the afternoon. He said he knew very little of what went on across the isthmus, but certainly something was under way. His cable inspired F. B. Loomis, the First Assistant to Secretary Hay, to send an unfortunate inquiry. He controlled his patience for an hour, and at 3:40 telegraphed to Felix Ehrman, the consul at Panama City: "Uprising on the isthmus reported. Keep Department promptly and fully informed." Ehrman, who was also close to the conspirators, replied that as yet there was no uprising but that one was due that night. It was this premature inquiry from Loomis, actually based on the report from Malmross, which led to the belief that the State Department had been in touch with the revolutionists and was in possession of their detailed plans.

A final change in plans by the excitable revolutionists scheduled the revolution for 8 o'clock that night, November 3, during a band concert on the plaza. Generals Tovar and Amaya were to be invited to the musical feast and then arrested. The rebellion, however, got out of hand. At about 5 o'clock the fire brigade began the distribution of weapons to the crowds in the streets. The two generals were escorted to police headquarters while a great crowd assembled, shouting *"Viva el Itmo libre!"* *"Vive Huertas!" "Viva el Presidente Amador!"* and shot off their guns, to the extreme peril of spectators. The hour of freedom was exactly 5:49 on November 3, 1903. Ehrman reported the revolution to Washington a few minutes later.

On the following morning Dr. Amador, soon to be President of Panama, directed that the troops which had taken part in the revolt be drawn up at the barracks. Somehow during the night funds had been obtained; according to one rumor by backing a mule cart up to the subtreasury in the city. In front of his expectant men stood General Huertas, and there was a moment of hushed silence.

"The world is astounded at our heroism!" said Amador. "Yesterday we were but the slaves of Colombia; today we are free. . . . President Roosevelt has made good. . . . Free sons of Panama, I salute you! Long live the Republic of Panama! Long live President Roosevelt! Long live the American Government!"

Then the president-elect suggested each of the heroes be given the $50 in gold which had been pledged. It was done, amid further cheers for America and Roosevelt. Later that day a demonstration was held in the plaza of Panama City. Huertas was carried aloft on an ornate chair, while the American consul, Ehrman, walked on one side with an American flag and Amador strutted on the other with the new emblem of Panama. The parade wound up at the Century Hotel, where Huertas was nearly drowned as bottle after bottle of champagne was poured over the warrior's head.

Nor did his countrymen deny to Huertas more substantial rewards. He was immediately paid $30,000 in silver and later received $50,000 additional in gold. Most of the junior officers received $10,000 each.

At Colón on November 4, while these jollifications went on across the isthmus, there was a moment of gravity. It was, however, as brief as the interval in Panama on the evening before when a Colombian gunboat had tossed a shell or two into the town and had killed a Chinaman. Colonel Torres was still outraged because he had been denied transportation to Panama City. He announced that he would kill every American in Colón unless his generals, still languishing in police headquarters, were released. Thereupon Commander Hubbard, no longer in doubt as to his function, landed some marines and announced that the troops could not, in any event, use the railroad. Torres calmed down. He assured Hubbard of his deep friendship for the United States and on November 5, in return for $8,000 advanced by Shaler, he consented to withdraw with his men. They sailed on the S.S. *Orinoco* as Shaler, always gallant, sent aboard two cases of champagne for Torres. On November 6, the Panamanian flag was raised at Colón.

All this excess of patriotism, flag-waving, and excitement must not obscure the real reasons for the Panama revolution—to preserve untouched the $40,000,000 of the New Panama Canal Company and to accelerate the construction of the canal across the isthmus. President Roosevelt was notified by Ehrman at 11:35 on the morning of November 6 that freedom had been finally and definitely accomplished. He thereupon acted with haste that was indecent, not to say unwise. At 12:51, hardly more than an hour later, Hay instructed the American consul at Panama City to recognize the de facto government. Identical instructions were sent to Beaupré at Bogotá and to Malmross at Colón. On November 10 Amador and Frederico Boyd were en route to the United States to sign a treaty.

Bunau-Varilla, actually a realist despite the romantic flavor of his writings, did not propose to wait for the arrival of the two Panamanians. The possibility loomed that the new republic, like Colombia, might grow dissatisfied with $10,000,000 and demand part of the $40,000,000 to be paid to the French stockholders. Bunau-Varilla did not intend to have all his labors thus undone, and he persuaded Roosevelt to receive him, as the minister from Panama, on November 13. The treaty was signed on November 17 by Hay and Bunau-Varilla. Amador, if he had any hope of raising the price, arrived too late.

"As for your poor old dad," sighed Hay in a letter to his daughter, "they are working him nights and Sundays."

To the protests from Colombia, forwarded by the too sympathetic Beaupré, the United States turned a deaf ear. Hay insisted, on behalf of Roosevelt, that the action had been "in the interest of peace and order." But American naval vessels, by now at Panama City as well as off Colón, had been used to prevent reprisals by Colombian troops. Roosevelt was determined that these should not take place. He gave instructions accordingly, and for a time it seemed as though there would certainly be fighting between the marines and the Colombian soldiers. This would have been war, and Roosevelt would have found it exceedingly difficult to defend before Congress. Ultimately, however, Colombia decided that it was hopeless to obtain justice by force, and she began the long and weary task of obtaining an indemnity by diplomatic representations.

Roosevelt's defense, as submitted in a message to Congress on January 4, 1904, and repeated on many subsequent occasions, was based, in essence, on the Treaty of 1846. Nothing could "be more erroneous," he said, than the interpretation that this agreement merely protected Colombia from revolution. The basic purpose had been to "assure the dedication of the isthmus to . . . free and unobstructed interoceanic transit, the consummation of which would be found in an interoceanic canal." The President then cited precedents to show that on many occasions the United States had intervened to preserve free transit, "with or without Colombia's consent." This message was written with the assistance of the Moore memorandum, advice from Bunau-Varilla, and suggestions from Oscar Straus [later secretary of commerce]. A more careful search of the precedents, or a more honest one, would have demonstrated to Roosevelt that, with one exception, American troops had been used on the isthmus only to put down revolts at the request of Colombia. The exception had been followed by a prompt apology offered through the State Department. Hay had no illusions regarding the action in Panama.

"Our intervention," he wrote to Roosevelt on September 13, 1904, "should not . . . *this time . . . be to the benefit, as heretofore,* of Bogotá."

In June, 1904, as Elihu Root prepared his summary of administration accomplishments for the 1904 convention, Roosevelt instructed him to tell about "Panama in all its details." The following year he declared that the United States had shown "a spirit not merely of justice but of generosity in its dealings with Colombia." These convictions of righteousness in "the most important action I took in foreign affairs" never deserted him. Pride in his achievement caused him to make indiscreet statements, however. On June 19, 1908, he referred to "taking Panama" in a letter to Sir George Trevelyan. The phrase in his memoirs was: "I took Panama without consulting the Cabinet.". . .

CHARLES LINDBERGH

&
the Spirit
of the 1920's

Charles Lindbergh's solo flight across the Atlantic Ocean to Paris in 1927 was perhaps the most sensational event in a sensation-laden decade. Acres of newsprint were devoted to this unassuming young man and his airplane. *The Spirit of St. Louis.* In an age used to media-induced events (then called "ballyhoo"), his daring inspired overwhelming popular enthusiasm with nary a press agent. Lindbergh himself was astonished at the public response, and contemporaries wondered just what chord he had touched in the American people. Although his flight was not newsworthy in the same sense as diplomatic meetings, political scandals, and court decisions, nonetheless people all over the world instantly grasped that something significant had happened.

Born in 1902, Charles Lindbergh grew up on a farm in Minnesota, the state his father represented in Congress for ten years. After high school Lindbergh entered the University of Wisconsin as a mechanical engineering student but soon withdrew to enroll in a flying school in Nebraska. In the early 1920's he did stunt flying; then he attended the United States Army flying school in Texas, from which he graduated in 1925. During 1926 and 1927, he flew mail from St. Louis to Chicago for a private company, pioneering in air mail travel and occasionally having to resort to a parachute. Attracted by the offer of a $25,000 prize for the first successful flight from New York to Paris, Lindbergh purchased a monoplane with a 223 h.p. motor, christened it *The Spirit of St. Louis,* and took

off from Roosevelt Field, Long Island, on May 20, 1927, landing at
Paris 33 hours and 29 minutes later. Lindbergh wanted to gain credit
and acclaim for air transportation—a cause in which he placed all his
faith—and his main concentration rested on the technical problems
of flight. His heroic reception obviously came as a surprise, and remained
one; the innocence of his achievement charmed the entire western world.

Lindbergh's feat brought him countless honors. He toured Central
and South America as goodwill ambassador and in 1929 flew over
Yucatan and Mexico, photographing Mayan ruins. He also flew to China
in 1931, a trip he made with his wife, who wrote *North to the Orient*
(1935) describing the adventure.

In addition to his devotion to flight, Lindbergh became interested in
medicine and helped Dr. Alexis Carrel design a circulating pump to keep
human organs alive outside the body. After the criminal kidnapping
and murder of his infant son in 1932, the famous pilot moved
to England and then to France with his family to escape the anguish of
publicity.

Lindbergh represented a most comfortable harbinger of the new age
that air transportation suggested, a pleasant ambassador between nations
as the world dramatically shrank in size. (Ironically, he later encouraged
a strong isolationist movement in the United States before World War II.)
Most of all, Lindbergh represented the paradoxical spirit of the twenties,
a spirit that aimed to hold to past certitudes even as it risked all on the
future. Americans in the 1920's talked incessantly about individualism,
but it was an era in which the federal bureaucracy, for example, grew
apace. While the nation's leaders talked isolationist rhetoric, they practiced
internationalism. And Lindbergh himself nicely catches the mixing of
nostalgia with grand visions of the future; that was why America thrilled
to the shy aviator who risked his life in the new machine.

"WE" (1927)
CHARLES LINDBERGH

*Lindbergh's own account of his flight, "WE," was received with almost
as much enthusiasm as the hero himself. Written and published immediately
after the heralded event, it went through twenty-seven printings by the
end of the year and continued to sell. Narrated in the first person, it
still seems remarkably unassuming, and it nicely communicates the
personality that so entranced the public in 1920's.*

AT NEW YORK we checked over the plane, engine and instruments, which
required several short flights over the field.

When the plane was completely inspected and ready for the trans-
Atlantic flight, there were dense fogs reported along the coast and over
Nova Scotia and Newfoundland, in addition to a storm area over the
North Atlantic.

On the morning of May 19th, a light rain was falling and the sky was
overcast. Weather reports from land stations and ships along the great
circle course were unfavorable and there was apparently no prospect of
taking off for Paris for several days at least. In the morning I visited the
Wright plant at Paterson, New Jersey, and had planned to attend a
theatre performance in New York that evening. But at about six o'clock
I received a special report from the New York Weather Bureau. A high
pressure area was over the entire North Atlantic and the low pressure
over Nova Scotia and Newfoundland was receding. It was apparent that
the prospects of the fog clearing up were as good as I might expect for
some time to come. The North Atlantic should be clear with only local
storms on the coast of Europe. The moon had just passed full and the
percentage of days with fog over Newfoundland and the Grand Banks was
increasing so that there seemed to be no advantage in waiting longer.

We went to Curtiss Field as quickly as possible and made arrangements for the barograph to be sealed and installed, and for the plane to
be serviced and checked.

We decided partially to fill the fuel tanks in the hangar before towing
the ship on a truck to Roosevelt, which adjoins Curtiss on the east, where
the servicing would be completed.

I left the responsibility for conditioning the plane in the hands of the
men on the field while I went into the hotel for about two and one-half

hours of rest; but at the hotel there were several more details which had to be completed and I was unable to get any sleep that night.

I returned to the field before daybreak on the morning of the twentieth. A light rain was falling which continued until almost dawn; consequently we did not move the ship to Roosevelt Field until much later than we had planned, and the take-off was delayed from daybreak until nearly eight o'clock.

At dawn the shower had passed, although the sky was overcast, and occasionally there would be some slight precipitation. The tail of the plane was lashed to a truck and escorted by a number of motorcycle police. The slow trip from Curtiss to Roosevelt was begun.

The ship was placed at the extreme west end of the field heading along the east and west runway, and the final fueling commenced.

About 7:40 A.M. the motor was started and at 7:52 I took off on the flight for Paris.

The field was a little soft due to the rain during the night and the heavily loaded plane gathered speed very slowly. After passing the half-way mark, however, it was apparent that I would be able to clear the obstructions at the end. I passed over a tractor by about fifteen feet and a telephone line by about twenty, with a fair reserve of flying speed. I believe that the ship would have taken off from a hard field with at least five hundred pounds more weight.

I turned slightly to the right to avoid some high trees on a hill directly ahead, but by the time I had gone a few hundred yards I had sufficient altitude to clear all obstructions and throttled the engine down to 1750 R.P.M. I took up a compass course at once and soon reached Long Island Sound where the Curtiss Oriole with its photographer, which had been escorting me, turned back.

The haze soon cleared and from Cape Cod through the southern half of Nova Scotia the weather and visibility were excellent. I was flying very low, sometimes as close as ten feet from the trees and water.

On the three hundred mile stretch of water between Cape Cod and Nova Scotia I passed within view of numerous fishing vessels.

The northern part of Nova Scotia contained a number of storm areas and several times I flew through cloudbursts.

As I neared the northern coast, snow appeared in patches on the ground and far to the eastward the coastline was covered with fog.

For many miles between Nova Scotia and Newfoundland the ocean was covered with caked ice but as I approached the coast the ice disappeared entirely and I saw several ships in this area.

I had taken up a course for St. Johns, which is south of the great Circle from New York to Paris, so that there would be no question of the fact that I had passed Newfoundland in case I was forced down in the north Atlantic.

I passed over numerous icebergs after leaving St. Johns, but saw no ships except near the coast.

Darkness set in about 8:15 New York time and a thin, low fog formed through which the white bergs showed up with surprising clearness. This fog became thicker and increased in height until within two hours I was just skimming the top of storm clouds at about ten thousand feet. Even at this altitude there was a thick haze through which only the stars directly overhead could be seen.

There was no moon and it was very dark. The tops of some of the storm clouds were several thousand feet above me and at one time, when I attempted to fly through one of the larger clouds, sleet started to collect on the plane and I was forced to turn around and get back into clear air immediately and then fly around any clouds which I could not get over.

The moon appeared on the horizon after about two hours of darkness; then the flying was much less complicated.

Dawn came at about 1 A.M. New York time and the temperature had risen until there was practically no remaining danger of sleet.

Shortly after sunrise the clouds became more broken although some of them were far above me and it was often necessary to fly through them, navigating by instruments only.

As the sun became higher, holes appeared in the fog. Through one the open water was visible, and I dropped down until less than a hundred feet above the waves. There was a strong wind blowing from the northwest and the ocean was covered with white caps.

After a few miles of fairly clear weather the ceiling lowered to zero and for nearly two hours I flew entirely blind through the fog at an altitude of about 1500 feet. Then the fog raised and the water was visible again.

On several more occasions it was necessary to fly by instrument for short periods; then the fog broke up into patches. These patches took on forms of every description. Numerous shorelines appeared, with trees perfectly outlined against the horizon. In fact, the mirages were so natural that, had I not been in mid-Atlantic and known that no land existed along my route, I would have taken them to be actual islands.

As the fog cleared I dropped down closer to the water, sometimes flying within ten feet of the waves and seldom higher than two hundred.

There is a cushion of air close to the ground or water through which a plane flies with less effort than when at a higher altitude, and for hours at a time I took advantage of this factor.

Also, it was less difficult to determine the wind drift near the water. During the entire flight the wind was strong enough to produce white caps on the waves. When one of these formed, the foam would be blown off, showing the wind's direction and approximate velocity. This foam remained on the water long enough for me to obtain a general idea of my drift.

During the day I saw a number of porpoises and a few birds but no ships, although I understand that two different boats reported me passing over.

The first indication of my approach to the European Coast was a small fishing boat which I first noticed a few miles ahead and slightly to the south of my course. There were several of these fishing boats grouped within a few miles of each other.

I flew over the first boat without seeing any signs of life. As I circled over the second, however, a man's face appeared, looking out of the cabin window.

I have carried on short conversations with people on the ground by flying low with throttled engine, shouting a question, and receiving the answer by some signal. When I saw this fisherman I decided to try to get him to point towards land. I had no sooner made the decision than the futility of the effort became apparent. In all likelihood he could not speak English, and even if he could he would undoubtedly be far too astounded to answer. However, I circled again and closing the throttle as the plane passed within a few feet of the boat I shouted, "Which way is Ireland?" Of course the attempt was useless and I continued on my course.

Less than an hour later a rugged and semi-mountainous coastline appeared to the northeast. I was flying less than two hundred feet from the water when I sighted it. The shore was fairly distinct and not over ten or fifteen miles away. A light haze coupled with numerous local storm areas had prevented my seeing it from a long distance.

The coastline came down from the north, curved over towards the east. I had very little doubt that it was the southwestern end of Ireland but in order to make sure I changed my course towards the nearest point of land.

I located Cape Valentia and Dingle Bay, then resumed my compass course towards Paris.

After leaving Ireland I passed a number of steamers and was seldom out of sight of a ship.

In a little over two hours the coast of England appeared. My course passed over Southern England and a little south of Plymouth; then across the English Channel, striking France over Cherbourg.

The English farms were very impressive from the air in contrast to ours in America. They appeared extremely small and unusually neat and tidy with their stone and hedge fences.

I was flying at about fifteen hundred foot altitude over England and as I crossed the Channel and passed over Cherbourg, France, I had probably seen more of that part of Europe than many native Europeans. The visibility was good and the country could be seen for miles around.

People who have taken their first flight often remark that no one knows what the locality he lives in is like until he has seen it from above. Countries take on different characteristics from the air.

The sun went down shortly after passing Cherbourg and soon the beacons along the Paris-London airway became visible.

I first saw the lights of Paris a little before ten P.M. or five P.M. New York time, and a few minutes later I was circling the Eiffel Tower at an altitude of about four thousand feet.

The lights of Le Bourget were plainly visible, but appeared to be very close to Paris. I had understood that the field was farther from the city, so continued out to the northeast into the country for four or five miles to make sure that there was not another field farther out which might be Le Bourget. Then I returned and spiralled down closer to the lights. Presently I could make out long lines of hangars, and the roads appeared to be jammed with cars.

I flew low over the field once, then circled around into the wind and landed.

After the plane stopped rolling I turned it around and started to taxi back to the lights. The entire field ahead, however, was covered with thousands of people all running towards my ship. When the first few arrived, I attempted to get them to hold the rest of the crowd back, away from the plane, but apparently no one could understand, or would have been able to conform to my request if he had.

I cut the switch to keep the propeller from killing some one, and attempted to organize an impromptu guard for the plane. The impossibility of any immediate organization became apparent, and when parts of the ship began to crack from the pressure of the multitude I decided to climb out of the cockpit in order to draw the crowd away.

Speaking was impossible; no words could be heard in the uproar and nobody apparently cared to hear any. I started to climb out of the cockpit, but as soon as one foot appeared through the door I was dragged the rest of the way without assistance on my part.

For nearly half an hour I was unable to touch the ground, during which time I was ardently carried around in what seemed to be a very small area, and in every position it is possible to be in. Every one had the best of intentions but no one seemed to know just what they were.

The French military flyers very resourcefully took the situation in hand. A number of them mingled with the crowd; then, at a given signal, they placed my helmet on an American correspondent and cried: "Here is Lindbergh." That helmet on an American was sufficient evidence. The correspondent immediately became the center of attraction, and while he was being taken protestingly to the Reception Committee via a rather devious route, I managed to get inside one of the hangars.

Meanwhile a second group of soldiers and police had surrounded the plane and soon placed it out of danger in another hangar.

The French ability to handle an unusual situation with speed and capability was remarkably demonstrated that night at Le Bourget.

Ambassador Herrick extended me an invitation to remain at his Embassy while I was in Paris, which I gladly accepted. But grateful as I was at the time, it did not take me long to realize that a kind Providence had placed me in Ambassador Herrick's hands. The ensuing days found me in situations that I had certainly never expected to be in and in which I relied on Ambassador Herrick's sympathetic aid.

These situations were brought about by the whole-hearted welcome to me—an American—that touched me beyond any point that any words can express. I left France with a debt of gratitude which, though I cannot repay it, I shall always remember. If the French people had been acclaiming their own gallant airmen, Nungesser and Coli, who were lost only after fearlessly departing in the face of conditions insurmountably greater than those that confronted me, their enthusiastic welcome and graciousness could not have been greater.

In Belgium as well, I was received with a warmth which reflected more than simply a passing curiosity in a trans-Atlantic flight, but which was rather a demonstration by the people of their interest in a new means of transportation which eventually would bring still closer together the new world and the old. Their welcome, too, will be a cherished memory for all time.

In England, I experienced one final unforgettable demonstration of friendship for an American. That spontaneous wonderful reception during my brief visit seemed typical of what I had always heard of the good sportsmanship of the English.

My words to all those friends in Europe are inadequate, but my feelings of appreciation are boundless.

Conclusion

When I was contemplating the flight to Paris I looked forward to making a short tour of Europe with especial regard to the various airports and aeronautical activities.

After I arrived, however, the necessity for returning to America in the near future became apparent and, after a consultation with Ambassador Houghton, who informed me that President Coolidge was sending the cruiser *Memphis* to Cherbourg for my return journey to America, I flew the "Spirit of St. Louis" to Gosport early one morning. There it was dismantled and crated, through the courtesy of the Royal Air Force which also placed a Woodcock pursuit plane at my disposal.

I returned to London in the Woodcock and a few days later flew to Paris in another R.A.F. machine of the same type.

I remained overnight in Paris, and early the next morning flew a French Breguet to Cherbourg where the cruiser *Memphis* was waiting.

Admiral Burrage met me at the dock, and after going aboard the *Memphis* I became acquainted with Captain Lackey and the officers of the ship. During the trip across they extended every courtesy and did everything within their power to make the voyage a pleasant one.

A description of my welcome back to the United States would, in itself, be sufficient to fill a larger volume than this. I am not an author by profession, and my pen could never express the gratitude which I feel towards the American people.

The voyage up the Potomac and to the Monument Grounds in Washington; up the Hudson River and along Broadway; over the Mississippi and to St. Louis—to do justice to these occasions would require a far greater writer than myself.

Washington, New York, and finally St. Louis and home. Each of these cities has left me with an impression that I shall never forget, and a debt of gratitude which I can never repay.

New York Stages Big Celebration (1927)
NEW YORK TIMES

The following selection from the New York Times, *May 22, 1927, describes the city's emotional response to Lindbergh's flight. New Yorkers, so often a peculiar breed, were in this case an epitome of the nation.*

NEW YORK BUBBLED all day yesterday with excitement and expectancy, first yearning for word of Captain Lindbergh, then half-doubting, gaining confidence as the afternoon progressed and finally acclaiming the victory of the young aviator with street demonstrations where the crowds were thickest, in which the ancient phrase, "I told you so," was often repeated. It was evident during the day that New York had confidence in the lad from the West.

On the streets and elsewhere Lindbergh was the one topic of conversation the whole day long. In the subway, on the elevated, in trains and cars, motion-picture houses, theatres, wherever a few had gathered, or even where one man could find another to talk to, one heard "Lindbergh—Lindbergh—Lindbergh."

And such expressions as this:

"He'll make it, all right."

"Some baby!"

"Well, if he's hit Ireland, he's safe anyway."

"He's away ahead of his time."

"What's the difference in time between here and there, anyway?"

To this latter question there were some amazing answers. One woman who had the aviator's running time mixed with the difference in time between New York and Paris solemnly informed her companion that there was thirty-six hours difference in time between the cities. She said it with an air which signified: "I don't mean maybe." A surprising number of persons insisted that the difference in time was three hours.

Early in the day, even before there was any good reason why there should be definite news, the interest of the people was demonstrated in two ways. At every news stand there were little groups scanning the headlines and buying newspapers. In every newspaper office the switchboards were literally swamped with inquiries. It was not sufficient that the operator said there was no word, or, later, that Lindbergh's plane had been seen over Ireland. The inquirers wanted specific information:

"Well, when will you get the first news?" they asked. And later:

"If he's over Ireland how long will it be before he gets to Paris?"

"Is he all right?". . .

But it wasn't always possible for the crowds to determine whether to be elated or not. The only really authentic reports were those telling of Lindbergh being seen over Ireland, and the later one in which The Associated Press announced that he was over France at 8 P.M., French time. These bulletins were received far apart and circulated rather slowly during the afternoon.

But in the meanwhile unconfirmed reports, and reports that were obviously erroneous, had been made the subject of headlines containing a flat statement of what purported to be a fact. Thus it was that a leather-lunged newsboy in the neighborhood of the Pennsylvania Station, in clarion tones that could be heard nearly a block away, announced, with absolute faith in the ability of his hearers to understand whom he meant:

"He's in Paris! He's in Paris! Extra! He's in Paris!"

The boy did a great business. But Lindbergh was not in Paris at that time, nor, in truth, had he yet succeeded in crossing the Channel. Even in the morning the crowd had been misled by one of those "unconfirmed reports" that Lindbergh was over the Channel and being escorted by a fleet of British army airplanes. The authentic report a little later, from Ireland, rather served to discount the Channel report, and the crowd became a little skeptical:

"I hope it's true, but you can't be sure."

"Why he simply couldn't be there by now."

"But he'll get there; he's a great kid."

"Some baby."

So it went for some hours during the afternoon. Where the crowds were large, as at the Times Building in Times Square, they remained extraordinarily quiet, waiting and growing in size as the afternoon progressed. Where smaller crowds gathered, as at the news stands, there was excited comment and speculation. But everywhere there was deep interest in the flight of the young fellow whose sheer nerve had aroused the admiration of apparently every man and woman in the city.

"I want that boy to win because he's a real sport. He got out and did this thing while other people were talking about it. He's going to win; I know he's going to win."

Scores of people said just about that, and repeated it often, not only along Broadway uptown, but downtown, where the Saturday afternoon quiet prevailed, where the people were few and only the groups at the news stands served to denote that something unusual was happening.

But there were other thoughts in the mind of the crowds than those of victory. At moments there were perceptibly solemn reactions and whispered ejaculations of earnest hope that nothing unfortunate would happen to the brave flier. This feeling found outward expression at a gathering of 1,500 school teachers in the Hotel Biltmore, who stood for a moment in silent prayer when a dispatch was read announcing that Lindbergh had safely passed the line of the French coast.

The late afternoon dragged. Newsboys were doing a rushing business. The authentic reports showed Lindbergh was nearing his goal. His victory seemed assured. But he was still in the air, a tired and weary man. Would something happen at the very end of the trip? The crowds tensed up. It was easy to sense a little anxiety, a little impatience. Five o'clock came. Here and there some speculated, calculating the flying time from Bayeux, on the French coast, to Paris. He should have been in Paris already, they argued. What was wrong? Why the delay?

It was half-past five, New York Daylight Saving Time, almost to the second when the word was passed that Lindbergh had landed. The announcement came exactly six minutes after the landing itself, which had been at 10:24, Paris time. Six minutes from the time Lindbergh's wheels touched the ground at Le Bourget the bulletin announcing the arrival was posted on a window of The Times Building on the Broadway side, where mounted police were endeavoring to keep vehicular traffic moving.

A shout and then a lot of little shouts, up and down Broadway, and a cheer that was prolonged, while again, for the second time, people in windows began throwing out torn paper to flutter downward and away in the light Spring breeze. Up and down the Great White Way automobile horns began an incessant tooting, creating an undercurrent for the cheering. Further away the autos took up the refrain and a low persistent roar spread through the adjoining streets. Men at the wheels of their cars grinned and tooted their horns continuously and the sound carried the message that Lindbergh had won and that he was safe.

Hardly a minute later, it seemed almost by prearrangement, the graceful giant dirigible Los Angeles poked her glistening nose through the haze over the northern part of Manhattan and sailed above Times Square with majestic steadiness into the setting sun, and the crowd in its exuberance, cheered her again and again.

The word of the actual arrival of Lindbergh traveled through the city with amazing swiftness. In police stations groups of policemen laughed and shouted, almost as if they had had some share in the feat. In movie houses the announcement was made and brought cheers. In fact, in some theatres the announcement came as an anti-climax, for in the Mark Strand the early "unconfirmed" report had been announced and the picture was stopped while the audience indulged itself in a few minutes of wild celebration.

Word of the arrival of the flier at Paris was conveyed to Mayor Walker by The Associated Press and he at once communicated with departments the plants of which have steam whistles, and within a few minutes there began a bedlam of whistles and sirens, the boats in the harbor being quick to take up the cue, so that the noise apprised every one who had not already heard that Lindbergh had reached Paris. Ferryboats, tugboats, liners, all the little boats and all the big boats that ply the waters of New York Harbor did honor to the man who had flown continuously over the largest stretch of water ever covered by an aviator.

Every fire company in the city sounded sirens during a five-minute interval. The firemen needed no prompting when the news of the gallant young flier's success was transmitted over the department telegraph. In an instant trucks were rolled out on the street and the sirens screamed their approval. If by that time there was any one in the city unaware of Lindbergh's success the shriek of fire sirens apprised them of something unusual and inquiry elicited the reason for the demonstration.

Broadway quickly took on even more of a holiday air than had marked the afternoon, flags were flung out here and there, and bunting displayed. The shower of paper, which had been intermittent in the afternoon, became a deluge. It reminded one of Armistice Day, though the hysteria was not as marked as on that occasion.

In the Paramount Theatre fifteen minutes had been devoted to one of those anticipatory celebrations and this was repeated later when definite news was received. So it was in the other picture houses, and the Schubert management announced that at the evening performances, at which prayers for Lindbergh had been said the night before, a brief speech would be made, to be followed by the singing of "The Star-Spangled Banner.". . .

Three radio stations broadcast the French and American national anthems soon after it became known that Lindbergh had landed at Le Bourget. The effect was striking on Broadway and wherever loud speakers were carrying programs outside radio supply stores. Men and women came to respectful attention, the men bareheaded, and remained like soldiers on parade until the last notes of the "Marsellaise" and "The Star-Spangled Banner" floated away—then they joined the cheering crowds.

The second evening performance at Roxy's Theatre last night evoked a demonstration during the showing of pictures of Lindbergh. By a recording device, the roar of Lindbergh's plane was heard as pictures of the ship leaving the ground were shown. The film and sound of the motor, together with the cheers of watchers in Roosevelt Field observing the plane ascend, made a powerful pull on the imagination of the audience, and more than 6,000 persons arose and cheered, drowning out the noise of the recording machine.

The Meaning of Lindbergh's Flight (1958)
JOHN WILLIAM WARD

John William Ward, a distinguished historian, probes the responses to Lindbergh's flight in an ingenious attempt to elicit the "meaning" it held for his contemporaries. The mixing of nostalgia with visions of the future that Ward discovers in these responses indicates the 1920's attitude toward the changes taking place so rapidly in the lives of Americans.

ON FRIDAY, May 20, 1927, at 7:52 A.M., Charles A. Lindbergh took off in a silver-winged monoplane and flew from the United States to France. With this flight Lindbergh became the first man to fly alone across the Atlantic Ocean. The log of flight 33 of "The Spirit of St. Louis" reads: "Roosevelt Field, Long Island, New York, to Le Bourget Aerodrome, Paris, France. 33 hrs. 30 min." Thus was the fact of Lindbergh's achievement easily put down. But the meaning of Lindbergh's flight lay hidden in the next sentence of the log: "(Fuselage fabric badly torn by souvenir hunters.)"

When Lindbergh landed at Le Bourget he is supposed to have said, "Well, we've done it." A contemporary writer asked "Did what?" Lindbergh "had no idea of what he had done. He thought he had simply flown from New York to Paris. What he had really done was something far greater. He had fired the imagination of mankind." From the moment of Lindbergh's flight people recognized that something more was involved than the mere fact of the physical leap from New York to Paris. "Lindbergh," wrote John Erskine, "served as a metaphor." But what the metaphor stood for was not easy to say. The *New York Times* remarked then that "there has been no complete and satisfactory explanation of the enthusiasm and acclaim for Captain Lindbergh." Looking back on the celebration of Lindbergh, one can see now that the American people were trying to understand Lindbergh's flight, to grasp its meaning, and through it, perhaps, to grasp the meaning of their own experience. Was the flight the achievement of a heroic, solitary, unaided individual? Or did the flight represent the triumph of the machine, the success of an industrially organized society? These questions were central to the meaning of Lindbergh's flight. They were also central to the lives of the people who made Lindbergh their hero. . . .

The parabola of the action was as clean as the arc of Lindbergh's flight. The drama should have ended with the landing of "The Spirit of St. Louis" at Le Bourget. That is where Lindbergh wanted it to end. In *"WE,"* written immediately after the flight, and in *The Spirit of St. Louis,* written twenty-six years later, Lindbergh chose to end his accounts there. But the flight turned out to be only the first act in the part Lindbergh was to play.

Lindbergh was so innocent of his future that on his flight he carried letters of introduction. The hysterical response, first of the French and then of his own countrymen, had been no part of his careful plans. In *"WE,"* after Lindbergh's narrative of the flight, the publisher wrote: "When Lindbergh came to tell the story of his welcome at Paris, London, Brussels, Washington, New York, and St. Louis he found himself up against a tougher problem than flying the Atlantic." So another writer completed the account in the third person. He suggested that "the reason Lindbergh's story is different is that when his plane came to a halt on Le Bourget field that black night in Paris, Lindbergh the man kept on going. The phenomenon of Lindbergh took its start with his flight across the ocean; but in its entirety it was almost as distinct from that flight as though he had never flown at all."

Lindbergh's private life ended with his flight to Paris. The drama was no longer his, it was the public's. "The outburst of unanimous acclaim was at once personal and symbolic," said the *American Review of Reviews.* From the moment of success there were two Lindberghs, the private Lindbergh and the public Lindbergh. The latter was the construction of the imagination of Lindbergh's time, fastened on to an unwilling person. The tragedy of Lindbergh's career is that he could never accept the role assigned him. He always believed he might keep his two lives separate. But from the moment he landed at Le Bourget, Lindbergh became, as the *New Republic* noted, *"ours . . . .* He is no longer permitted to be himself. He is US personified. He is the United States." Ambassador Herrick introduced Lindbergh to the French, saying, "This young man from out of the West brings you better than anything else the spirit of America," and wired to President Coolidge, "Had we searched all America we could not have found a better type than young Lindbergh to represent the spirit and high purpose of our people." This was Lindbergh's fate, to be a type. A writer in the *North American Review* felt that Lindbergh represented "the dominant American character," he "images the best" about the United States. And an ecstatic female in the *American Magazine,* who began by saying that Lindbergh "is a sort of symbol. . . . He is the dream that is in our hearts," concluded that the American public responded so wildly to Lindbergh because of "the thrill of possessing, in him, our dream of what *we* really and truly want to be." The act of possession was so complete that articles since have attempted to discover the "real" Lindbergh, that enigmatic and taciturn figure behind the public mask. But it is no less difficult to discern the features of the public Lindbergh, that symbolic figure who presented to the imagination of his time all the yearnings and buried desires of its dream for itself.

Lindbergh's flight came at the end of a decade marked by social and political corruption and by a sense of moral loss. The heady idealism of the First World War had been succeeded by a deep cynicism as to the war's real purpose. The naïve belief that virtue could be legislated was violated by the vast discrepancy between the law and the social habits of prohibition. A philosophy of relativism had become the uneasy rationale of a nation which had formerly believed in moral absolutes. The newspapers agreed that Lindbergh's chief worth was his spiritual and moral value. His story was held to be "in striking contrast with the sordid unhallowed themes that have for months steeped the imaginations and thinking of the people." Or, as another had it, "there is good reason why people should hail Lindbergh and give him honor. He stands out in a grubby world as an inspiration."

Lindbergh gave the American people a glimpse of what they liked to think themselves to be at a time when they feared they had deserted their own vision of themselves. The grubbiness of the twenties had a good deal to do with the shining quality of Lindbergh's success, especially when one remembers that Lindbergh's flight was not as unexampled as our national memory would have it. The Atlantic was not unconquered when Lindbergh flew. A British dirigible had twice crossed the Atlantic before 1919 and on May 8 of that year three naval seaplanes left Rockaway, New York, and one, the NC-4 manned by a crew of five, got through to Plymouth, England. A month later, Captain John Alcock, an Englishman, with Arthur W. Browne, an American, flew the first heavier-than-air land plane across the Atlantic nonstop, from Newfoundland to Ireland, to win twice the money Lindbergh did, a prize of $50,000 offered by the London *Daily Mail*. Alcock's and Browne's misfortune was to land in a soft and somnolent Irish peat bog instead of before the cheering thousands of London or Paris. Or perhaps they should have flown in 1927.

The wild medley of public acclaim and the homeric strivings of editors make one realize that the response to Lindbergh involved a mass ritual in which America celebrated itself more than it celebrated Lindbergh. Lindbergh's flight was the occasion of a public act of regeneration in which the nation momentarily rededicated itself to something, the loss of which was keenly felt. It was said again and again that "Lindy" taught America "to lift its eyes up to Heaven." Heywood Broun, in his column in the *New York World*, wrote that this "tall young man raised up and let us see the potentialities of the human spirit." Broun felt that the flight proved that, though "we are small and fragile," it "isn't true that there is no health in us." Lindbergh's flight provided the moment, but the meaning of the flight is to be found in the deep and pervasive need for renewal which the flight brought to the surface of public feeling. When Lindbergh appeared at the nation's capital, the *Washington Post* observed, "He was given that frenzied acclaim which comes from the depths of the people." In New York, where 4,000,000 people saw him, a reporter wrote that the dense and vociferous crowds were swept, as Lindbergh passed, "with an emotion tense and inflammable." The *Literary Digest* suggested that the answer to the hero-worship of Lindbergh would "throw an interesting light on the psychology of our times and of the American people."

The *Nation* noted about Lindbergh that "there was something lyric as well as heroic about the apparition of this young Lochinvar who suddenly came out of the West and who flew all unarmed and all alone. It is the kind of stuff which the ancient Greeks would have worked into a myth and the medieval Scots into a border ballad. . . . But what we have in the case of Lindbergh is an actual, an heroic and an exhaustively exposed experience which exists by suggestion in the form of poetry." The *Nation* quickly qualified its statement by observing that reporters were as far as possible from being poets and concluded that the discrepancy between the fact and the celebration of it was not poetry, perhaps, but "magic on a vast scale." Yet the *Nation* might have clung to its insight that the public meaning of Lindbergh's flight was somehow poetic. The vast publicity about Lindbergh corresponds in one vital particular with the poetic vision. Poetry, said William Butler Yeats, contains opposites; so did Lindbergh. Lindbergh did not mean one thing, he meant many things. The image of itself which America contemplated in the public person of Lindbergh was full of conflict; it was, in a word, dramatic.

To heighten the drama, Lindbergh did it alone. He was the "lone eagle" and a full exploration of that fact takes one deep into the emotional meaning of his success. Not only the *Nation* found Sir Walter Scott's lines on Lochinvar appropriate: "he rode all unarmed and he rode all alone." Newspapers and magazines were deluged with amateur poems that vindicated one rhymester's wry comment, "Go conquer the perils/That lurk in the skies—/And you'll get bum poems/Right up to your eyes." The *New York Times,* that alone received more than two hundred poems, observed in trying to summarize the poetic deluge that "the fact that he flew alone made the strongest impression." Another favorite tribute was Kipling's "The Winners," with its refrain, "He travels the fastest who travels alone." The others who had conquered the Atlantic and those like Byrd and Chamberlin who were trying at the same time were not traveling alone and they hardly rode unarmed. Other than Lindbergh, all the contestants in the transAtlantic race had unlimited backing, access to the best planes, and all were working in teams, carrying at least one co-pilot to share the long burden of flying the plane. So a writer in the New York *Sun,* in a poem called "The Flying Fool," a nickname that Lindbergh despised, celebrated Lindbergh's flight: ". . . no kingly plane for him;/No endless data, comrades, moneyed chums;/No boards, no councils, no directors grim—/He plans ALONE . . . and takes luck as it comes."

Upon second thought, it must seem strange that the long distance flight of an airplane, the achievement of a highly advanced and organized technology, should be the occasion for hymns of praise to the solitary unaided man. Yet the National Geographic Society, when it presented a medal to Lindbergh, wrote on the presentation scroll, "Courage, when it goes alone, has ever caught men's imagination," and compared Lindbergh to Robinson Crusoe and the trailmakers in our own West. But Lindbergh and Robinson Crusoe, the one in his helmet and fur-lined flying coat and the other in his wild goatskin, do not easily co-exist. Even if Robinson Crusoe did have a tidy capital investment in the form of a well-stocked shipwreck, he still did not have a ten thousand dollar machine under him.

Lindbergh, in nearly every remark about his flight and in his own writings about it, resisted the tendency to exploit the flight as the achievement of an individual. He never said "I," he always said "We." The plane was not to go unrecognized. Nevertheless, there persisted a tendency to seize upon the flight as a way of celebrating the self-sufficient individual, so that among many others an Ohio newspaper could describe Lindbergh as this "self-contained, self-reliant, courageous young man [who] ranks among the great pioneers of history." The strategy here was a common one, to make Lindbergh a "pioneer" and thus to link him with a long and vital tradition of individualism in the American experience. Colonel Theodore Roosevelt, himself the son of a famous exponent of self-reliance, said to reporters at his home in Oyster Bay that "Captain Lindbergh personifies the daring of youth. Daniel Boone, David Crocket [sic], and men of that type played a lone hand and made America. Lindbergh is their lineal descendant." In *Outlook* magazine, immediately below an enthusiastic endorsement of Lindbergh's own remarks on the importance of his machine and his scientific instruments, there was the statement, "Charles Lindbergh is the heir of all that we like to think is best in America. He is of the stuff out of which have been made the pioneers that opened up the wilderness, first on the Atlantic coast, and then in our great West. His are the qualities which we, as a people, must nourish." It is in this mood that one suspects it was important that Lindbergh came out of the West and rode all alone.

Another common metaphor in the attempt to place Lindbergh's exploit was to say that he had opened a new "frontier." To speak of the air as a "frontier" was to invoke an interpretation of the meaning of American history which had sources deep in American experience, but the frontier of the airplane is hardly the frontier of the trailmakers of the old West. Rather than an escape into the self-sufficient simplicity of the American past, the machine which made Lindbergh's flight possible represented an advance into a complex industrial present. The difficulty lay in using an instance of modern life to celebrate the virtues of the past, to use an extreme development of an urban industrial society to insist upon the significance of the frontier in American life.

A little more than a month after Lindbergh's flight, Joseph K. Hart in *Survey* magazine reached back to Walt Whitman's poem for the title of an article on Lindbergh: "O Pioneer." A school had made Lindbergh an honorary alumnus but Hart protested there was little available evidence "that he was educated in *schools*." "We must look elsewhere for our explanation," Hart wrote and he looked to the experience of Lindbergh's youth when "everything that he ever did . . . he did by himself. He lived more to himself than most boys." And, of course, Lindbergh lived to himself in the only place conceivably possible, in the world of nature, on a Minnesota farm. "There he developed in the companionship of woods and fields, animals and machines, his audaciously natural and simple personality." The word, "machines," jars as it intrudes into Hart's idyllic pastoral landscape and betrays Hart's difficulty in relating the setting of nature upon which he wishes to insist with the fact that its product spent his whole life tinkering with machines, from motorcycles to airplanes. But except for that one word, Hart proceeds in uncritical nostalgia to show that "a lone trip across the Atlantic was not impossible for a boy who had grown up in the solitude of the woods and waters." If Lindbergh was "clear-headed, naif, untrained in the ways of cities," it was because he had "that 'natural simplicity' which Fenimore Cooper used to attribute to the pioneer hero of his Leatherstocking Tales." Hart rejected the notion that any student "bent to all the conformities" of formal training could have done what Lindbergh did. "Must we not admit," he asked, "that this pioneering urge remained to this audacious youth because he had never submitted completely to the repressions of the world and its jealous institutions?"

Only those who insist on reason will find it strange that Hart should use the industrial achievement of the airplane to reject the urban, institutionalized world of industrialism. Hart was dealing with something other than reason; he was dealing with the emotion evoked by Lindbergh's solitude. He recognized that people wished to call Lindbergh a "genius" because that "would release him from the ordinary rules of existence." That way, "we could rejoice with him in his triumph, and then go back to the contracted routines of our institutional ways [because] ninety-nine percent of us must be content to be shaped and moulded by the routine ways and forms of the world to the routine tasks of life." It is in the word, "must," that the pathos of this interpretation of the phenomenon of Lindbergh lies. The world had changed from the open society of the pioneer to the close-knit, interdependent world of a modern machine-oriented civilization. The institutions of a highly corporate industrial society existed as a constant reproach to a people who liked to believe that the meaning of its experience was embodied in the formless, independent life of the frontier. Like Thomas Jefferson who identified American virtue with nature and saw the city as a "great sore" on the public body, Hart concluded that "certainly, in the response that the world—especially the world of great cities—has made to the performance of this mid-western boy, we can read of the homesickness of the human soul, immured in city canyons and routine tasks, for the freer world of youth, for the open spaces of the pioneer, for the joy of battling with nature and clean storms once more on the frontiers of the earth."

The social actuality which made the adulation of Lindbergh possible had its own irony for the notion that America's strength lay in its simple uncomplicated beginnings. For the public response to Lindbergh to have reached the proportions it did, the world had by necessity to be the intricately developed world of modern mass communications. But more than irony was involved. Ultimately, the emotion attached to Lindbergh's flight involved no less than a whole theory about American history. By singling out the fact that Lindbergh rode alone, and by naming him a pioneer of the frontier, the public projected its sense that the source of America's strength lay somewhere in the past and that Lindbergh somehow meant that America must look backward in time to rediscover some lost virtue. The mood was nostalgic and American history was read as a decline, a decline measured in terms of America's advance into an urban, institutionalized way of life which made solitary achievement increasingly beyond the reach of ninety-nine per cent of the people. Because Lindbergh's ancestors were Norse, it was easy to call him a "Viking" and extend the emotion far into the past when all frontiers were open. He became the "Columbus" of another new world to conquer as well as the "Lochinvar" who rode all alone. But there was always the brute, irreducible fact that Lindbergh's exploit was a victory of the machine over the barriers of nature. If the only response to Lindbergh had been a retreat to the past, we would be involved with a mass cultural neurosis, the inability of America to accept reality, the reality of the world in which it lived. But there was another aspect, one in which the public celebrated the machine and the highly organized society of which it was a product. The response to Lindbergh reveals that the American people were deeply torn between conflicting interpretations of their own experience. By calling Lindbergh a pioneer, the people could read into American history the necessity of turning back to the frontier past. Yet the people could also read American history in terms of progress into the industrial future. They could do this by emphasizing the machine which was involved in Lindbergh's flight.

Lindbergh came back from Europe in an American man-of-war, the cruiser *Memphis*. It seems he had contemplated flying on, around the whole world perhaps, but less adventurous heads prevailed and dictated a surer mode of travel for so valuable a piece of public property. The *New Republic* protested against bringing America's hero of romance home in a warship. If he had returned on a great liner, that would have been one thing. "One's first trip on an ocean-liner is a great adventure—the novelty of it, the many people of all kinds and conditions, floating for a week in a tiny compact world of their own." But to return on the *Memphis,* "to be put on a gray battleship with a collection of people all of the same stripe, in a kind of ship that has as much relation to the life of the sea as a Ford factory has! We might as well have put him in a pneumatic tube and shot him across the Atlantic." The interesting thing about the *New Republic*'s protest against the unromantic, regimented life of a battleship is that the image it found appropriate was the Ford assembly line. It was this reaction against the discipline of a mechanized society that probably led to the nostalgic image of Lindbergh as a remnant of a past when romance was possible for the individual, when life held novelty, and society was variegated rather than uniform. But what the Ford Assembly Line represents, a society committed to the path of full mechanization, was what lay behind Lindbergh's romantic success. A long piece in the Sunday *New York Times,* "Lindbergh Symbolizes the Genius of America," reminded its readers of the too obvious fact that "without an airplane he could not have flown at all." Lindbergh "is, indeed, the Icarus of the twentieth century; not himself an inventor of his own wings, but a son of that omnipotent Daedalus whose ingenuity has created the modern world." The point was that modern America was the creation of modern industry. Lindbergh "reveres his 'ship' as a noble expression of mechanical wisdom. . . . Yet in this reverence . . . Lindbergh is not an exception. What he means by the Spirit of St. Louis is really the spirit of America. The mechanical genius, which is discerned in Henry Ford as well as a Charles A. Lindbergh, is in the very atmosphere of [the] country." In contrast to a sentiment that feared the enforced discipline of the machine there existed an attitude of reverence for its power.

Lindbergh led the way in the celebration of the machine, not only implicitly by including his plane when he said "we," but by direct statement. In Paris he told newspapermen, "You fellows have not said enough about that wonderful motor." Rarely have two more taciturn figures confronted one another than when Lindbergh returned to Washington and Calvin Coolidge pinned the Distinguished Flying Cross on him, but in his brief remarks Coolidge found room to express his particular delight that Lindbergh should have given equal credit to the airplane. "For we are proud," said the President, "that in every particular this silent partner represented American genius and industry. I am told that more than 100 separate companies furnished materials, parts or service in its construction."

The flight was not the heroic lone success of a single daring individual, but the climax of the co-operative effort of an elaborately interlocked technology. The day after Coolidge's speech, Lindbergh said at another ceremony in Washington that the honor should "not go to the pilot alone but to American science and genius which had given years of study to the advancement of aeronautics.". . . "The flight," concluded Lindbergh, "represented American industry. "

The worship of the machine which was embodied in the public's response to Lindbergh exalted those very aspects which were denigrated in the celebration of the flight as the work of a heroic individual. Organization and careful method were what lay behind the flight, not individual self-sufficiency and daring romance. One magazine hailed the flight as a "triumph of mechanical engineering." "It is not to be forgotten that this era is the work not so much of brave aviators as of engineers, who have through patient and protracted effort been steadily improving the construction of airplanes." The lesson to be learned from Lindbergh's flight, thought a writer in the *Independent,* "is that the splendid human and material aspects of America need to be organized for the ordinary, matter of fact service of society." The machine meant organization, the careful rationalization of activity of a Ford assembly line, it meant planning, and, if it meant the loss of spontaneous individual action, it meant the material betterment of society. Lindbergh meant not a retreat to the free life of the frontier past but an emergence into the time when "the machine began to take first place in the public mind—the machine and the organization that made its operation possible on a large scale." A poet on this side of the matter wrote, "All day I felt the pull / Of the steel miracle." The machine was not a devilish engine which would enthrall mankind, it was the instrument which would lead to a new paradise. But the direction of history implicit in the machine was toward the future, not the past; the meaning of history was progress, not decline, and America should not lose faith in the future betterment of society. An address by a Harvard professor, picked up by the *Magazine of Business,* made all this explicit. "We commonly take Social Progress for granted," said Edwin F. Gay, "but the doctrine of Social Progress is one of the great revolutionary ideas which have powerfully affected our modern world." There was a danger, however, that the idea "may be in danger of becoming a commonplace or a butt of criticism." The speaker recognized why this might be. America was "worn and disillusioned after the Great War." Logically, contentment should have gone with so optimistic a creed, yet the American people were losing faith. So Lindbergh filled an emotional need even where a need should have been lacking. "He has come like a shining vision to revive the hope of mankind." The high ideals of faith in progress "had almost come to seem like hollow words to us—but now here he is, emblematic of heroes yet to inhabit this world. Our belief in Social Progress is justified symbolically in him."

It is a long flight from New York to Paris; it is a still longer flight from the fact of Lindbergh's achievement to the burden imposed upon it by the imagination of his time. But it is in that further flight that lies the full meaning of Lindbergh. His role was finally a double one. His flight provided an opportunity for the people to project their own emotions into his act and their emotions involved finally two attitudes toward the meaning of their own experience. One view had it that America represented a brief escape from the course of history, an emergence into a new and open world with the self-sufficient individual at its center. The other said that America represented a stage in historical evolution and that its fulfillment lay in the development of society. For one, the meaning of America lay in the past; for the other in the future. For one, the American ideal was an escape from institutions, from the forms of society, and from limitations put upon the free individual; for the other, the American ideal was the elaboration of the complex institutions which made modern society possible, an acceptance of the discipline of the machine, and the achievement of the individual within a context of which he was only a part. The two views were contradictory but both were possible and both were present in the public's reaction to Lindbergh's flight.

ELEANOR ROOSEVELT

&

the Changing Role of Women

Anna Eleanor Roosevelt, social reformer, humanitarian, newspaper and magazine columnist, intrepid visitor to coal mines, battlefields, inaccessible kingdoms, and scenes of natural disaster, stands foremost among the First Ladies of American history. Although Mrs. Roosevelt gained prominence because she was the wife of President Franklin D. Roosevelt, she influenced others in her own right through a network of organizational and personal relationships with major reform and charitable groups. At one time or another, she was involved with settlement work, the National Consumers' League, the NAACP, and various international charity and peace organizations.

Born in 1884 and orphaned at nine, Eleanor grew up in New York City with her grandmother. She studied and traveled in England for three years with a French tutoress, and after returning to America at eighteen, she worked in a settlement house in New York. Her marriage to Franklin in 1905 ended her public work for a time. When they moved to Washington, D.C., in 1913, she once more entered social and public activity, and during the 1920's, while living again in New York City, she joined the League of Women Voters and worked in the Todhunter School, teaching current events and history. When she became First Lady, her activities, closely followed by the press, showed up in popular cartoons and in the routines of comedians much as do the foibles of a president. Her wide interests and personal popularity led

her to write many articles and books, including a syndicated daily
newspaper column, "My Day," and an autobiography, *This I Remember.*
After her husband's death in 1945, she further increased the range and
depth of her activities and was appointed United States resspresentative
to the United Nations. She died in 1962 at the age of seventy-eight.

As a child, Eleanor Roosevelt had been extremely shy and awkward.
Never at home in the fashionable society into which she had been born,
she nevertheless was dominated by its standards and its narrow definition
of the role of women. As she became involved in work of her own,
especially during and after World War I, she became increasingly
self-assured. She was no longer simply Franklin's wife but a strong and
effective personality in her own right. During her years as the First Lady
women hardly existed in political circles; but she expressed her views
on many subjects, often whether or not they coincided with those of the
president. Much of the criticism directed at her was simply resentment
at her presumptuousness; after all, she was only a woman and drew
attention largely because she was the president's wife. But the humanitarian
causes she publicized, including those related to women, benefited from
her activities.

For the feminist movement, the image she projected of political
leadership, personal vigor, and humanitarian concern was itself a huge
boost. Beyond that, Eleanor Roosevelt's desire to expand the power of
women was a lifelong passion. Her support for the Women's Trade
Union League and other progressive women's groups continued throughout
her long career. She was active in behalf of women during the depression,
as Tamara Hareven explains below. During World War II she interceded
frequently for the millions of women employed in defense industries,
trying to provide them with adequate day care services and generally
to facilitate their new lives as workers. Later, in her activities as a
private citizen and with the United Nations, she continually concerned
herself with women's causes. She did, however, oppose the bills for
an Equal Rights Amendment that women's groups introduced in Congress
annually beginning in the 1920's, because she was against defining the
rights of women as a distinct group. She preferred to press for piecemeal
legislation and judicial interpretation to remove women's legal
liabilities. Today her feminism seems distinctly that of an earlier
generation: she retained some of the Victorian presumption that a woman
should work to raise men to her own level and should concentrate on
improving the lives of all citizens rather than women's lives alone.
The limits of the unquestionably noble tradition within which she acted
became obvious to the newer feminists who emerged in the 1960's. But
for her time, Eleanor Roosevelt was indeed something of a radical.

This Is My Story (1937)
ELEANOR ROOSEVELT

In addition to the well-known volume This I Remember, *Eleanor Roosevelt published an autobiographical book entitled* This Is My Story. *It is in the classic mold of progressive and liberal memoirs: the story of a member of the privileged classes discovering the problems of the unfortunate and at the same time discovering her own self and role in the world. In the passages below we see how naively dependent she was in the early days and how she gradually developed her own knowledge and individual assertion. Her story is affecting for its very artlessness, as the mature Eleanor Roosevelt experienced with fresh astonishment the depths of her innocence in the days before the world opened to her reach. The selection begins with Franklin and Eleanor on vacation in Britain shortly after their marriage, then moves to Washington during World War I when Franklin was assistant secretary of the navy. It ends in New York after the war when Franklin had returned to his law practice.*

ONE AFTERNOON AT TEA [in Scotland in 1905] I was alone with Lady Helen [Ferguson], when she suddenly asked me a devastating question: "Do tell me, my dear, how do you explain the difference between your national and state governments? It seems to us so confusing."

I had never realized that there were any differences to explain. In fact, I had never given a thought to the question. I knew that we had state governments, because Uncle Ted [Theodore Roosevelt] had been Governor of New York State. My heart sank, and I wished that the ground would open up and swallow me. Luckily, Sir Ronald and my husband appeared at that moment for tea, and I could ask Franklin to answer her question. He was adequate, and I registered a vow that once safely back in the United States I would find out something about my own government.

We had to be home for the opening of the Columbia Law School, so our holiday, or second honeymoon, had come to an end. My mother-in-law had taken a house for us within three blocks of her own. It was at 125 East 36th Street. She had furnished it and engaged our servants, and everything was almost in order for us. We were to spend the first few days with her on landing until we could put the finishing touches on our house.

I was beginning to be an entirely dependent person—no tickets to buy, no plans to make, someone always to decide everything for me. . . .

The edge of my shyness was gradually wearing off through enforced contact with many people. I still suffered but not so acutely, and I was beginning to be conscious of the fact that it was rare that you could not establish some kind of a relationship with your neighbor at dinner or at any social gathering.

Either Maude or Pussie [her aunts] once told me that if I were stuck for conversation I should take the alphabet and start right through it. "A—Apple. Do you like apples, Mr. Smith? B—Bears. Are you afraid of bears, Mr. Jones? C—Cats. Do you have the usual feeling, Mrs. Jellyfish, about cats? Do they give you the creeps even when you do not see them?" And so forth all the way down the line, but some time had passed since anything as desperate as this had had to be done for conversational purposes. As young women go, I suppose I was fitting pretty well into the pattern of a fairly conventional, quiet, young society matron. . . .

A Changing Existence

That autumn [of 1917], back in Washington, real work began in earnest, and all my executive ability, which had been more or less dormant up to this time, was called into play. The house must run more smoothly than ever, we must entertain and I must be able to give less attention to it than ever before. The children must lead normal lives; Anna must go to the Eastman school every day, and James and Elliott must go to the Cathedral school, which was out in the opposite direction. All this required organization.

My mother-in-law used to laugh at me and say I could provide my chauffeur with more orders to be carried out during the day than anyone else she had ever listened to, but this was just a symptom of developing executive ability. My time was now completely filled with a variety of war activities, and I was learning to have a certain confidence in myself and in my ability to meet emergencies and deal with them.

One afternoon of every week I gave out wool from my own house and took in finished articles. Marie de Laboulaye and I went over them, for she volunteered to help in American war work, feeling that that was a way of showing her gratitude for the help which our Government was giving her country. Mrs. Charles Munn was a young and very pretty bride at that time and drove her own car. She collected the bundles of knitted garments and delivered them to their destination.

Two or three shifts a week I spent in the Red Cross canteen in the railroad yards. During the winter I took chiefly day shifts in the canteen, for I was obliged to be at home, if possible, to see my children before they went to bed, and I frequently had guests for dinner. I can remember one or two occasions when I arrived in my uniform as my guests arrived, and I think it was during this period that I learned to dress with rapidity, a habit which has stayed with me ever since. We had some wonderful women in charge of the canteen and were very fortunate in the direction which they gave us. Miss Mary Patten worked on a number of shifts with me and I would often stop for her in the car, so I came to know her very well, and I grew to have great affection and respect for her character and willingness to work.

Everyone in the canteen, however, was expected to do any work that was necessary, even mopping the floor, and no one remained long a member of this Red Cross unit who could not do anything that was asked of her. I remember one lady who came down escorted by her husband to put in one afternoon. I doubt if she had ever done any manual labor before in her life, and she was no longer young. The mere suggestion that she might have to scrub the floor filled her with horror and we never again saw her on a shift.

We had an army kitchen in a little tin building where we made coffee. We cut the bread with the cutting machine, spread it with jam, and wrapped the finished sandwiches in paper. Large caldrons of coffee and large baskets of sandwiches were ready for the trainloads of men as they went through.

I had one disastrous experience with the bread-cutting machine. On a particularly busy day, rather early on my shift, I cut part of my finger almost to the bone. There was no time to stop, so I wrapped something tightly around it and proceeded during the day to wrap more and more handkerchiefs around it, until it finally stopped bleeding. When I got home late in the afternoon, I sent for the doctor, and asked him if I should have it sewed up; he said it would probably be too painful so long after cutting it, and though it might leave a scar, it would heal. The doctor bandaged it and left it as it was and I still have the scar!

We sold post cards, candy and cigarettes to the boys and we had to censor the cards so they would not give any forbidden information. Later on, as the warm weather came, we had some showers in a building near us, a very make-shift arrangement, but very welcome, as the heat increased, to the boys who had spent days and nights on trains.

Once a week I visited the Naval Hospital and took flowers, cigarettes and any little thing that might cheer the men who had come back from overseas. There were a number of Navy units stationed in different parts of France; for instance, those who went with our Navy guns; those stationed at Dunkirk and various other places on the coasts of Europe; those with the destroyers and the transports, besides our Marines who fought with the Second Division in some of the hottest fighting of the war, in Belleau Wood and the Argonne.

The Naval Hospital filled up very rapidly and we finally took over one building in St. Elizabeth's Hospital for the so-called shell-shocked patients. The doctors, of course, explained that these were men who had been submitted to great strain and cracked under it. Some of them came back to sanity, others remained permanently in our veterans' hospitals for mental care.

St. Elizabeth's was the one Federal hospital for the insane in the country and I had never seen it before. A fine man was at the head of it, but he always had been obliged to run his institution on an inadequate appropriation, and as yet the benefits of occupational therapy were little understood in the treatment of the insane. I did, however, know that in some hospitals this work was being done with a measure of success for the patients.

I visited our naval unit there and had my first experience of going into a ward of people who, while they were not violent, were more or less incalculable because they were not themselves. Those who were not under control were kept in padded cells or in some kind of confinement.

When the doctor and I went into the long general ward where the majority of men were allowed to move about during the daytime, he unlocked the door and locked it again after us. We started down that long room, speaking to different men on the way. Quite at the other end stood a young boy with fair hair. The sun in the window placed high up, well above the patients' heads, touched his hair and seemed almost like a halo around his head. He was talking to himself incessantly and I inquired what he was saying. "He is giving the orders," said the doctor, "which were given every night in Dunkirk, where he was stationed." I remembered my husband telling me that he had been in Dunkirk and that every evening the enemy planes came over the town and bombed it and the entire population was ordered down into the cellars. This boy had stood the strain of the nightly bombing until he could stand it no longer, then he went insane and repeated the orders without stopping, not being able to get out of his mind the thing which had become an obsession.

I asked what chances he had for recovery and was told that it was fifty-fifty, but that in all probability he would never again be able to stand as much strain as before he had had this illness.

The doctor told me that many of our men in the Naval Hospital unit were well enough to go out every day, play games and get air and exercise, and that we had sufficient attendants to do this; in the rest of the hospital, however, they were so short of attendants since the war that the other patients practically never got out. The doctor also told me that in spite of the fact that wages had gone skyrocketing during this period, the hospital had never been able to pay its attendants more than thirty dollars a month and their board, which was low wages in comparison with what men were getting in other occupations.

I drove through the grounds and was horrified to see poor demented creatures with apparently very little attention being paid them, gazing from behind bars or walking up and down on enclosed porches.

This hospital was under the Department of the Interior, so I could hardly wait to reach Secretary Lane, to tell him that I thought an investigation was in order, and that he had better go over and see for himself. He confided to me that the last thing he wanted to see was a hospital for the insane. He did, however, appoint a committee which later appeared before Congress and asked for and obtained an increased appropriation. I believe this action of the secretary enabled Doctor White to make this hospital what every Federal institution in Washington should be—a model of its kind which can be visited with profit by interested people from the various parts of our country.

In the meantime, I was so anxious that our men should have a meeting place that I went to the Red Cross and begged them to build one of their recreation rooms, which they did. Then, through Mrs. Barker, I obtained five hundred dollars from the Colonial Dames, which started the occupational-therapy work, and in a short time they were able to see what they produced and to buy new materials for themselves.

In the Naval Hospital I was seeing many tragedies enacted. There was a woman who sat for days by the bed of her son who had been gassed and had tuberculosis. There was a chance that he might be saved if he could get out West. She could not afford to go with him but we finally obtained permission to send a nurse. Only a few years ago I had a letter from her reminding me of our contact in the hospital and telling me that her boy had died.

Another boy from Texas, with one leg gone, wanted so much to get home; finally, with the help of the Daughters of the Confederacy, some of whom were our most faithful workers, he achieved his desire and I think became self-supporting.

These are just examples of the many things touching the lives of individuals which came to all of us in those days; and so far as I was concerned, they were a liberal education. Some of the stories were sordid, all of them filled with a mixture of the heroism in human nature and its accompanying frailties.

I think I learned then that practically no one in the world is entirely bad or entirely good, and that motives are often more important than actions. I had spent most of my life in an atmosphere where everyone was sure of what was right and what was wrong, and as life has progressed I have gradually come to believe that human beings who try to judge other human beings are undertaking a somewhat difficult job. When your duty does not thrust ultimate judgments upon you, perhaps it is as well to keep an open and charitable mind, and to try to understand why people do things instead of condemning the acts themselves.

Out of these contacts with human beings during the war I became a more tolerant person, far less sure of my own beliefs and methods of action, but I think more determined to try for certain ultimate objectives. I had gained a certain assurance as to my ability to run things, and the knowledge that there is joy in accomplishing a good job. I knew more about the human heart, which had been somewhat veiled in mystery up to now. . . .

The Budding of a Life of My Own

I did not look forward to a winter of four days in New York with nothing but teas and luncheons and dinners to take up my time. [This was in 1920, when Eleanor and Franklin were spending part of the week in New York City and part in Hyde Park.] The war had made that seem an impossible mode of living, so I mapped out a schedule for myself. I decided that I would learn to cook and I found an ex-cook, now married, who had an apartment of her own, and I went twice a week and cooked an entire meal which I left with her for her family to criticize. I also attended a business school, and took a course in typewriting and shorthand every day that I was in New York.

Before I had been in New York many days I was visited by Mrs. Frank Vanderlip, who was at that time chairman of the League of Women Voters for New York State. She asked if I would join the board and be responsible for reports on national legislation. I explained that I had little or no contact in Washington with national legislation, that I had listened a great deal to the talk that went on around me, and that I would be interested but doubted my ability to do this work. Mrs. Vanderlip said she was sure that I had absorbed more than most of the New York members of the board knew, and that I would have the assistance of a very able woman lawyer, Miss Elizabeth Read. She would take the Congressional Record, go through it and mark the bills which she thought were of interest to the league, send for them and even assist me to understand them if I required any assistance.

With this assurance, I finally agreed that I would attempt to do the work. I decided that I would go to Miss Read's office one morning a week and devote that time to the study of legislation and bring home the bills that needed further study before I wrote my monthly reports.

I felt very humble and very inadequate to the job when I first presented myself to Elizabeth Read, but I liked her at once and she gave me a sense of confidence. It was the beginning of a friendship with her and with her friend, Miss Esther Lape, which was to be a lasting and warm friendship from then on. Elizabeth and Esther had a small apartment together. Esther has a brilliant mind and a driving force, a kind of nervous power. Elizabeth seemed calmer, more practical and domestic, but I came to see that hers was a keen and analytical mind and in its way as brilliant as Esther's. I have for years thought that Providence was particularly wise and farseeing when it threw these two women together, for their gifts complement each other in a most extraordinary way. From their association has come much good work which has been of real service in a good many causes. Gradually I think they came to feel an affection and a certain respect for me because I was willing really to work on these reports and not to expect them to do my work for me.

My husband was working hard; he went occasionally to men's dinners, and I remember many a pleasant evening spent with Elizabeth and Esther in their little apartment. Their standards of work and their interests played a great part in what might be called "the intensive education of Eleanor Roosevelt" during the next few years.

My mother-in-law was distressed and felt that I was not always available, as I had been when I lived in New York before. I joined the Monday Sewing Class of which she had always been a member. It is now more of a social and charitable institution than an actual sewing group. Some of the ladies still take home sewing, but most of them pay their dues and give the work to women who need it. The garments made are distributed to charity. The ladies lunch together every Monday and enjoy one another's company. It pleased my mother-in-law to have me with her and it gave us a definite engagement together once a week.

I had long since ceased to be dependent on my mother-in-law, and the fact that my cousin, Mrs. Parish, suffered from a long illness, lasting several years, had made me less dependent on her. I wrote fewer letters and asked fewer questions and gave fewer confidences, for I had begun to realize that in my development I was drifting far afield from the old influences. I do not mean to imply that I was the better for this. Far from it, but I was thinking things out for myself and becoming an individual. Had I never done this, perhaps I might have been saved some difficult experiences, but I have never regretted even my mistakes. They all added to my understanding of other human beings, and I came out in the end a more tolerant, understanding and charitable person. It has made life and the study of people more interesting than it could have been if I had remained in the conventional pattern.

Equal Pay for Equal Work (1933)
ELEANOR ROOSEVELT

Equal pay for equal work sounds like a conservative enough program. Yet in 1933, when Mrs. Roosevelt wrote It's Up to the Women, *from which the following selection was taken, pay scales for women were sharply lower than for men in similar jobs—and this was perfectly legal. ᵒday, while pay scales for women are still lower than for men, such crimination is now illegal and the differential is gradually being reduced. anor Roosevelt, here as in so many places, was a pioneer.*

THIS IS A TIME when working conditions for both men and women are undergoing very violent changes. It has usually been an accepted fact that women should be paid less than men. The original theory on which this idea was based, I imagine, was that men were physically stronger than women, could work more hours and do heavier work. But since machinery has so largely come to be the order of the day, this has changed. Women in factories and in shops find themselves quite able to do the same work that a man does if they go into the work at all. This being the case, it would seem advisable that the principle of equal pay for equal work should be accepted, otherwise employers who wish to keep down the cost of production will largely employ women and pay them less than they would have to pay men. It would be natural to wonder why women are willing to work for less than men. There are a number of reasons and perhaps the main one is that women employed in industry generally do not expect to work all their lives, but look forward to the day when they will be married, and therefore are not so deeply concerned with wages or working conditions outside their own homes. This is all very well and for the unscrupulous employer very satisfactory, but it is not good for labor in general, not good for men who work and not good for women who may have to continue to work throughout their entire lives.

Great efforts have been made to make working women realize the necessity for union organizations but very little result in the way of actual organizations can be seen. Now and then you will find women are organized in some trade, but it is very apt to be a trade where they are allowed to enter the same union with the men and where the men's union had already been established.

One would think that enough women of intelligence would have recognized this problem and educated the great body of working women. This, however, does not seem to be the case and women in industry continue, largely because of their own lack of initiative, to receive lower wages than men and to pull down the wage scale of the men as well as their own.

In occupations where the higher type of women with a better education is employed, they are more nearly getting to an equality and I think before many years in the professions and the more skilled trades and more executive jobs, we shall see very little difference in the earning capacity of women as compared with men. Women should receive equal pay for equal work and they should also work the same hours and insist on the same good working conditions and the same rights of representation that the men have. If they accept longer hours and unsanitary working conditions, they injure the cause of labor. This may mean, however, if they are not allowed to join the men's unions, the forming of a union of their own, but I hope it will not be as difficult in the future as it has been in the past to awaken them to the necessity of organization. I think women have a right to demand equality as far as possible but I think they should still have the protection of special legislation regarding certain special conditions of their work and until we actually have equal pay and are assured of a living wage for both men's and women's work, I believe in minimum wage boards and regulating by law the number of hours women may work. They should also be allowed a certain number of days off before and after the birth of a child. This legislation is primarily necessary because as yet women are not as well organized or as able to negotiate for themselves with the employers. but it is also necessary in the interests of the state, which must concern itself with the health of the women because the future of the race depends upon their ability to produce healthy children. The new codes aim to accomplish many of these things, but the codes must be enforced and public opinion must insist on this. . . .

. . . I feel that the modern woman should take a particular interest in the conditions under which all women are going to work because the basis of much of our present day unrest is the discontent of the working class generally with the returns which they receive for their labor. If we women who are usually the ones most concerned in keeping peace, whether it is peace between nations or peace between the employer or employee, do not concern ourselves with working conditions as they affect the social conditions of our day, then we can hardly expect that any advance toward a satisfactory solution of these problems will be made in the future.

Eleanor's Press Conferences (1971)
JOSEPH P. LASH

In her own subdued way, Eleanor Roosevelt helped raise the status of women and projected an image of an activist female reaching into public life rather than retiring into remote corners of the White House. This selection from the major biography by Joseph Lash shows clearly what a national departure she made in the role of First Lady. The two selections following this one focus specifically on Eleanor's activities in behalf of women.

THE MOST RADICAL BREAK with precedent was her decision to hold press conferences, the first ever given by a First Lady, in the White House, on the record. The contrast with Mrs. Hoover could not have been more marked. That silvery-haired, kindly woman had shielded herself from public notice. The handful of women who were assigned to keep track of her, who were known as the "Green Room girls," were permitted to observe her only at a distance at official receptions, teas, tree plantings, charity bazaars, and public appearances with the president. The few occasions on which she appeared in the press in her own right were in connection with the Girl Scouts. Behind the screen of protocol, within the confines of the White House, there was a motherly human being whose warmth, had the nation been permitted to share it, would have done something to relieve the impression of severity the Hoovers created. But only in the final days of the campaign did the Hoover managers realize that it had been a mistake to keep Mrs. Hoover at arms' length from friendly reporters. On the Roosevelt campaign train, Mrs. Roosevelt was talking daily to Lorena Hickok of the Associated Press, and out of the blue Bess Furman, the redheaded AP correspondent traveling with the Hoover campaign special, was told she could interview Mrs. Hoover, the only interview she was granted in four years of covering the First Lady. The ground rules, Mrs. Hoover informed her, were that she should not be directly quoted; Miss Furman would have to write about the biographical details Mrs. Hoover would now furnish her as if she had obtained them from a library.

Mrs. Hoover had conformed to a pattern of behavior established for First Ladies from the time of Martha Washington. It was not a model Eleanor Roosevelt could follow without stultifying herself, and it was not a model she thought appropriate in a democratic society where the channels of communication between the people in the White House and the people in the country should, she felt, be open, lively, and sympathetic. So when Hick suggested that she hold press conferences, Eleanor agreed, and Bess Furman, whom she consulted, approved enthusiastically—as did Franklin and Louis [Howe, a presidential aide]. On Monday, March 6, two days before her husband's first press conference, an astonished and somewhat disapproving Ike Hoover [chief usher], or so Eleanor thought, accompanied her into the Red Room, where thirty-five women reporters had assembled. The conference had been restricted to women, she explained, in order to encourage the employment of newspaper women and to make it more comfortable to deal with subjects of interest primarily to women. To further emphasize that she was in no way encroaching upon Franklin's domain, she had stipulated that no political questions could be asked. She brought with her a large box of candied fruits which she passed around—to hide her nervousness, she later claimed. The first news conference did not produce much news, but the women were elated, although some of them, especially May Craig of the *Portland* (Maine) *Press Herald,* having fought hard to break down masculine professional barriers, were uncomfortable that men were excluded. However, the attitude of the men was "Why in the world would we want to come to Mrs. Roosevelt's conferences?" Byron Price, the manager of the AP, predicted that the institution would last less than six months. However, a few weeks later, when a bill to legalize 3.2 beer went up to Congress, Roosevelt was asked at his news conference whether beer should be served at the White House if the bill were passed; that would have to be answered by his wife, he replied off the record. Eleanor was on her way to New York, so Ruby Black of the United Press raced out to catch her at the airport. Would she, a tee-totaler, permit beer to be served at the White House? "You'll have to ask my husband," was Eleanor's guarded reply. Told that the president had referred the press to her, she burst into laughter. She would have a state-ment for them at her next news conference, she promised. By Monday, when the women reporters trooped in for their meeting with Eleanor, masculine scorn had turned to anguish, and some of the men begged the women to fill them in later.

Beer would be served at the White House to those who desire it, Eleanor's mimeographed announcement read. She herself did not drink anything with an alcoholic content, but she would not dream of imposing her convictions on others. She hoped, however, that the availability of beer might lead to greater temperance, and to a reduction in the bootlegger's trade.

The scoffing ceased. Eleanor proved to be such a good news source that Emma Bugbee, who had been sent by the *New York Herald Tribune* to report on the First Lady's inauguration activities, was kept in Washington by her Republican employers for four months. "Well, if it's going to be like that," Emma's office said, after their reporter had lunched with Mrs. Roosevelt and had been taken through the living quarters of the president's family, something Mrs. Hoover had not done until the final months of her husband's regime, "you had better stay down." Another Monday the press conference became a classroom in diets—patriotic, wholesome, and frugal; the women learned the recipe for Martha Washington's crab soup and for dishes that Andrew Jackson ate in the days "when the onion and herb were as important as the can opener." Sheila Hibben, the culinary historian whom Eleanor had invited to the news conference, even ventured a theory of history about White House menus: "The more democratic our Presi-dents have been, the more attention they paid to their meals." The lecture on the wholesome, inexpensive dishes that other First Ladies had served their husbands led up to an announcement that with the help of Flora Rose of Cornell, Eleanor had served "a 7-cent luncheon" at the White House— hot stuffed eggs with tomato sauce, mashed potatoes, prune pudding, bread, and coffee. In London a woman read this menu and exclaimed to a friend that "if Mrs. Roosevelt can get her kitchen staff to eat three-penny, ha-penny meals, she can do more than I can with mine!"

"Oh, I don't know what she gives the servants," the friend replied. "She gives them to the President—and he eats them like a lamb."

Malnutrition, Eleanor concluded, was not only a result of a lack of food, but often of a lack of knowledge of menus that cost little and had high nu-tritional value. She thought the White House should set an example in the use of simple and nourishing foods. "Perhaps because of the depression we may teach people how really to feed their children."

Bess Furman contrasted the news-conference styles of president and First Lady: "At the President's press conference, all the world's a stage; at Mrs. Roosevelt's, all the world's a school."

Eleanor's ban on political subjects did not mean a ban on issues of consequence and controversy. She hit out at sweatshops. She urged women to patronize the merchants who provided decent working conditions. She called for the elimination of child labor and urged more money for teachers' salaries. When in April the foreign dignitaries came flocking to the White House to confer with the president on the forthcoming World Economic Conference, she startled her press conference with the passion of her anti-isolationist plea. "We ought to be able to realize what people are up against in Europe. We ought to be the ready-to-understand ones, and we haven't been. . . . We've got to find a basis for a more stabilized world. . . . We are in an ideal position to lead, if we will lead, because we have suffered less. Only a few years are left to work in. Everywhere over there is the dread of this war that may come." She spoke, wrote Emma Bugbee, with "an intensity her hearers had never seen in her before."

With many of her press-conference regulars, what began as a professional relationship soon ripened into friendship. Before the inauguration, Ruby Black (Mrs. Herbert Little) had shown Eleanor a photograph of her fourteen-month-old daughter. Eleanor had said she would love to see the child, and Ruby had thought it was an expression of courtesy rather than of intent. A week after she was in the White House, however, Eleanor telephoned her—could she come the next day to visit Ruby? She did, driving her little blue roadster to Ruby's house and making friends with the child. Newswomen found themselves being given lifts in the White House car, receiving Easter lilies from the White House greenhouses, lunching at the White House table, being invited to Hyde Park. Eleanor's gestures of thoughtfulness were not matters of calculation, of "being nice to the press"; one natural act of friendliness led to another. But friendship did not encroach upon journalistic responsibility. The women asked the questions to which they or their editors felt the public was entitled to know the answers. When a reporter cautioned the First Lady that an answer might get her into trouble, her colleagues made their displeasure known; the First Lady could take care of herself, they felt. And she did.

"Sometimes I say things," she said to her press conference,

which I thoroughly understand are likely to cause unfavorable comment in some quarters, and perhaps you newspaper women think I should keep them off the record. What you don't understand is that perhaps I am making these statements on purpose to arouse controversy and thereby get the topics talked about and so get people to thinking about them.

Political Sisterhood (1971)
JOSEPH P. LASH

THERE WAS ANOTHER SIGN of her intense practicality—the way she backed up her exhortations to women to take leadership in the fight against war and social injustice with hard-headed political organization. Many women held important positions in the Roosevelt administration, she noted in *It's Up to the Women,* and were, therefore, in a stronger position to shape policy than ever before. The book did not say what insiders in Washington knew, that at the center of this growing New Deal political sisterhood was Eleanor Roosevelt.

"About the most important letter I ever wrote you!" Molly Dewson scribbled on the margin of a seven-page enclosure she sent Mrs. Roosevelt a few weeks after the Roosevelts arrived in Washington. The letter reported on Molly's talk with James Farley, the postmaster general, about women's patronage. He would make no appointments of women, Farley assured Molly, without consulting Eleanor, so Molly felt safe about the lists she had left with him, which described the jobs the Democratic women wanted in categories of descending urgency. "Imperative recognition" covered the four appointments to the staff of the Democratic National Committee, followed by the names of fourteen women who warranted "Very Important Recognition" and twenty-five for whom jobs were sought under the classification of "Very Desirable Recognition." Postmasterships and comparable minor appointments were listed under the heading of "Worthy of Lesser Recognition."

"I think they are '100 percent' friendly toward recognizing the work of the Women and that they will probably do it," Molly's letter continued. But she cautioned Eleanor that the men were lobbying for jobs so insistently "that continuous pressure will have to be brought on Mr. Farley on behalf of the women. I mean continuous in the sense of pressure on behalf of one woman today and another woman tomorrow."

Mrs. Roosevelt and Molly Dewson were determined that women's voices should be heard at every level of the new administration, and they worked as a team to bring this about, although as far as the world knew Molly was the chief dispenser of the New Deal's feminine patronage. The relationship between Eleanor and Molly was harmonious and sympathetic. They had a common conception of the importance of building party organization and of using the influence of women to achieve the objectives of the New Deal.

Eleanor persuaded Farley to make the women's division a full-time functioning department of the Democratic National Committee, and then she

and the president prevailed upon Molly Dewson to come to Washington
to head the department. On January 15, 1934, despite her ban on political
subjects, Eleanor presented Molly at her press conference to describe the
new setup of the women's Democratic organization. When Molly said that
women Democrats had long hoped for such an organization and were now
about to achieve it "for many reasons," Ruby Black of the United Press,
who knew Mrs. Roosevelt's decisive role behind the scenes, mischievously
blurted out, "name three." Eleanor gave her a humorously reproving
glance, and Molly, after a pause, said, "This Democratic party really
believes in women, and the plan was presented to it properly." Molly
arrived in the capital with the names of sixty women qualified on the basis
of their work in the campaign and their past records to hold high government positions. By April, 1935, the Associated Press reported that there
were more than fifty women in such positions, and many of them made
public pronouncements under Eleanor's auspices. Secretary of Labor
Frances W. Perkins announced the establishment of camps for unemployed
women at one of Eleanor's press conferences. It was in Eleanor's sitting
room that Mrs. Mary Harriman Rumsey, the chairman of the NRA Consumer's Advisory Board, described her group's efforts to combat rising
prices through local consumer organization. And the plans of the Civil
Works Administration to provide 100,000 jobs for women were first disclosed by the new director of the CWA's women's work, Mrs. Ellen S.
Woodward, at a joint press conference with the First Lady.

"I do happen to know, from my close connections with the business and
professional women, of the resentment felt against Hoover because he did
not recognize women," Judge Florence E. Allen of the Ohio supreme court
wrote Eleanor in expressing her pleasure in the new administration's appointment of women. Such recognition did not come automatically—not
even in the New Deal. Molly fought vigorously to enlarge the number of
positions open to women. Sometimes she won her point on her own, but
if not, she went to Eleanor, and Eleanor, if she ran into difficulty, turned
to Louis or Franklin. Occasionally nothing worked. When Secretary of
State Hull recommended the appointment of Lucile Foster McMillin to
the place on the Civil Service Commission that traditionally had gone to
a woman, Molly complained to Eleanor, "Don't you really think that
Secretary Hull has enough recognition and power in his own job not to
take away from the regular organization women the few jobs that have
always been marked out for them?" Why didn't he appoint Mrs. McMillin
to a diplomatic post? But then, she added apologetically, "Of course, I
realize I may be asking more from you than is possible at this stage of
woman's development." Hull had his way and Mrs. McMillin was named
Civil Service commissioner, but several years later he did name two women
as American ministers—"the first time in our history that women had been
named to head diplomatic missions," he would proudly write, adding with
male condescension, "They both proved competent, and made excellent
records."

Harry Hopkins was much more receptive to the wishes of the women, especially Eleanor. He was as passionate a reformer as she and just as ready for bold experimentation. He cultivated her interest in the Civil Works Administration and encouraged her to take the lead in setting up the women's end of the CWA. "You may be sure that under the new Civil Works program women will not be overlooked," Eleanor assured a woman correspondent who was upset that the president's announcement of the CWA omitted specific mention of women. A program for unemployed women was hammered out at a White House conference called and keynoted by Eleanor and attended by the leading figures in the field of social welfare. By the end of 1933, 100,000 women had CWA jobs.

The irascible and aggressive Harold L. Ickes was tougher to deal with. When Eleanor went to him with a request, she was usually careful to preface it with the statement that the president had asked her to do so. This was the case when she urged that the post of assistant commissioner of education, "which is now held by a woman [should] be retained by a woman" and that under the plan to provide work for unemployed teachers, half the positions should be allotted to women. Ickes agreed on both points.

While she sought patronage to build up the women's division of the party. Eleanor insisted that appointments had to be on the basis of merit, not just party loyalty, particularly as she felt that "during the next few years, at least, every woman in public office will be watched far more carefully than a man holding a similar position." Farley, under pressure from a female party worker for one of the top jobs in the administration, turned to Eleanor, who noted that "as head of the Children's Bureau, she [the woman in question] would be appalling. . . . I imagine she is entitled to something if it can be had and I also imagine that she needs the money badly, but I would not sacrifice a good job for her."

While pressing for the appointment of Democratic women, Eleanor would not agree to the removal of outstanding women who happened to be Republican. The head of the Children's Bureau, Grace Abbott, a Republican, had been one of the three top-ranking women in Washington under Hoover. Although she militantly championed children's rights, ambitious Democrats tried to use Miss Abbott's party affiliation as an excuse for Farley to force her out. Eleanor advised Farley to write the woman who was after Dr. Abbott's job "that no change is being made in the Children's Bureau and that Miss Abbott has the backing of most of the organized groups of women interested in child welfare."

Although she wanted the Democrats to become the majority party, which it was not in 1932, Eleanor did not hesitate to urge women to be ready to reject the party and its candidates "when the need arises."

This will not be disloyalty but will show that as members of a party they are loyal first to the fine things for which the party stands and when it rejects those things or forgets the legitimate objects for which parties exist, then as a party it cannot command the honest loyalty of its members.

Basically what she hoped might result from the inclusion of women was a humanization of government services and programs.

At a dinner honoring the new secretary of labor, Eleanor stressed that the post had been given to Frances Perkins "not only because there was a demand on the part of the women that a woman should be given a place in the Cabinet, but because the particular place which she occupies could be better filled by her than by anyone else, man or woman, with whom the President was acquainted." But beyond that, Miss Perkins exemplified the new type of public servant who was being brought to Washington by the New Deal.

> When Frances Perkins says "I can't go away because under the new industrial bill [NIRA] we have a chance to achieve for the workers of this country better conditions for which I have worked all my life," she is not staying because she will gain anything materially for herself or her friends, but because she sees an opportunity for government to render a permanent service to the general happiness of the working man and woman and their families. This is what we mean as I see it by the "new deal."

If this attitude toward public service struck people as new, "the women are in part responsible for it."

· Louis Howe, who shared Eleanor's view that women were in the forefront of the revolution in thinking that was back of the New Deal, believed that revolution would soon make it possible to elect a woman president. "If the women progress in their knowledge and ability to handle practical political and governmental questions with the same increasing speed as they have during the last ten years, within the next decade, not only the possibility but the advisability of electing a woman as President of the United States will become a seriously argued question," he wrote, adding that if politics continued to divide along humanitarian-conservative lines and the people decided they wanted a New Deal approach to such issues as education, recreation, and labor, "it is not without the bounds of possibility that a woman might not only be nominated but elected to that office on the grounds that they better understand such questions than the men."

Louis was so persuaded that the country might in the not-too-distant future say "Let's try a woman" that one day he came up into Eleanor's sitting room, propped himself cross-legged on a daybed, and said, "Eleanor, if you want to be President in 1940, tell me now so I can start getting things ready."

One politician in the family was enough, was her reply to such proposals, seriously meant or not. She did not deceive herself about the real attitude of the country, and doubted that the election of a woman was as imminent as Louis thought. "I do not think it would be impossible to find a woman who could be President, but I hope that it doesn't happen in the near future. . . . I do not think we have yet reached the point where the majority of our people would feel satisfied to follow the leadership and trust the judgment of a woman as President." Some day it might come to pass "but I hope it will not be while we speak of a 'woman's vote.' I hope it only becomes a reality when she is elected as an individual, because of her capacity and the trust which a majority of the people have in her integrity and ability as a person."

Women would have to learn that no amount of masculine chivalry was going to give them leadership if they could not actually "deliver the goods." They should leave their "womanly personalities" at home and "disabuse their male competitors of the old idea that women are only 'ladies in business.'" Women must stand or fall "on their own ability, on their own character as persons. Insincerity and sham, whether in men or in women, always fail in the end in public life."

It's Up to the Women, which came out in November, 1933, was her first book, and like most first authors she soon was inquiring of her publisher, Frederick A. Stokes, how well it was going. "The book is not running away but is selling very steadily," he replied. Eleanor wanted to be successful, and she cared about her influence. Women leaders were conscious that the New Deal meant that more women were involved in government, that more strongholds of masculine privilege were being infiltrated, and that Eleanor Roosevelt was at the hub of this movement. "For some time I have had a collection of statesmen hanging upon my wall," wrote Carrie Chapman Catt [the women's suffrage advocate], "but under the new administration, I have been obliged to start a new collection and that is one of stateswomen. Now it is ready and you are the very center of it all."

Fundamentally Eleanor was neither stateswoman, politician, nor feminist. She was a woman with a deep sense of spiritual mission. Like Saint Theresa, she not only "had a powerful intellect of the practical order" but was a woman of extravagant tenderness and piety. There was always some prayer in her purse to recall her to her Christian vocation. Christ's story was a drama that re-enacted itself repeatedly in her thoughts and feelings. Amid the worldliness, the pomp, and the power of Washington she managed to hold vivid and intimate communion with Christ with a child's innocence and simplicity. Christ's life in this world, she wrote in a Christmas message,

> lasted only a short thirty-three years. This life began in a manger surrounded by poverty and the only thing apparently which the Christ Child was given was an abundance of love. All his life was spent in want as far as material things were concerned. And, yet from that life there has sprung the Christian religion and what we know as Christian civilization. . . .
>
> Christ died a horrible death, probably at the time it was looked upon as a death of shame. He was buried by those who loved him in a borrowed tomb for he had never acquired any property of his own and yet from that death of shame and that borrowed tomb, has come to us all the

teaching which has made progress possible in the love of human beings, one for another.

What a tolerant person Christ was! He rarely condemned any one. Only when the money changers desecrated his Temple did he allow himself to drive them out.

To those who were weak, however, and to those who had aspirations or a desire to do better, he was the understanding and forgiving master.

Her greatest admiration, she wrote in *It's Up to the Women,* went to the women in all ages "whose hearts were somehow so touched by the misery of human beings that they wanted to give their lives in some way to alleviate it." Preaching and exhortation were of little value unless followed up by living example. "The reason that Christ was such a potent preacher and teacher was because He lived what He preached," and missionaries—social as well as religious—"who want to accomplish the double task not only of alleviating human suffering but of giving faith to the people with whom they come in contact, must show by their own way of living what are the fruits of their faith." She did so every hour of every day.

Women During the Depression (1968)
TAMARA HAREVEN

FROM THE BEGINNING of the depression, Mrs. Roosevelt concerned herself with the "forgotten woman" who was roaming the streets and parks and sleeping in subways at night. She tried not only to secure employment for women through the FERA but to assure their equal treatment. In a private conversation, Harry Hopkins promised Mrs. Roosevelt equality for women on relief. Subsequently, Mrs. Roosevelt called the White House Conference on the Emergency Needs for Women for the purpose of defining their problems and needs and suggesting possibilities for their constructive employment. The delegates represented various ranges of experience and areas of activity in social work, education, and government service.

In their respective speeches, both Harry Hopkins and Mrs. Roosevelt expressed their concern for the needs of thirty thousand to 400,000 unemployed women. "We must see to it," said Hopkins, "that they have a place to sleep at night, a decent bed, and good food while they are looking for jobs." He complained about the lack of imagination on the part of state administrators in allotting jobs for women. Carrying on along Hopkins' lines, Mrs. Roosevelt said, "In talking to Mr. Hopkins the other day we came to two conclusions: one was that it would be necessary to tell people in different places that either a certain number of jobs must be found for a certain number of women, or that a certain amount of money allotted must be used for giving the women work." The suggestion that state administrators be instructed to employ a minimal number of women was not immediately followed. Nevertheless, first attempts were made. Mrs. Roosevelt issued a call to each state to arrange meetings of representatives from national and state agencies to discuss immediately the steps for the employment of women. Subsequently, the states called conferences.

By December 17, 1933, about 100,000 women were among the 2,610,451 workers under the FERA and the Civil Works Administration (CWA), and Hopkins planned for the employment of an additional 300,000. Mrs. Woodward, who took charge of women's projects in the CWA in addition to the FERA, reported at Mrs. Roosevelt's press conference that thirty-five states had appointed women directors to head work projects for women. At Mrs. Roosevelt's insistence, Hopkins issued recommendations to include women wherever possible in the re-employment program. He suggested that they be given clerical jobs, even if this meant transferring men from such positions to other jobs.

Mrs. Roosevelt served as the clearing house for proposals for women's projects under the FERA, CWA, and later the Works Progress Administration (WPA). Proposals came streaming in from all directions. Some reflected the true needs of the community, others the imagination of concerned, responsible individuals, and still others the selfish interests of those seeking to establish themselves through the inauguration of such projects. When referring the suggestions to Mrs. Woodward, Mrs. Roosevelt endorsed the ones that seemed most reasonable. They revealed a variety of local needs and much imagination. For instance, Kansasville, Tennessee, was unable to maintain its thousand-book library serving five hundred people. Upon Mrs. Roosevelt's suggestion, it was incorporated into a book repair project. Likewise, a children's museum in Duluth, Minnesota, which could not support itself, was maintained as a works project.

With her efforts to serve both communities and unemployed women by creating projects, Mrs. Roosevelt also insisted on a fair pay rate to women on relief. At her press conference she voiced the demands of the Women's Trade Union League that women on relief jobs be given the same pay as men; that differentiation should be made between skilled and unskilled workers, or between women in different kinds of jobs, rather than between men and women.

In 1933, while attempting to integrate women into the federal work relief system, Mrs. Roosevelt, with Frances Perkins, Secretary of Labor, planned to establish resident camps for unemployed girls patterned after the Civilian Conservation Corps (CCC). Such camps would not only provide necessary work but would offer the "girl with the worn-out shoes" an opportunity for recreation before she went out again to hunt for jobs. Women in reforestation camps could work in tree nurseries and receive instruction in horticulture. The feminine counterpart of the CCC camps —nicknamed by newspapermen "She, She, She"—did not materialize. But Mrs. Roosevelt kept the principle of women's camps alive and secured the support of Harry Hopkins for work and educational camps for unemployed women under the FERA. At a White House conference on camps and resident schools for unemployed women called by the First Lady, seventy-five representatives of government departments and organizations in charge of women's works outlined plans for the project. Hilda Smith of the FERA said after the conference that it was Mrs. Roosevelt's leadership that helped the group reach "a definite plan of action and a unified purpose."

According to the plans of Mrs. Roosevelt and Hilda Smith, between two thousand and five thousand women were to spend the summer in forty resident schools and educational camps planned as joint federal and state projects. The distribution of camps would be determined by areas where the needs of women were greatest and where states indicated a readiness to cooperate. The first twenty-eight camps were established in the summer of 1934 under the direction of Hilda Smith. Eighteen hundred women, ranging in age from twenty to forty-five, passed through them in the first year. By May 1936 a total of 6,400 women from thirty-three states had benefited from the eighty-six camps established. In the summer of 1935 the camps were transferred to the National Youth Administration, but they followed the same pattern as in their initial stage, because Miss Smith continued to supervise them. The camps came close to Mrs. Roosevelt's idea of combining relief with education. The girls admitted were required to prove that they had no source of income. Unlike the men in CCC camps, they did not receive full payment. Each girl earned fifty cents a week in addition to maintenance, medical care, and travel expenses. The girls spent their mornings working in the installations servicing the camps and at various handicrafts. The major part of the day was devoted to education. The curriculum included workers' education, vocational guidance, training in home economics, and health education. In addition, the girls engaged in various other recreation projects.

Taking a personal interest in the camps, Mrs. Roosevelt adopted Camp Tera in Bear Mountain Park, New York, as her favorite. Originally founded by the New York Temporary Relief Administration, it was incorporated into the federal system and served as a model. Mrs. Roosevelt visited the camp often, helped administrators settle difficulties, and participated in the various activities with the girls. Part of the $3,000 which she donated to the New York relief fund went to equip this camp. It was typical of Mrs. Roosevelt's attitude to send a radio as soon as she discovered that the girls missed one.

Whichever project the First Lady endorsed received immediate publicity, often out of proportion to its importance. This made it automatically a target for public attacks. First the American Legion branded Camp Tera as a hotbed of communism; then criticisms were directed against government expenditures. To the American Legion Mrs. Roosevelt replied that a healthy group getting its courage back was far from being a disintegrating element susceptible to communism. Countering those who objected to the cost, she insisted that the investment was worth while because it would save the government higher expenditures in the long run. Not only should the camps be maintained; they should be expanded to year-round residences. The facts spoke for themselves, she said: girls who arrived weak and exhausted regained their health and went out with renewed energy. The vocational guidance they received helped them toward a new feeling of social responsibility. Those who had been stripped of a sense of belonging and felt no civic responsibility were now trained in citizenship through their daily involvement with others. In a circular to state administrators, Harry Hopkins admitted that the camps "proved an interesting educational experiment during the past summer." In one letter, thirteen girls from South Carolina wrote Mrs. Roosevelt about the reunion they held: "The group led discussions in which each girl told something of what she had been doing since her return from camp, and how helpful camp life has been to her in obtaining a job. We wish to see other NYA camps organized for the benefit of girls who didn't get to attend these camps and also those of us who would like to go back to camp."

JOSEPH R. MCCARTHY

&

the Cold War

Joe McCarthy (as he called himself after 1951) gave his name to an era and an attitude as surely as did Jefferson and Jackson. McCarthyism was built upon the foreign policy dilemmas of the Cold War. Despairing of explaining the intricacies of its policy to the American people, the Truman administration wrapped itself in the blanket of anti-Communism as an all-sufficient justification of its assorted and varying diplomatic activities the world over. Overseas, China had fallen to the Communists, and the Soviet Union had exploded its first atomic bomb. The issue of internal security was quite real: spies did work in government, and secrets, including information on the construction of nuclear weapons, had been passed to Soviet agents. In response to a few notorious spy cases, President Truman had instituted loyalty investigations for federal employees, and the sensational Alger Hiss case had been tried.

At this point, on February 9, 1950, in a speech at Wheeling, West Virginia, Senator McCarthy from Wisconsin claimed to have a "list of names that were made known to the Secretary of State as being members of the Communist Party and who nevertheless are still working and shaping policy in the State Department." At first he asserted that the list contained 205 names, then he settled on 57—as many as Heinz had varieties of pickles and condiments. For the next four years, until the Senate cracked down on him in 1954, McCarthy managed to keep the country in a broth with charges of Communists in the armed forces, in the churches, in the newspaper and movie industries. Typically characterized as a bully, McCarthy played rough indeed, making incredible public accusations, intimidating witnesses before his investigative subcommittee, and unleashing forces that damaged the careers of many people. But unlike the stereotype of the neighborhood bully, McCarthy threatened both the weak and the strong with grand impartiality.

McCarthy grew up in the Irish Catholic farm area of Outagamie County, Wisconsin. Born in November 1908, the fifth of seven children, Joseph R. McCarthy was raised on a 142-acre farm in an atmosphere of hard work, frugality, and self-reliance. He went to school in a one-room schoolhouse. Perhaps it was a combination of a father's harsh discipline and a mother's ambition for her favorite son that drove him to spend his time reading and made him shun not only adults but also the companionship of other children. With school behind him at fourteen, McCarthy started a chicken farm, renting an acre of land from his father. When he was nineteen his chicken business failed because no one could care for the brood when he became ill, and he moved to Manawa, where he got a job as manager of a chain grocery store.

At twenty McCarthy returned to school in Manawa, going to class with thirteen- and fourteen-year-olds and taking an advanced mathematics correspondence course from the University of Wisconsin. He finished high school in one year. McCarthy then entered the engineering school at Marquette University, where he received attention from fellow students as a boxer and joined the debating club. After two years McCarthy turned to the law. He ran for class president and, on a second vote, won by two points—the result of voting for himself rather than for his opponent as they had supposedly agreed.

Six hours after becoming a member of the Wisconsin bar, McCarthy set up a law practice in Waupaca. He supported himself mainly by playing poker and joined fraternal clubs to help him on his way to a political career. He lost his race for district attorney on the Democratic ticket in 1936 but was elected circuit judge soon after. During World War II McCarthy joined the Marines as a first lieutenant and voluntarily flew bombing missions. While still in the service, he attempted to win a U.S. Senate seat from Wisconsin; he managed to get an impressive number of votes but lost. Soon after, he resigned from the Marines and returned to his job as circuit judge. Late in 1945, he began a campaign that landed him the Republican nomination for U.S. Senator in a primary election that gave him a margin of only 5,000 votes over Robert M. LaFollette, Jr. In 1946 he was in Washington as duly elected Senator, and four years later he began his hunt for Communists. After the Senate finally censured him in 1954, McCarthy turned to heavy drinking and died in 1957.

McCarthy became strong because he built his hysterical visions out of real materials, much as a nightmare elaborates the realities of waking experience. The clue to the puzzle of McCarthyism lies not in how many "subversives" he or anyone else unearthed, but in why millions of Americans, both the powerful and the powerless, responded as they did to the menacing accusations of Joe McCarthy.

The Marshall-Acheson
Strategy for the Future (1951)
JOSEPH R. MC CARTHY

*The Cold War, a new situation of twilight struggle, went against every
assumption of a nation conditioned to ask for unconditional surrender.
McCarthy, as this speech to the Senate suggests, impaled the Truman
administration and its foreign policy leaders, Secretary of Defense
George C. Marshall and Secretary of State Dean Acheson, on their own
rationale: if Communism were so dangerous a threat, why did we
engage in half-measures, compromises, and evasions of what to McCarthy
meant a central obligation to attack and defeat it directly? McCarthy's
explanation appeared plausible to millions of Americans, and many
who thought they knew better found reasons not to engage McCarthy
in debate.*

THE NEXT APPEARANCE of Marshall in a position of supreme influence
over our affairs came only in September 1950. It was a black day for
America when this Senate voted to set aside a law it had passed to guard
against lesser calamities to allow Marshall to become Secretary of Defense.
We were not on guard, we were not vigilant. We fell short on that day
and I repentantly accept my share of the blame. I was recorded against
the bill but opposition was hopeless because Marshall was still wearing
the halo placed upon his head by the alchemy of liberal-leftist propaganda.

I wondered then why this venerable soldier, who had received the
world's honors, who had served as the first man in the President's Cabinet,
should be willing to return to the wars. I no longer wonder.

What is our strategy now?

It is to abandon American interest in the Far East, surrendering Formosa
to the grasp of a United Nations strewn with our enemies and wanting
nothing so much, under the leadership of the Socialist Government of
Britain and the racist, totalitarian Government of India, as to thrust the
United States out of the Far East.

It is because he differed with that policy that General MacArthur was
recalled from the Far East. He stood as a barrier to the final fulfillment of
the Marshall policy for China. That is why, when Marshall took office,
Eisenhower was rushed to Europe and the great debate over the extent of

our participation in the defense of Europe was provoked. That was the diversionary trick of a carnival prestidigitator. What had changed in Europe during last summer and early fall? What new sign was there that we faced attack from Russia in that quarter? The whole procedure was without meaning in any objective sense, yet it had meaning in the mind of the man referred to by the Democrats at Denver as "a master of global strategy."

Let us examine Marshall's strategy in Europe. Some feel that the problem of defending Europe can be settled merely by the decision whether we shall send an additional six or eight or ten American divisions to Western Europe. Would that it were that simple. The group which is doing the planning for Western Europe is the identical group which has been doing the disastrous planning for Asia; the same group that did the planning for the sellout of Poland and China.

When General Eisenhower appeared before the joint session of the Congress, he said he was unable to discuss the use of German manpower until the politics of the situation were cleared up by the diplomats. And for five years those diplomats have done nothing to clear up the situation. Periodically, our State Department has talked of rearming Western Germany to counter the powerful "peoples" army built up by the Russians in East Germany. We have had nothing but talk, apparently planned to lull the American people into a sense of security that we are going to do something in West Germany to counter the threat of Russia in East Germany.

When Eisenhower went to Europe to plan the defense of Western Europe, he was not even allowed to visit the greatest potential source of manpower for a Western European army—a country that has long been dedicated to fighting communism—Spain. I shall not argue that Spain has or has not the kind of government of which we should approve. I am not going to argue that we should or should not love the 48,000,000 people of Western Germany. But it takes no argument, it follows as the night follows the day, that there is no way to defend the industrial heart of Europe unless we use those two great wells of tough anti-Communist manpower, Western Germany and Spain. . . .

We have embraced Yugoslavia. Dean Acheson has served notice upon the Kremlin that an attack upon Communist Yugoslavia will mean war with us. At whose bidding and by whose authority did Acheson speak— Acheson so meek in the Far East, so willing to surrender Formosa, to make peace on the thirty-eighth parallel and admit Communist China into the United Nations? Whose bidding was he following? Was it the British Socialist Government which, pursuing what Winston Churchill has called a sectarian and isolationist policy, has sought to strengthen all left-wing governments this side of the Iron Curtain and weaken all others? Was it the British Labor Party's desire for a socialized Europe that prompted Acheson to give his guaranty to Tito?

The policy of the United States with reference to the global pressures of Russia was ambiguous enough even before Marshall reentered the picture in September 1950. With Marshall again at Acheson's side, their captive President between them, there has been little doubt that we were treading the old path of appeasement of Russia.

Marshall's friends, the liberals of Yenan, shouldered their way into the war in Korea in December 1950. In January this Government agreed to the most abject poltroonery, the cease-fire offer to Peking which, had it been accepted, would have resulted in our departure from Korea, the seating of the Chinese Reds in the United Nations, and placing the disposition of Formosa at the hazard of a commission weighted three to one against us. What saved us then I do not know.

Our escape was, however, only temporary.

After Marshall resumed his place as mayor of the palace in September 1950, with Acheson as captain of the palace guard and that weak, fitful, bad-tempered and usable Merovingian in their custody, the outlines of the defeat they meditated grew even plainer. The weakness of the United States in relation to the growing power of Soviet imperialism became clearer. And our weakness has become plain to the simplest citizen, the farthest removed from the seat of Government in Washington, and would have been evident even without the shameless doubts of the President that we could win a war with Russia and the self-satisfied revelations of our poor estate as a world power by Marshall and his palace men before the Russell Committee.

The feeling of America's weakness is in the very air we breathe in Washington. It derives not only from the moral debility of the highest echelons of the administration, from the flabbiness and lack of resolve upon the part of the palace guard and their minions. It comes from the objective facts of the situation.

During the summer of 1945 America stood at what Churchill described as the "highest pinnacle of her power and fame." The President and the man who was to be his Secretary of Defense commanded the greatest military instrumentality on land, sea and in the air that the world had ever seen. Our forces had fought victoriously on every continent except the American—in Africa, in Europe, in Asia, and above, on and over the seven seas. The Soviet empire, which would have fallen before the Nazis but for our assistance, was nursing its wounds, but glowering, self-confident and on the march from its own weakness. Britain had declined into the incompetent, self-righteous and doctrinaire hands of its Labor Party. Britain was economically prostrated, its empire was dwindling and was to dwindle further.

Only the United States among the great powers found its economic strength undiminished, its Territories uninvaded and unswept by war, its full powers still unflexed. Everywhere America had friends, everywhere its power suggested friendship to others. In terms of the division of the world into spheres of interest, the United States, at the head of the coalition of the West, exercised friendly influence over nearly all the masses of the earth. The Soviet Union's own people and the few millions in the bordering satellites upon which it was already laying its hands constituted a small minority of the earth's peoples.

What do we find in the winter of 1951? The writs of Moscow run to lands which, with its own, number upward of 900 millions of people—a good forty per cent of all men living. The fear of Russia or the subservience that power inspires inclines many hundreds of other millions, as in India, toward Moscow. The fear of Russia, plus other reasons, the chief of which is the supine and treacherous folly of our own policies, places other hundreds of millions in a twilight zone between the great poles of Moscow and Washington.

The United States stands today virtually alone as it faces its greatest trials. Where have we loyal allies? In Britain? I would not stake a shilling on the reliability of a Government which, while enjoying billions in American munificence, rushed to the recognition of the Chinese Red regime, traded exorbitantly with the enemy through Hong Kong and has sought to frustrate American interest in the Far East at every turn. Let us not blame our long-time friends, the British people. They have their Attlee and Morrison directing their foreign policy. We have our Marshall. We have our Acheson. Or perhaps I should say their Acheson.

What of Western Europe generally? Have we a constant friend in that quarter? The Marshall Plan has mystified and alienated while it enriched them; the Marshall strategy, which threatens to turn Western Europe into another devastated Korea, has rightfully terrified them and encouraged among them a neutralism which sees the coming world struggle as one between two reeling giants, Russia and the United States, in which they seek to avoid a part.

In Europe we have snubbed our friends, the heroic Greeks and Turks and the thoroughly indoctrinated anti-Communists of Spain; and because of our servility toward Russia in Eastern Europe we have discouraged the gallant souls behind the Iron Curtain who might have waited upon our deliverance of them, as the peoples oppressed by the Nazis did, only to find themselves betrayed to an equal tyranny by our appeasement. What do we find in Asia? We reject the friendship of the Chinese of Formosa and the millions on the mainland struggling to be free of the monstrous usurpation that overwhelms them. The new Japan may be our friend but the governments of India, of Pakistan, of Burma, of Indonesia—all of which rose from and owe their existence to our defeat of the Japanese empire—belong to the league of those who want to deprive us of our strategical interests in the western Pacific.

The will to resist Russia here at home is vitiated. Gone is the zeal with which we marched forth in 1941 to crush the dictatorships. The leftist-liberals who preached a holy war against Hitler and Tojo are today seeking accommodation with the senior totalitarianism of Moscow. Is this because we are today arrayed against, to recall the phrase of General Bradley, "the wrong enemy" in the "wrong war"? We were on Russia's side in the last war—our strategy after the first Quebec conference might as well have been dictated in the Kremlin and teletyped to the Pentagon—and is that why the Marshall who prosecuted World War II with bloodthirsty zeal, eager to storm fortified shores, sat this one out?

The administration preached a gospel of fear and Acheson and Marshall expounded a foreign policy in the Far East of craven appeasement. The President threatens the American people with Russian-made atomic bombs. What is the purpose of such actions and utterances? Is it to condition us to defeat in the Far East, to soften us up so that we shall accept a peace upon the Soviet empire's terms in Korea; a peace which would put the enemy one step nearer to Alaska? And how did Russia acquire the technical secrets, the blueprints, the know-how to make the bombs with which the administration seeks to terrify us? I have yet to hear a single administration spokesman raise his voice against the policy of suppression, deceit, and false witness with which this administration has protected the Soviet agents who have abstracted those secrets from us.

The people, I am convinced, recognize the weakness with which the administration has replaced what was so recently our great strength. They are troubled by it. And they do not believe that the decline in our strength from 1945 to 1951 just happened. They are coming to believe that it was brought about, step by step, by will and intention. They are beginning to believe that the surrender of China to Russia, the administration's indecently hasty desire to turn Formosa over to the enemy and arrive at a cease-fire in Korea instead of following the manly, American course prescribed by MacArthur, point to something more than ineptitude and folly. They witness the conviction of Hiss, which would not have happened had he not brought a private suit for damages against Whittaker Chambers; they follow the revelations in the Remington case, the Marzani case, and the others which have disclosed at the heart of Government active Soviet agents influencing policy and pilfering secrets; they note the policy of retreat before Soviet assertion from Yalta to this day, and they say: this is not because these men are incompetents, there is a deeper reason.

How can we account for our present situation unless we believe that men high in this Government are concerting to deliver us to disaster? This must be the product of a great conspiracy, a conspiracy on a scale so immense as to dwarf any previous such venture in the history of man.

Who constitutes the highest circles of this conspiracy? About that we cannot be sure. We are convinced that Dean Acheson, who steadfastly serves the interests of nations other than his own, who supported Alger Hiss in his hour of retribution, who contributed to his defense fund, must be high on the roster. The President? He is their captive. I have wondered, as have you, why he did not dispense with so great a liability as Acheson to his own and his party's interests. It is now clear to me. In the relationship of master and man, did you ever hear of man firing master? President Truman is a satisfactory front. He is only dimly aware of what is going on.

[There follows a long catalogue of Marshall's actions from 1942 to 1951, designed to show that he too was part of the conspiracy.]

If Marshall were merely stupid, the laws of probability would have dictated that at least some of his decisions would have served this country's interest. Even if Marshall had been innocent of guilty intention, how could he have been trusted to guide the defense of this country further? We have declined so precipitously in relation to the Soviet Union in the last six years, how much swifter may be our fall into disaster with Marshall's policies continuing to guide us? Where will all this stop? This is not a rhetorical question; ours is not a rhetorical danger. Where next will Marshall's policies, continued by Acheson, carry us?

What is the objective of the conspiracy? I think it is clear from what has occurred and is now occurring: to diminish the United States in world affairs, to weaken us militarily, to confuse our spirit with talk of surrender in the Far East and to impair our will to resist evil. To what end? To the end that we shall be contained and frustrated and finally fall victim to Soviet intrigue from within and Russian military might from without. Is that far-fetched? There have been many examples in history of rich and powerful states which have been corrupted from within, enfeebled and deceived until they were unable to resist aggression.

In the Witness Chair (1953)
JAMES A. WECHSLER

In mid-1953 James A. Wechsler, then managing editor of the
New York Post, *appeared before the McCarthy committee, ostensibly as part of the committee's inquiry into the operation of government overseas libraries. The* Post *was one of the most liberal newspapers in the country and under Wechsler's editorship had consistently opposed McCarthy. And Wechsler seemed fair game, because during his undergraduate days in the thirties he had been a member of the Young Communist League (YCL), an auxiliary of the Communist Party. Wechsler had resigned from the YCL in 1937 at the age of twenty-two, but*

McCarthy, in his questioning, expressed his doubts about the sincerity of that resignation. In the following selection Wechsler carefully analyzes his ordeal in the witness chair.

THE HEARING had been scheduled to begin at 3 o'clock, but it did not actually get under way until seventy minutes later. I spent the interval pacing the corridor of the Senate Office Building with Shannon and wondering whether the delay was a stratagem designed to try the nerves of the witness. That suspicion proved unfounded: the delay was a result of Wayne Morse's refusal to permit unanimous consent for a committee hearing while the Senate was in session.

This was an executive session, and the press and public were barred. When I walked into the spacious hearing room McCarthy was seated at the head of the table. At his side was Roy Cohn looking like a precocious college sophomore visiting Washington during spring recess. Nearby was [Hearst reporter Howard] Rushmore, slouched uncomfortably in a chair that, like most chairs, was too small to hold him. My seat was at the opposite end of the table, facing McCarthy. On my left, a few feet back, as if keeping at a respectful distance from McCarthy, were G. David Schine and Don Surine, neither of whom uttered a word throughout the proceedings. On my right was the only conceivably friendly face in the room—Senator Henry Jackson, a former Representative just elected to the Senate from the State of Washington.

When I entered McCarthy stood up stiffly and motioned me to the witness chair. Disarmingly, he asked me how I pronounced my last name. I was tempted to respond that he had pronounced it correctly on television but I resolved to fight such temptation. I answered the question.

Then McCarthy began in his low, unprovocative voice: "Mr. Wechsler, we are sorry we kept you waiting but there originally was an objection to this committee sitting this afternoon by Senator Morse, and we had to wait for permission to sit."

I replied that I understood.

"I may say," he continued, speaking quite swiftly and softly so that I almost had difficulty hearing him, "the reason for your being called today is that you are one of the many authors of books whose books have been used in the Information Program in various libraries, and we would like to check into a number of matters. Mr. Cohn will do the questioning."

Cohn took over briefly for a review of the names and dates of my published works. He elicited the fact that two of the books—*Revolt on the Campus* and *War Our Heritage*—were written when I was a member of the YCL. Then he jumped quickly to nonliterary fields and, during most of the remainder of the two hearings, little attention was devoted to the ostensible subject of the hearings—the books I had written. First he established that I had used the name "Arthur Lawson" on my YCL membership card.

"Let me add," I said, "that it was a name I was given when I joined and that I never used it again."

Cohn dropped the subject. Now he wanted to know how long I had been a member of the YCL. I gave him the answer and added that the whole chronology had already been published in the *Congressional Record* in the statement that Senator Lehman had inserted at my request.

The committee's researchers were apparently unaware of the existence of the document and wanted to know the date.

McCarthy seemed only mildly interested in Cohn's questioning; he was getting ready to take over himself. After another moment, he jumped in.

"May I interrupt, Mr. Cohn?" McCarthy asked and, without waiting for an answer, he interrupted at length, while Cohn maintained a sulky silence, like a star pupil whom teacher has pushed aside.

"Mr. Wechsler, do you have any other people who are members of the Young Communist League, who were or are members of the Young Communist League, working for you on your newspaper?"

The fight was beginning rather sooner than I had expected, and on ground I had hardly expected him to invade so casually.

This was the first of many questions that I answered fully despite my belief that they were far beyond the scope of the committee's authorized inquiry. I had resolved much earlier that silence was suicidal in dealing with McCarthy. I know some thoughtful people differ with me, and that there are some who believe I should have refused to answer any questions dealing with the policies and personnel of the newspaper I edit. But I was persuaded then, and I have not changed my opinion, that McCarthy was hoping I would refuse to testify so that he could use my silence to charge that I had something to hide. I was not trying to "convince" McCarthy of anything; I was trying to write a record that could be read intelligibly by bemused Americans who might still believe that McCarthy was interested in truth. To put it simply, I did not believe that my answers would tend to incriminate or degrade me but I was quite certain that silence would.

"I will say that I am going to answer that question because I believe it is a citizen's responsibility to testify before a Senate committee whether he likes the committee or not," I said.

"I know you do not like this committee," McCarthy interjected tonelessly, as if to assure me at once that he was impervious to personal offense and as if he had forgotten that he had repeatedly refused to testify before a Senate committee because he considered it hostile to him.

"I want to say that I think you are now exploring a subject which the American Society of Newspaper Editors might want to consider at some length," I continued.

"I answer the question solely because I recognize your capacity for misinterpretation of a failure to answer. I answer it with the protest signified.

To my knowledge there are no communists on the staff of the New York *Post* at this time."

What about former communists, McCarthy wanted to know. I identified them. There were four, and in each case they were men whose past affiliations were as well known as their present anti-communism.

Thus, in less than five minutes, an investigation allegedly directed at my work as an author of books in use by United States Information Service libraries had become an examination of the staff of the *Post*. There had been no indication as to what books of mine were found overseas, or any discussion of their content.

Now McCarthy got to his real point:

"You see your books, some of them, were paid for by taxpayers' money. They are being used, allegedly, to fight communism. Your record, as far as I can see it, has not been to fight communism. You have fought every man who has ever tried to fight communism, as far as I know. Your paper, in my opinion, is next to and almost paralleling the *Daily Worker*. We are curious to know, therefore, why your books were purchased. We want to know how many communists, if any, you still have working for you."

This was quite a speech; it was a summary of everything that he had to say in that hearing and the one that followed. Listening to it I had to resist the competing emotions of anger and hopelessness. But I had brought with me a document that I naively considered a devastating rebuttal. Since McCarthy had delivered what almost sounded like his summation before the hearing had barely begun, I decided to use it at once.

So I asked permission to insert in the record of the hearing the statement issued on December 28, 1952, by the National Committee of the Communist Party reviewing the previous election and especially the failure of the Progressive Party ticket to roll up a meaningful vote: it had in fact obtained only a small fraction of the disappointing Wallace vote of 1948. In the course of this analysis the communist chieftains declared:

> Support of the pro-war measures of the Truman administration; acceptance and propagation of the "Big Lie" of the external and internal "communist menace" disarmed the workers, blocked the path to independent political action by labor and its allies and paved the way for a Republican victory.
>
> The major responsibility for this policy and its consequences rests squarely with the reformist and Social Democratic trade-union officialdom. This was the content of the policies of the Reuthers, Dubinskys, Wechslers et al who paralyzed independent political action by projecting the myth that Stevenson was an obstacle to the advance of reaction. They pursued these policies despite the fact that the Democratic Party administration, operating with bipartisan support, originated and unfolded the current war program in behalf of Wall Street.

This communist jargon was simply a way of affirming what I had long believed—that the most effective opponents of communism in America have been the liberals and labor leaders associated with the non-communist Left. Offering the document as an exhibit, I said: "I am rather fond of this tribute, and it may perhaps have some bearing on your comment that I have not been active in fighting communism."

In a cold, casual voice McCarthy responded quickly:

"Did you have anything to do with the passage of that resolution? Did you take any part in promoting the passage of that resolution?"

I thought I had expected anything, but my imagination had been inadequate. His words registered slowly. I must have looked baffled as well as astonished, almost incapable of trusting my own senses.

"Is that a serious question?" I asked.

McCarthy turned briskly to the stenographer.

"Will you read the question to the witness?"

His voice was harder and tougher. In this strange proceeding he alternately played the role of prosecutor and judge, and now he was definitely the prosecutor. The stenographer read the question.

I knew I was making an obvious effort to keep my voice down as I answered, and I am sure my hands trembled a little:

"Sir, I have not been in any way affiliated with the communist movement since late 1937, as I believe your investigation will show. That resolution was adopted by the Communist Party as a tribute to the militant and vigorous anti-communism of the New York *Post* which has, in my judgment, been more effective in leading people away from communism, Senator, than those who prefer to identify liberalism with communism."

He let me finish and then, in the same flat tone, he said:

"Now will you answer the question?"

"The answer is no, Senator," I replied.

"The answer is no. Do you know whether anyone on your staff took part in promoting the passage of that resolution?"

"Senator, to the best of my knowledge, no one on my staff is a member of the Central Committee of the Communist Party or identified with it in any way."

"Now will you answer the question? Will you read the question to the witness?"

"I have answered it as best I can."

"You have said that you did not think anyone on your staff was a part of the committee. That was not the question. Read the question to the witness."

The stenographer read it. The faint smile which McCarthy had exhibited earlier was gone now. Once again, in a voice that must have sounded quite spiritless, I answered the question.

"I do not know that anyone on my staff took any part in promoting the passage of that resolution," I said. He had astounded me, and he knew it.

Thus, within ten minutes after the hearing had begun, I found myself in the preposterous position of denying under oath that I had inspired the long series of communist attacks against me, climaxed by the denunciation of the Central Committee.

With that single stroke of what Philip Graham, publisher of the Washington *Post,* later described as "brute brilliance," McCarthy thus virtually ruled out the whole structure of evidence which I had wide-eyedly assumed would resolve the issue once and for all. Here indeed was a daring new concept in which the existence of evidence of innocence becomes the damning proof of guilt. This is the way it must feel to be committed to a madhouse through some medical mistake; everything is turned upside down. What had heretofore constituted elementary reasonableness is viewed by everyone else as a quaint eccentricity; the most absurd remark becomes the commonplace.

McCarthy reverted to the same thesis several times. Each time he did so with total blandness, as though only the dullest or most subversive mind could detect anything extraordinary in his approach.

He had at last spelled out the formula under which our whole society could be transformed into a universe of suspicion. What a man had said or done could no longer be accepted as bearing the slightest relationship to what he was or what he believed. More likely, it was a disguise to conceal his hidden allegiances to exactly the reverse of what he claimed to stand for. At the second hearing he was to develop this theme even more spectacularly. . . .

Had I ever talked to the FBI [McCarthy asked]? The answer was yes; whenever an FBI agent came to see me about someone I had known applying for a Government post, I gave as much information as I had; I always emphasized that I had no first-hand knowledge extending beyond 1937 and cautioned that others might have changed their views as decisively as I had.

I know there are some former communists who have conscientiously declined to give any information about others than themselves. I confronted that problem a long time ago and the answer I reached was that there was no justification for a vow of silence. The communist movement was not an amiable secret society to which one owed a personal loyalty after abandoning membership in it. There is abundant evidence that it is a tough, disciplined world-wide movement dedicated to the destruction of free society. I am willing to defend its right to conduct public propaganda functions because I believe there is ample margin of safety in our system and because I am convinced that communist ideas can best be met and overcome in open debate. But to defend that principle of open expression is not to argue that there is an obligation to protect communists seeking strategic positions in Government. Liberals who maintain this opinion would have been the first, I think, to rebuke a professed ex-Nazi who declined to identify his former associates in Government at a time when Nazism was sweeping over Europe.

McCarthy seemed impatient as I responded:

"Where I have been asked about people I knew at that time [of my communist membership], I answered freely and fully. If I knew today that someone who had been in the Young Communist League with me was in a strategic Government post, I would certainly communicate that information. There has never been any question in my mind as to a citizen's responsibility on that point, and I do not believe the FBI would suggest that I have been unco-operative in the discussion of such cases."

But had I ever given the FBI a full list of everyone I had known?

The answer was that no such dragnet question, I am glad to say, had ever been asked me by the FBI. In 1948 I had given Louis Nichols, now the Deputy Chief of the FBI, a detailed statement of my own past connections; I had done so because of an incident involving Nancy which revealed that the FBI file on us was seriously incomplete. She had been serving as counsel for the Truman Committee on Civil Rights when a question was abruptly raised about her past membership in the YCL—a point she had fully discussed with an FBI agent after she went to work for the Government. When I heard that had been raised again, I went to see Nichols and we talked it out and the matter was cleared up.

"Do you know any of those Young Communists who are in any Government position today?" McCarthy asked.

"No, I do not."

"Do you know Bernard De Voto?"

"I trust this is not a sequitur," I replied.

"Pardon?"

"I trust this is not a sequitur."

"It is a question."

"I believe I may have met Bernard De Voto. I can't recall the occasion on which I did. I regret to say that he is not a close personal friend of mine."

"You regret to say that?"

"Yes, sir."

"You did not collaborate with him in writing the article in which he advocated that Americans not talk to the FBI?"

"No, sir, I thought that was a very bad article."

"You do not agree with that?"

"I don't agree with that."

This exchange compressed into half a minute a whole range of McCarthy devices. First there was the sudden introduction of De Voto's name into a discussion dealing with the identity of former communists; he happens to be a distinguished American scholar who never roamed into communist territory. Then there was the intimation that De Voto's article on the FBI was proof he was a traitor and that I not only sanctioned the article but had helped him write it (presumably in that spare time when I was not writing communist denunciations of myself). It was almost a case of guilt by non-association.

Then McCarthy announced:

"We are going to ask you, Mr. Wechsler, to prepare a list and submit it to the committee and consider it to be submitted under oath, of all the Young Communist Leaguers that you knew as such, or the communists."

This was the final gambit. I had characterized myself as a "responsible but not friendly witness." From the start, whether rightly or wrongly, I had believed that what McCarthy was seeking was the chance to walk out of the hearing room and tell the press that I had "balked." Once he was able to do that, I would be engaged in the hopeless pursuit of headlines describing me as just another reluctant witness. And from that point on McCarthy would proceed to discredit the *Post* because I had refused to testify freely before a Senate committee.

There may be some splendor in such a role but on the whole it escapes me. By and large liberals have believed in giving wide scope to congressional committees. Moreover, there is in the American tradition a very real belief that the man who has nothing to conceal will speak up when spoken to; muteness has not often been equated with valor. Back in 1947, in an article in the *Guild Reporter,* I had written:

> It would be nice if the world were prettier, but it isn't; espionage and sabotage are facts of modern life. I have no grief for anybody who refuses to testify before a congressional committee; no matter how foolish or fierce the committee, an American ought to be prepared to state his case in any public place at any time.

Believing this, I had gone along answering everything and now I faced what McCarthy undoubtedly regarded as the great question. I am sure that he knew enough about me to guess the reluctance with which I would give such a list to a man like him. I am also confident that he would have felt he had finally cornered me if I now refused to give it to him. Then, and for many days after, it was a rather strange duel. For McCarthy knew I would have been happier not to give him any list and I knew he would have been delighted if I had taken that stand.

All this, let me add, was clearer to me after the hearing than at that moment. The demand for the list was an almost parenthetical remark; my answer was an oblique comment about the obvious absurdity of asking a man to remember everyone whom he had known in a different context nearly sixteen years before.

"I don't know that you would be able to do very well with a similar list of any organization that you were connected with sixteen years ago," I said.

"Well, we are asking for the list. You say you have severed your connection. I am not going to, at this time, try to—"

"Senator, you are raising that point," I interrupted.

He went on as if I were inaudible.

"—pass on whether that is true or not. I know that you never testified in a case against an ex-communist. I know that none of the men you have named here as anti-communists ever testified in a case against communists. I know that they and you have been consistently and viciously attacking anyone who does testify against communists, anyone that exposes communists—"

"Senator, that is not true."

"Let me finish. You may have all the time in the world to talk. So you cannot blame the average person who questions whether you ever did break with the party."

There it was again, and not for the last time; and each time he said it I had a feeling of rage tinged with futility. Senator Jackson was listening attentively, with manifest concern, and at various points along the way he helped me clarify the record; but how could one break through the ring of fantasy that McCarthy was constructing? If each exhibit of my anti-communism were merely additional evidence that I had led a truly gigantic political double life, what remained to be said that had any meaning? . . .

That morning, before I left home, Nancy had admonished me to keep my temper, a plea I have not always heeded. Now, I must confess, I was rather impressed with my demeanor. I asked to introduce a series of additional exhibits, including the chapter from my biography of John L. Lewis dealing with his relations with the communists, my statement of resignation when I left *PM* and the attacks on me published by the *Daily Worker* while I was on *PM*.

The chairman admitted the exhibits and then, in a tone of simulated objectivity, as though talking about someone a thousand miles away, he said:

"Mr. Wechsler, let me ask you this. If you or I were a member of the Communist Party and we wanted to advance the communist cause, perhaps the most effective way of doing that would be to claim that we deserted the party and, if we got in control of the paper, use that paper to attack and smear anybody who actually was fighting communism. Now, without saying whether you have done it, you would agree that would be a good tactic, would you not?"

I replied that I doubted very much that this was one of the stratagems used by the communists. I questioned, for example, whether the presence of Rushmore as a staff member of his committee conclusively proved that the communists had successfully infiltrated the McCarthy operation.

At this point Senator Jackson expressed surprise that there was an ex-communist on the staff, and McCarthy hastened to explain that Rushmore was a very different breed of former communist because he had repeatedly volunteered to testify before congressional committees. Howard, in short, had won his varsity M.

"Rushmore does not spend his time, you see, trying to smear and tear down the people who are really fighting communism," McCarthy said, while Howard tried not to beam.

The chairman let me comment on the point: "Senator, let's face it. You

·are saying that an ex-communist who is for McCarthy is a good one and an ex-communist who is against McCarthy is a suspect. I will stand on that distinction."

That was incorrect, said McCarthy. The true test of an ex-communist was how many of his former associates he helped to expose. . . .

Throughout the interrogation the grand inquisitor was by turns truculent, contemptuous and bland. Yet I rarely had any feeling of authentic personal animosity. He acted like the gangster in a B-movie who faces the unpleasant necessity of rubbing out someone who has gotten in his way: he would really like the victim to feel that there is nothing personal about it and that he rather regrets the exorbitant demands of duty. At no time did I have the feeling that I was confronted by a fanatic. McCarthy is a poker player, not a zealot, a cold-blooded operator in a big game. There were a few off-the-record asides when he almost seemed to be saying: "Look, don't get excited, old man, we've all got our rackets." This detachment may be his greatest strength; at moments it endows him with a certain cold charm.

When I challenged him sharply, he sometimes assumed the pose of a stern schoolmaster, but even then there seemed to be an element of play-acting. He seemed to enjoy my references to him, as though he at last found my words interesting because they concerned the only truly interesting subject on earth. I am sure some lunatics on the rightist fringe genuinely consider me subversive; at no time did I believe that McCarthy was overcome by that theory. I think he is one of the least passionate demagogues I have ever encountered. I am certain that he would have been happy to shake my hand and forget the whole thing if I had merely indicated that I had misjudged him and was prepared henceforth to write kinder things about him.

What I could not quite determine was whether Roy Cohn had achieved an equivalent cynicism at the age of twenty-six or whether he really believed he was saving the republic. He seemed rather out of things anyway.

It looked as though we were nearing the end.

"As I recall, and I may misquote this, because I do not read your sheet," McCarthy said, "I understand that you have been disturbed by the unfair treatment witnesses received before this committee. Do you feel you were unfairly treated?"

He asked the question almost clinically, like a doctor asking a patient whether the needle he had just administered was really painful.

"Senator, I question the basic nature of this proceeding, of course I do," I replied.

"You feel you were unfairly treated?"

"I regard this proceeding as the first in a long line of attempts to intimidate editors who do not equate McCarthyism with patriotism."

Again he betrayed no resentment over the use of the word "McCarthyism"; I think he is rather proud to be an ism as well as a Senator.

"You have not been intimidated, have you?" he persisted.

"Senator, I am a pretty tough guy," I responded with a certain vanity.

"I say you have not been intimidated, have you?"

"I say this is the first of a long line of attempts to do so," I answered.

"Answer my question. Have you been intimidated?"

"You are not going to win this argument, Senator. We will go back and forth all afternoon."

It was getting to be a comic colloquy, but he wasn't smiling. He seemed genuinely absorbed in the line of questioning. I think one of his true delights is the constant rediscovery of his own strength. For public purposes he may have wanted to wrest a statement that I had not been terrorized, yet I think he would have been equally happy to hear me say that I had been.

"Have you been intimidated?" he repeated in the same phlegmatically insistent voice.

"Sir, I have been taken away from my work. I have not even had a chance to write a word about Senator McCarthy today."

He smiled then; the picture of anyone writing about him could not be unattractive. He hammered back:

"You have not been intimidated at all, have you? You mean you have been inconvenienced. The question is: 'Have you been intimidated?' "

He was provoking me into a speech.

"I am fully aware this is a proceeding designed to smear the New York *Post,*" I said. "I recognize that, Senator. We are both grown up. But this is a free country and I am going to keep fighting."

"So will the *Daily Worker* and every other communist-line paper," he responded. "But have you been intimidated?"

"I am afraid that is a question we would have to discuss with doctors and get all sorts of expert testimony."

"In other words, you cannot answer that question?"

It was like being a small child and having the town bully ask you whether you have had enough. No answer you can give him is satisfactory to yourself; for if you say that you haven't been frightened, you may re-enforce his sense of virtue, and if you say that you have been he can walk away triumphant. So I clung to the evasive answer.

"I say there is no doubt that this is an attempt to intimidate me. I trust that I have the moral courage to stand up under it. I trust that other editors will."

He would not let go.

"Do you feel that you may have been intimidated? Is there a doubt in your mind as to whether you have been intimidated?"

"We will not know, Senator, until we see whether as editor of the *Post* I keep on fighting just as hard for the things I believe as I have been. I think I will."

"Do you think you have been intimidated?" he asked monotonously.

"I have great confidence in myself, so at the moment, Senator, I feel I have not been intimidated."

"Do you feel you have been abused?"

"Why of course I have been abused. The suggestion that my break with communism was not authentic is the greatest affront you could recite anywhere. I have fought this battle a long time, longer than you have, Senator, and I have taken plenty of beatings from the communists in the course of that fight. So I feel very strongly about this."

Now he spoke in the accents of a judge who, having listened to the devastating words of the prosecutor, delivers his verdict:

"I may say, so that there is no doubt in your mind, so that you need not say that Senator McCarthy intimated or insinuated that you have not broken: I have been following your record, not as closely perhaps as I would if you were in Government, but I have been following you somewhat. I am convinced that you have done exactly what you would do if you were a member of the Communist Party, if you wanted to have a phony break and then use that phony break to the advantage of the Communist Party. I feel that you have not broken with Communist ideals. I feel that you are serving them very, very actively. Whether you are doing it knowingly or not, that is in your own mind. I have no knowledge as to whether you have a card in the party."

I had vowed not to explode; I said as derisively as I could:

"I appreciate that concession."

He ignored the sarcasm; he was very much the judge now, handing down the decision in favor of the prosecutor (who happened to be himself) and untroubled by any murmuring in the courtroom.

"I think you are doing tremendous damage to America," he continued; "when I find books by authors like yourself being purchased by the Information Program we are going to check into them. I say this so you need not say that McCarthy intimated or insinuated. McCarthy did not intimate, he said that he thinks Wechsler is still very, very valuable to the Communist Party."

He was shuffling the papers in front of him and getting ready to depart. My own peroration was inadequate.

"Senator, I should like to say before you leave that under the standards you have established here this afternoon, the only way that I could in your view prove my devotion to America and the validity of my break with communism would be to come out in support of Senator McCarthy. This I do not plan to do."

He was on his feet, his face preoccupied. He was a man who had much more justice to mete out before the day was done and who regarded the present defendant as belonging to the past.

"That I am not asking you to do," he said. "If you ever did that, I would be worried about myself."

Then he walked out.

For the record I delivered a last statement:

"Just one further thing. The *Post* has been fighting Senator McCarthy for a long time. Our editorial page, I am happy to say, has never wavered on this point. It is not going to change now. . . . I answered freely here today because I do not believe that I have anything to hide or that the *Post* has anything to hide.

"I regard this inquiry as a clear invasion of what used to be considered the newspaper's right to act and function independently. I am hopeful that there will be voices raised by newspapers throughout the country in protest against this inquiry, but I repeat again that, rather than give Senator McCarthy the opportunity to distort my stand . . . I have answered all questions to the best of my knowledge and recollection."

There was a perfunctory aftermath. Senator Jackson asked me a few additional questions that enabled me to introduce the remaining exhibits I had brought with me. Roy Cohn got around to asking me about Reed Harris, and I gave the unsatisfactory answer he had anticipated; anything I had to say about Harris was favorable, and Cohn didn't labor the inquiry.

With McCarthy gone the spirit had left the hearing. To debate with Roy Cohn appeared to be the climactic foolishness of the fantastic afternoon. Senator Jackson did not need additional documentation. His problem was how to deal with Joe McCarthy.

It was all over at 5:40, ninety minutes after we had begun.

When we got outside the reporters were there. I told them as accurately as I could the substance of what had occurred and said I would ask that a transcript of the hearing be made public. I also said I would ask the American Society of Newspaper Editors to study the document, since it seemed clear that I had been questioned, not as the author of some undesignated book found in some library overseas, but as the editor of a newspaper that had been fighting Joe McCarthy.

I was dead tired; no ordeal is more exacting than the systematic suppression of one's temper. And there was also an element of despair. Often the communists had said democratic debate is a sham because reaction owns all the weapons. I was too old to believe that nonsense. But for a moment I had to fight the awful fear that this was the century of the demagogues, and that only eighteenth-century romantics could believe that truth always triumphs in the end.

Views of McCarthyism (1967)
MICHAEL PAUL ROGIN

*The history of how scholars and observers have understood McCarthy
is almost as interesting as the events of McCarthy's career. Why did he
succeed? Why did so many people support him, and why were so
many afraid of him? The answers to these questions also reveal
contemporary America's view of itself, especially of its political life.
Michael Paul Rogin, a political scientist, discusses the way American
thinkers have attempted to understand McCarthyism.*

WHEN MC CARTHY first became prominent, most liberals interpreted the
danger he posed in fairly straightforward terms. To them McCarthy was
simply the most successful of a number of conservative Republicans capitalizing on the Communist threat to attack the New Deal at home and the
Fair Deal abroad. "McCarthyism" was a synonym for smear attacks on
liberals, its roots were in traditional right-wing politics, and its principal
targets were innocent individuals and liberal political goals. Liberals hardly
minimized McCarthy's political importance, although they had little difficulty explaining either his roots or the danger he posed.

But to many writers such traditional analysis failed to account for
McCarthy's strength. In their eyes, McCarthy was getting support not
from the established groups with which traditional conservatism had been
associated but rather from the dispossessed and discontented. One had to
wonder about any inevitable association between popular discontent and
support for progressive movements of economic reform. Moreover,
McCarthy continually appealed to the mass of people for direct support
over the heads of their elected leaders. And the established eastern elite,
unsympathetic to the Wisconsin senator, was one of his important targets.
All this suggested that popular democracy constituted a real threat to the
making of responsible political decisions. McCarthy appeared not in the
guise of a conservative smearing innocent liberals but in the guise of a
democrat assaulting the political fabric.

If faith in democracy suffered from the McCarthy period, sympathy for
radicalism hardly fared better. Both the more orthodox liberal analysis of
McCarthyism and those with the newer view recognized that McCarthy
dominated America while traditional radical movements lay dormant. To
the old-fashioned liberals, McCarthyism symbolized the death of radical

protest in America. In the newer view, McCarthy was the bearer of the historical radical mission—challenging, like earlier radicals, the established institutions of American society. The McCarthy years thus ushered in a new fear of radicalism among growing numbers of intellectuals. One can date from the McCarthy period the rise of such terms as "radical Right" to go with radical Left. and left-wing "fundamentalism" to coincide with right-wing extremism.

In this new view, McCarthyism was a movement of the radical Left. For traditional liberals, the New Deal and contemporary liberalism had grown out of the protest of the pre-Roosevelt years. The newer view produced a very different history. Left-wing protest movements, democratic in their appeal to the popular masses, radical in the discontent they mobilized, had borne fruit in McCarthyism. To some, McCarthy was directly descended from an alliance between traditional conservatism and agrarian radicalism.

The term agrarian radicalism refers to the movements of rural protest that flourished between the end of the Civil War and the New Deal epoch —the Grangers, the Greenbacks, the Farmers' Alliances, the Populists, the progressives, and the Non-Partisan League. Not all these movements were exclusively rural. Progressivism in particular had an important urban wing, although it is well to remember that in state and national politics progressives most continually triumphed in rural areas.

Aside from being predominantly rural, pre-New Deal protest movements had important geographic sources of continuity. Outside the South, these movements flourished along the settled frontier. From the 1880's to the 1930's, left-wing protest politics were strongest in the West and the western Middle West. Populism outside the South received most of its support from the plains states and those bordering on them. The Non-Partisan League of 1916 to 1924 had been strongest there too. Pre- and post-World War I progressivism tended to be strong in the Middle West and weak in the East.

Agrarian radicalism thus flourished in the states of the trans-Mississippi West. Political leaders in these states were most vociferous in their support of McCarthy and supplied him with most of his votes against the senatorial censure resolution of 1954. In particular, senators from states that had supported the Populist presidential candidate in 1892 or La Follette for President in 1924 disproportionately voted against the McCarthy censure.

Certainly the geographic coincidence of support for McCarthyism and agrarian radicalism can be exaggerated. The South opposed both La Follette and McCarthy, but party loyalty was more crucial than ideological commitment. Since the Populist revolt, agrarian radicalism was not strong in the eastern Middle West; but this area produced strong Republican support for McCarthy. The trans-Mississippi West, however, supported both McCarthyism and agrarian radicalism. A look at the map thus provides concrete evidence linking McCarthy to agrarian radicalism. The interpretation of McCarthy as radical democrat appears persuasive. The new view of politics implied by that interpretation seems supported by the evidence.

The present study challenges the notion that McCarthy had agrarian radical roots. Examination of the empirical evidence finds no correlation between support for agrarian radicals and support for McCarthy; consideration of the reform tradition uncovers no unique reform appeals on which McCarthy capitalized. Investigation of the McCarthy movement discloses no agrarian radical flavor but rather a traditional conservative heritage. . . .

The pluralists [1] justify their ahistorical view of rural politics because they detect a moralistic thread running through its progressive and conservative phase. Populism, progressivism, and McCarthyism were all in the pluralist view mass moralistic protests against industrialization.

The first difficulty with this view arises when the "mass" character of the movements is examined. A close look at the "mass" nature of McCarthyism and agrarian radicalism suggests the gulf that separates these phenomena rather than the bonds that unite them. The difference between McCarthyism and agrarian radicalism at the grass roots is striking. McCarthy mobilized little specific organizational support outside the grass roots Republican Party organizations. He encountered little opposition from local elites. He gave little evidence of exerting a mass appeal that uprooted voters from their traditional loyalties. Agrarian radical movements, on the other hand, held hundreds of meetings, organized at the grass roots for innumerable electoral campaigns, and created new voting patterns that often influenced events after the movements themselves had disappeared. Although these mass movements had a salutary effect on American politics, they exhibited many of the effects of mass activity that the pluralists fear. McCarthyism exhibited few of these effects. It neither split apart existing coalitions nor created an organized, active mass following. If Populism was a mass movement in the sense of its grass roots appeal and McCarthyism was not, McCarthyism had "mass" characteristics, such as contempt for the rule of law and generalized hostility to cosmopolitan values, that were lacking in agrarian radicalism. But such anomic characteristics were found more among political leaders and local elites than among masses. Since McCarthyism cannot be explained by the "mass" preoccupations of the masses, one must examine the support for McCarthy among certain elite groups and the tolerance or fear of him among others. The pluralists' preoccupation with mass movements as threats to a stable, democratic group life prevents them from analyzing McCarthyism in this fashion.

When the relevant political issues are closely examined, the anti-indus-

---

[1] The author's term for liberal social scientists of the 1950's, 1960's, and 1970's who analyze American politics in terms of bargaining between interest groups, a tradition that still dominates much of American social science and political commentary. —Eds.

trial character of McCarthyism and agrarian radicalism—and therefore the alleged connection between them—also evaporates.

Like the agrarian protest movements, McCarthy drew sustenance from concrete political issues; but his issues were not the agrarian radical issues. Populism, La Follette progressivism, and the Non-Partisan League attacked industrial capitalists, not industrialization. They proposed concrete and practical economic reforms. McCarthy focused on the political not the economic order. While many McCarthy activists were in rebellion against modern industrial society, this society included—and was in their eyes dominated by—New Deal reforms of the type agrarian radicals had favored. This was a very different society from that of the "trusts" and the "robber barons" at the turn of the twentieth century, against which agrarian radicals directed their fire. Moreover, most of McCarthy's supporters on public opinion polls cared more about communism, Korea, and the cold war than they did about modern industrial society. McCarthyism could not have flourished in the absence of these foreign policy concerns.

If no direct links are sustained by the evidence, the pluralists may still retreat to the general argument that McCarthy utilized a peculiarly moralistic, agrarian radical, political style. They point to an alleged agrarian radical tendency to seek moral solutions to practical problems. As Hofstadter explains, "We are forever restlessly pitting ourselves against [the evils of life], demanding changes, improvements, remedies, but not often with sufficient sense of the limits that the human condition will in the end insistently impose upon us." The pluralists argue that as the agrarian radical world of moral certainty disappeared, this progressive optimism became frustrated. Former agrarian radicals sought scapegoats to explain their defeats. It was an easy step, for example, from the progressive belief that only special interests stood in the way of reforms to the McCarthy certainty that only treason could explain the failures of American foreign policy.

Consider, as evidence for this interpretation, the career of Tom Watson. Watson, the leading southern Populist of the 1890's, supported the political organization and economic demands of the southern Negro farmer. He made a reasoned analysis of the causes of rural misery and opposed economic panaceas. But out of frustration generated by the defeat of Populism, Watson became an anti-Negro, anti Catholic, anti-Semitic, southern demagogue. For the pluralists, Watson's career symbolizes the development of McCarthyism. . . .

The Populist tradition could produce antidemocratic and even neofascist figures, but given the nature of American society and the absence of strong elite backing for these figures, they had little success in national politics. Tom Watson, who combined anti-Semitism with sympathy for the Soviet Union, was clearly a product of Populism gone sour; McCarthy was not.

McCarthy and the agrarian radicals came from two contrasting political traditions. Both traditions stressed self-help, but the Populists did not attack bureaucracies indiscriminately. Agrarian radicals sought to meet the threat of private bureaucracies by increasing the role of the state. The agrarian radical tradition was anti-Wall Street, anti-vested interests, anti-industrial capitalist. This tradition has been dying out as the role of left-wing protest politics has passed to the cities. Its evolution has produced Tom Watsons and Burton Wheelers, but sophisticated, humanitarian liberals like Quentin Burdick and George McGovern have been equally prominent. Perhaps their independence from Johnson on the Vietnamese war owes something to the agrarian radical heritage. McCarthy's ideological conservative tradition was anti-intellectual, antistatist, antibureaucratic, and antiforeign. Locally prestigious and wealthy elites have dominated this politics, generally attracting widespread popular support as well. McCarthy, the son of a poor farmer. was marginally outside this conservative tradition. He effectively exploited this marginality, but without the support of the conservative tradition he would have made little impact.

Behind the pluralist misinterpretation of McCarthyism and fear of agrarian radicalism lies a legitimate suspicion of mass movements. But this fear, fed by the triumph of totalitarianism in Russia, Italy, and Germany, obscures the differences among mass movements. To find radical roots for McCarthy's support is to underestimate the middle-class diversity of the American populace. For the pluralists, McCarthyism and agrarian radicalism were united by their petit bourgeois character. But in America the *petit bourgeois* class is both enormous and diverse. Different political movements can call on support from different segments of that class; their support can be *petit bourgeois* without being significantly related. It is a mistake to identify mass movements with authoritarianism and pressure groups with democracy. Rather there are authoritarian and democratic mass movements, just as there are authoritarian and democratic pressure groups. The Populist mass movement operated within the established constitutional framework of the republic; it was not a threat to democracy.

The danger of McCarthyism, on the other hand, while real, was not the danger of a mass movement. McCarthy had powerful group and elite support. He did not mobilize the masses at the polls or break through existing group cleavages. McCarthy's power was sustained only in part by the vague discontents of frustrated groups. Communism and the Korean War played crucial roles. The real danger posed by McCarthy should not distort our understanding of agrarian radical movements in America, nor should the pluralist criticisms of mass movements blind us to the real nature of McCarthyism.

MARTIN LUTHER KING, JR.

&

the Civil Rights Movement

The black civil rights movement long antedates Martin Luther King, Jr., and it has survived his tragic death by assassination on April 4, 1968. Yet one phase of the movement—direct nonviolent protest—coincides with King's public career; and this is what many people remember as the civil rights movement. Under King the movement held far more drama than earlier legal efforts that led to the school desegregation decision of 1954, *Brown v. Board of Education of Topeka, Kansas*. Graced with more unity and a higher sense of moral authority, it inspired a support that has not been enjoyed by various succeeding attempts to gain black political power and economic advancement. Thus the epic days of civil rights marches and demonstrations have become covered with a haze of nostalgia.

Martin Luther King's early years were spent in Atlanta, Georgia, where he was born on January 15, 1929. The son of a Baptist minister and his schoolteacher wife, King had the middle-class background not uncommon for many blacks in a southern city. He graduated from Morehouse College in 1948 and three years later received a bachelor of divinity degree from Crozer Theological Seminary in Chester, Pennsylvania. He then entered the Graduate School of Theology at Boston University, and in 1953 married Coretta Scott, a music student from Antioch College studying at the New England Conservatory of Music. In 1954, still working on his doctorate (he would receive the degree in 1955), King returned to the South and became pastor of a church in Montgomery, Alabama, a post he held until 1960. During these years King embraced the goal of civil rights for blacks. And it was here, in Montgomery, that King startled the nation during the year-long bus boycott of 1955–1956.

Martin Luther King, Jr., was a man of words. A minister and, as he wrote to his fellow ministers, "the son, the grandson, and the great-grandson of preachers," he used an astonishing rhetoric including Old Testament prophecy and devices employed by generations of black preachers; to these he added a large store of allusions to theologians, philosophers, and moralists gained from his studies. Yet King was more than a man of words; he devised a way to turn words into acts. Just when the strategy of legal challenge to laws enforcing segregation reached its climax in the *Brown* case, he stumbled upon nonviolent protest and quickly developed it into a strategy and a morality to demolish the edifice of legal segregation.

To accomplish this task, in 1957 King organized a group later called the Southern Christian Leadership Conference. He moved back to Atlanta three years later primarily to direct the civil rights work of the SCLC, although he also held the position of co-pastor in his father's church there. The March on Washington in 1963 received its leadership and impetus from King; the following year he was awarded the Nobel Peace Prize. King, the other leaders of the movement, and their millions of followers accomplished their goal in a series of civil rights laws passed in 1964, 1965, 1966, and 1968, but in so doing they instantly discovered the sharp limits of their achievement.

Toward the end of his life, King faced the challenges of de facto segregation in Northern cities, the black power movement within his own community, and the Vietnam war. He bravely split the old civil rights coalition in 1967 when he became one of the first prominent opponents of the Vietnam war. He continued to believe that his tactics could be made to work, although he recognized the difficulties surrounding him at every turn. Most of all, King accepted the need to form some new coalition to advance beyond "issues of personal dignity . . . to programs that impinge upon the basic system of social and economic control." He reached out for an economic base of white and black poor, and his trip to Memphis in support of striking sanitation workers is an example of that strategy. King's assassination there left all the questions about his new dreams unanswered.

The Montgomery Bus Boycott (1958)
MARTIN LUTHER KING, JR.

King's public career began with the Montgomery, Alabama, boycott in
1955–1956, when blacks protested the rule that they had to sit in the
rear of public buses. This first campaign—as was true of many later ones
—was not initiated by King. That was done by Mrs. Rosa Parks, who
refused to surrender her seat to a white passenger when ordered to by
a bus driver. Nor did King conceive the idea of a boycott. E. D. Nixon, a
long-time local civil rights leader, did. But King, who had been a
Montgomery minister for less than two years, assumed leadership of
the newly formed Montgomery Improvement Association and held the
black community of the city to the bus boycott for over a year despite
considerable intimidation and harassment. Desegregation came, finally,
ordered by a federal court in a case prepared by the National
Association for the Advancement of Colored People.

ON DECEMBER 1, 1955, an attractive Negro seamstress, Mrs. Rosa Parks, boarded the Cleveland Avenue Bus in downtown Montgomery. She was returning home after her regular day's work in the Montgomery Fair—a leading department store. Tired from long hours on her feet, Mrs. Parks sat down in the first seat behind the section reserved for whites. Not long after she took her seat, the bus operator ordered her, along with three other Negro passengers, to move back in order to accommodate boarding white passengers. By this time every seat in the bus was taken. This meant that if Mrs. Parks followed the driver's command she would have to stand while a white male passenger, who had just boarded the bus, would sit. The other three Negro passengers immediately complied with the driver's request. But Mrs. Parks quietly refused. The result was her arrest.

There was to be much speculation about why Mrs. Parks did not obey the driver. Many people in the white community argued that she had been "planted" by the NAACP in order to lay the groundwork for a test case, and at first glance that explanation seemed plausible, since she was a former secretary of the local branch of the NAACP. So persistent and persuasive was this argument that it convinced many reporters from all over the country. Later on, when I was having press conferences three times a week—in order to accommodate the reporters and journalists who came to Montgomery from all over the world—the invariable first question was: "Did the NAACP start the bus boycott?"

But the accusation was totally unwarranted, as the testimony of both Mrs. Parks and the officials of the NAACP revealed. Actually, no one can understand the action of Mrs. Parks unless he realizes that eventually the cup of endurance runs over, and the human personality cries out, "I can take it no longer." Mrs. Parks's refusal to move back was her intrepid affirmation that she had had enough. It was an individual expression of a timeless longing for human dignity and freedom. She was not "planted" there by the NAACP, or any other organization; she was planted there by her personal sense of dignity and self-respect. She was anchored to that seat by the accumulated indignities of days gone by and the boundless aspirations of generations yet unborn. She was a victim of both the forces of history and the forces of destiny. She had been tracked down by the *Zeitgeist*—the spirit of the time. . . .

After a heavy day of work, I went home late Sunday afternoon [December 4] and sat down to read the morning paper. There was a long article on the proposed boycott. Implicit throughout the article, I noticed, was the idea that the Negroes were preparing to use the same approach to their problem as the White Citizens Councils used. This suggested parallel had serious implications. The White Citizens Councils, which had had their birth in Mississippi a few months after the Supreme Court's school decision, had come into being to preserve segregation. The Councils had multiplied rapidly throughout the South, purporting to achieve their ends by the legal maneuvers of "interposition" and "nullification." Unfortunately, however, the actions of some of these Councils extended far beyond the bounds of the law. Their methods were the methods of open and covert terror, brutal intimidation, and threats of starvation to Negro men, women, and children. They took open economic reprisals against whites who dared to protest their defiance of the law, and the aim of their boycotts was not merely to impress their victims but to destroy them if possible.

Disturbed by the fact that our pending action was being equated with the boycott methods of the White Citizens Councils, I was forced for the first time to think seriously on the nature of the boycott. Up to this time I had uncritically accepted this method as our best course of action. Now certain doubts began to bother me. Were we following an ethical course of action? Is the boycott method basically unchristian? Isn't it a negative approach to the solution of a problem? Is it true that we would be following the course of some of the White Citizens Councils? Even if lasting practical results came from such a boycott, would immoral means justify moral ends? Each of these questions demanded honest answers.

I had to recognize that the boycott method could be used to unethical and unchristian ends. I had to concede, further, that this was the method used so often by the White Citizens Councils to deprive many Negroes, as well as white persons of good will, of the basic necessities of life. But certainly, I said to myself, our pending actions could not be interpreted in this light. Our purposes were altogether different. We would use this method to give birth to justice and freedom, and also to urge men to comply with the law of the land; the White Citizens Councils used it to perpetuate the reign of injustice and human servitude, and urged men to defy the law of the land. I reasoned, therefore, that the word "boycott" was really a misnomer for our proposed action. A boycott suggests an economic squeeze, leaving one bogged down in a negative. But we were concerned with the positive. Our concern would not be to put the bus company out of business, but to put justice in business.

As I thought further I came to see that what we were really doing was withdrawing our coöperation from an evil system, rather than merely withdrawing our economic support from the bus company. The bus company, being an external expression of the system, would naturally suffer, but the basic aim was to refuse to coöperate with evil. At this point I began to think about Thoreau's *Essay on Civil Disobedience*. I remembered how, as a college student, I had been moved when I first read this work. I became convinced that what we were preparing to do in Montgomery was related to what Thoreau had expressed. We were simply saying to the white community, "We can no longer lend our coöperation to an evil system."

Something began to say to me, "He who passively accepts evil is as much involved in it as he who helps to perpetrate it. He who accepts evil without protesting against it is really coöperating with it." When oppressed people willingly accept their oppression they only serve to give the oppressor a convenient justification for his acts. Often the oppressor goes along unaware of the evil involved in his oppression so long as the oppressed accepts it. So in order to be true to one's conscience and true to God, a righteous man has no alternative but to refuse to coöperate with an evil system. This I felt was the nature of our action. From this moment on I conceived of our movement as an act of massive noncoöperation. From then on I rarely used the word "boycott."

Public Statement by Eight White Alabama Clergymen (1963)

Nonviolent protest required clear-cut moral issues to succeed. Applied to obvious indignities—segregated buses, "colored" signs in waiting rooms,

*lunch counters off limits to blacks—it could stir outrage and force
people in authority to obey the law or to bring existing laws into
conformity with constitutional guarantees. Martin Luther King, Jr.,
helped lead numerous demonstrations in the South protesting the
segregation of restaurants, hotels, and department stores. In 1963 he was
arrested in Birmingham, Alabama, for leading a protest march in defiance
of a court order. A group of Birmingham clergymen sought to put an
end to the demonstrations by issuing the following statement.*

WE THE UNDERSIGNED CLERGYMEN are among those who, in January, issued "An Appeal for Law and Order and Common Sense," in dealing with racial problems in Alabama. We expressed understanding that honest convictions in racial matters could properly be pursued in the courts, but urged that decisions of those courts should in the meantime be peacefully obeyed.

Since that time there had been some evidence of increased forbearance and a willingness to face facts. Responsible citizens have undertaken to work on various problems which cause racial friction and unrest. In Birmingham, recent public events have given indication that we all have opportunity for a new constructive and realistic approach to racial problems.

However, we are now confronted by a series of demonstrations by some of our Negro citizens, directed and led in part by outsiders. We recognize the natural impatience of people who feel that their hopes are slow in being realized. But we are convinced that these demonstrations are unwise and untimely.

We agree rather with certain local Negro leadership which has called for honest and open negotiation of racial issues in our area. And we believe this kind of facing of issues can best be accomplished by citizens of our own metropolitan area, white and Negro, meeting with their knowledge and experience of the local situation. All of us need to face that responsibility and find proper channels for its accomplishment.

Just as we formerly pointed out that "hatred and violence have no sanction in our religious and political traditions," we also point out that such actions as incite to hatred and violence, however technically peaceful those actions may be, have not contributed to the resolution of our local problems. We do not believe that these days of new hope are days when extreme measures are justified in Birmingham.

We commend the community as a whole, and the local news media and law enforcement officials in particular, on the calm manner in which these demonstrations have been handled. We urge the public to continue to show restraint should the demonstrations continue, and the law enforcement officials to remain calm and continue to protect our city from violence.

We further strongly urge our own Negro community to withdraw support from these demonstrations, and to unite locally in working peacefully for a better Birmingham. When rights are consistently denied, a cause should be pressed in the courts and in negotiations among local leaders, and not in the streets. We appeal to both our white and Negro citizenry to observe the principles of law and order and common sense.

Signed by:

C. C. J. CARPENTER, D.D., LL.D., Bishop of Alabama

JOSEPH A. DURICK, D.D., Auxiliary Bishop, Diocese of Mobile-Birmingham

RABBI MILTON L. GRAFMAN, Temple Emanu-El, Birmingham, Alabama

BISHOP PAUL HARDIN, Bishop of the Alabama–West Florida Conference of the Methodist Church

BISHOP NOLAN B. HARMON, Bishop of the North Alabama Conference of the Methodist Church

GEORGE M. MURRAY, D.D., LL.D., Bishop Coadjutor, Episcopal Diocese of Alabama

EDWARD V. RAMAGE, Moderator, Synod of the Alabama Presbyterian Church in the United States

EARL STALLINGS, Pastor, First Baptist Church, Birmingham, Alabama

Letter from Birmingham City Jail (1963)
MARTIN LUTHER KING, JR.

King responded to the Birmingham clergymen's challenge to his moral authority in this letter, one of the most impressive literary products of the civil rights movement. His attack on the "white moderate" who counseled patience quickly became a significant theme of the movement, as the difficult coalition between white and black activists and politicians began to come apart.

MY DEAR FELLOW CLERGYMEN,   While confined here in the Birmingham City Jail, I came across your recent statement calling our present activities "unwise and untimely." Seldom, if ever, do I pause to answer criticism of my work and ideas. If I sought to answer all of the criticisms that cross my desk, my secretaries would be engaged in little else in the course of the day and I would have no time for constructive work. But since I feel that you are men of genuine good will and your criticisms are sincerely set forth, I would like to answer your statement in what I hope will be patient and reasonable terms. . . .

You deplore the demonstrations that are presently taking place in Birmingham. But I am sorry that your statement did not express a similar concern for the conditions that brought the demonstrations into being. I am sure that each of you would want to go beyond the superficial social analyst who looks merely at effects, and does not grapple with underlying causes. I would not hesitate to say that it is unfortunate that so-called demonstrations are taking place in Birmingham at this time, but I would say in more emphatic terms that it is even more unfortunate that the white power structure of this city left the Negro community with no other alternative.

In any nonviolent campaign there are four basic steps: (1) collection of the facts to determine whether injustices are alive; (2) negotiation; (3) self-purification; and (4) direct action. We have gone through all of these steps in Birmingham. There can be no gainsaying of the fact that racial injustice engulfs this community. Birmingham is probably the most thoroughly segregated city in the United States. Its ugly record of police brutality is known in every section of this country. Its unjust treatment of Negroes in the courts is a notorious reality. There have been more unsolved bombings of Negro homes and churches in Birmingham than any city in this nation. These are the hard, brutal, and unbelievable facts. On the basis of these conditions Negro leaders sought to negotiate with the city fathers. But the political leaders consistently refused to engage in good faith negotiation.

Then came the opportunity last September to talk with some of the leaders of the economic community. In these negotiating sessions certain promises were made by the merchants—such as the promise to remove the humiliating racial signs from the stores. On the basis of these promises Reverend [Fred] Shuttlesworth and the leaders of the Alabama Christian Movement for Human Rights agreed to call a moratorium on any type of demonstrations. As the weeks and months unfolded we realized that we were the victims of a broken promise. The signs remained. As in so many experiences of the past, we were confronted with blasted hopes, and the dark shadow of a deep disappointment settled upon us. So we had no alternative except that of preparing for direct action, whereby we would present our very bodies as a means of laying our case before the conscience of the local and national community. We were not unmindful of the difficulties involved. So we decided to go through a process of self-purification. We started having workshops on nonviolence and repeatedly asked ourselves the questions, "Are you able to accept blows without retaliating?" "Are you able to endure the ordeals of jail?"

We decided to set our direct action program around the Easter season, realizing that, with the exception of Christmas, this was the largest shopping period of the year. Knowing that a strong economic withdrawal program would be the by-product of direct action, we felt that this was the best time to bring pressure on the merchants for the needed changes. Then it occurred to us that the March election was ahead, and so we speedily decided to postpone action until after election day. When we discovered that Mr. [Eugene "Bull"] Connor was in the run-off, we decided again to postpone action so that the demonstrations could not be used to cloud the issues. At this time we agreed to begin our nonviolent witness the day after the run-off.

This reveals that we did not move irresponsibly into direct action. We too wanted to see Mr. Connor defeated; so we went through postponement after postponement to aid in this community need. After this we felt that direct action could be delayed no longer.

You may well ask, "Why direct action? Why sit-ins, marches, etc.? Isn't negotiation a better path?" You are exactly right in your call for negotiation. Indeed, this is the purpose of direct action. Nonviolent direct action seeks to create such a crisis and establish such creative tension that a community that has constantly refused to negotiate is forced to confront the issue. It seeks so to dramatize the issue that it can no longer be ignored.

I just referred to the creation of tension as a part of the work of the nonviolent resister. This may sound rather shocking. But I must confess that I am not afraid of the word tension. I have earnestly worked and preached against violent tension, but there is a type of constructive nonviolent tension that is necessary for growth. Just as Socrates felt that it was necessary to create a tension in the mind so that individuals could rise from the bondage of myths and half-truths to the unfettered realm of creative analysis and objective appraisal, we must see the need of having nonviolent gadflies to create the kind of tension in society that will help men rise from the dark depths of prejudice and racism to the majestic heights of understanding and brotherhood. So the purpose of the direct action is to create a situation so crisis-packed that it will inevitably open the door to negotiation. We, therefore, concur with you in your call for negotiation. Too long has our beloved Southland been bogged down in the tragic attempt to live in monologue rather than dialogue.

One of the basic points in your statement is that our acts are untimely. Some have asked, "Why didn't you give the new administration time to act?" The only answer that I can give to this inquiry is that the new administration must be prodded about as much as the outgoing one before it acts. We will be sadly mistaken if we feel that the election of Mr. [Albert] Boutwell will bring the millennium to Birmingham. While Mr. Boutwell is

much more articulate and gentle than Mr. Connor, they are both segrega-
tionists dedicated to the task of maintaining the status quo. The hope I see
in Mr. Boutwell is that he will be reasonable enough to see the futility of
massive resistance to desegregation. But he will not see this without pressure from the devotees of civil rights.

My friends, I must say to you that we have not made a single gain in
civil rights without determined legal and nonviolent pressure. History is
the long and tragic story of the fact that privileged groups seldom give up
their privileges voluntarily. Individuals may see the moral light and voluntarily give up their unjust posture; but as Reinhold Niebuhr has reminded
us, groups are more immoral than individuals.

We know through painful experience that freedom is never voluntarily
given by the oppressor; it must be demanded by the oppressed. Frankly I
have never yet engaged in a direct action movement that was "well timed,"
according to the timetable of those who have not suffered unduly from the
disease of segregation. For years now I have heard the word "Wait!" It
rings in the ear of every Negro with a piercing familiarity. This "wait" has
almost always meant "never.". . .

I must close now. But before closing I am impelled to mention one other
point in your statement that troubled me profoundly. You warmly commended the Birmingham police force for keeping "order" and "preventing
violence." I don't believe you would have so warmly commended the police
force if you had seen its angry violent dogs literally biting six unarmed,
nonviolent Negroes. I don't believe you would so quickly commend the
policemen if you would observe their ugly and inhuman treatment of Negroes here in the city jail; if you would watch them push and curse old
Negro women and young Negro girls; if you would see them slap and kick
old Negro men and young Negro boys; if you will observe them, as they
did on two occasions, refuse to give us food because we wanted to sing
our grace together. I'm sorry that I can't join you in your praise for the
police department.

It is true that they have been rather disciplined in their public handling
of the demonstrators. In this sense they have been rather publicly "nonviolent." But for what purpose? To preserve the evil system of segregation.
Over the last few years I have consistently preached that nonviolence demands that the means we use must be as pure as the ends we seek. So I
have tried to make it clear that it is wrong to use immoral means to attain
moral ends. But now I must affirm that it is just as wrong, or even more
so, to use moral means to preserve immoral ends. Maybe Mr. Connor and
his policemen have been rather publicly nonviolent, as Chief Prichett was
in Albany, Georgia, but they have used the moral means of nonviolence
to maintain the immoral end of flagrant racial injustice. T. S. Eliot has said
that there is no greater treason than to do the right deed for the wrong
reason.

I wish you had commended the Negro sit-inners and demonstrators of

Birmingham for their sublime courage, their willingness to suffer, and their amazing discipline in the midst of the most inhuman provocation. One day the South will recognize its real heroes. They will be the James Merediths,[1] courageously and with a majestic sense of purpose, facing jeering and hostile mobs and the agonizing loneliness that characterizes the life of the pioneer. They will be old, oppressed, battered Negro women, symbolized in a 72-year-old woman of Montgomery, Alabama, who rose up with a sense of dignity and with her people decided not to ride the segregated buses, and responded to one who inquired about her tiredness with ungrammatical profundity: "My feets is tired, but my soul is rested." They will be young high school and college students, young ministers of the gospel and a host of the elders, courageously and nonviolently sitting in at lunch counters and willingly going to jail for conscience sake. One day the South will know that when these disinherited children of God sat down at lunch counters they were in reality standing up for the best in the American dream and the most sacred values in our Judeo-Christian heritage, and thus carrying our whole nation back to great wells of democracy which were dug deep by the founding fathers in the formulation of the Constitution and the Declaration of Independence.

Never before have I written a letter this long (or should I say a book?). I'm afraid that it is much too long to take your precious time. I can assure you that it would have been much shorter if I had been writing from a comfortable desk, but what else is there to do when you are alone for days in the dull monotony of a narrow jail cell other than write long letters, think strange thoughts, and pray long prayers? . . .

Yours for the cause of Peace and Brotherhood,

M. L. KING, JR.

I Have a Dream (1963)
MARTIN LUTHER KING, JR.

The famous "March on Washington for Jobs and Freedom" which took place on August 28, 1963, was initiated by A. Philip Randolph, long-time

[1] In the fall of 1962 Meredith became the first black to enroll at the University of Mississippi. —Eds.

president of the Brotherhood of Sleeping Car Porters and senior statesman of the civil rights movement. The first truly massive peaceable demonstration in American history, the March succeeded in assembling about one quarter million people at the Lincoln Memorial to hear the songs of Bob Dylan, Odetta, and Marian Anderson and the speeches of many civil rights leaders. The day will live in American memory because of King's speech.

I AM HAPPY to join with you today in what will go down in history as the greatest demonstration for freedom in the history of our nation.

Five score years ago, a great American, in whose symbolic shadow we stand, signed the Emancipation Proclamation. This momentous decree came as a great beacon light of hope to millions of Negro slaves who had been seared in the flames of withering injustice. It came as a joyous daybreak to end the long night of captivity.

But one hundred years later the Negro is still not free. One hundred years later, the life of the Negro is still sadly crippled by the manacles of segregation and the chains of discrimination. One hundred years later, the Negro lives on a lonely island of poverty in the midst of a vast ocean of material prosperity. One hundred years later, the Negro is still languished in the corners of American society and finds himself an exile in his own land. So we have come here today to dramatize a shameful condition.

In a sense we have come to our Nation's Capital to cash a check. When the architects of our Republic wrote the magnificent words of the Constitution and the Declaration of Independence, they were signing a promissory note to which every American was to fall heir. This note was a promise that all men, yes, black men as well as white men, would be guaranteed the unalienable rights of life, liberty, and the pursuit of happiness.

It is obvious today that America has defaulted on this promissory note insofar as her citizens of color are concerned. Instead of honoring this sacred obligation, America has given the Negro people a bad check; a check which has come back marked "insufficient funds." But we refuse to believe that the bank of justice is bankrupt. We refuse to believe that there are insufficient funds in the great vaults of opportunity of this nation. So we have come to cash this check—a check that will give us upon demand the riches of freedom and the security of justice. We have also come to this hallowed spot to remind America of the fierce urgency of now. This is no time to engage in the luxury of cooling off or to take the tranquilizing drug of gradualism. Now is the time to rise from the dark and desolate valley of segregation to the sunlit path of racial justice. Now is the time to lift our nation from the quicksands of racial injustice to the solid rock of brotherhood. Now is the time to make justice the reality for all of God's children.

It would be fatal for the nation to overlook the urgency of the moment.

This sweltering summer of the Negro's legitimate discontent will not pass until there is an invigorating autumn of freedom and equality. 1963 is not an end, but a beginning. Those who hope that the Negro needed to blow off steam and will now be content will have a rude awakening if the Nation returns to business as usual. There will be neither rest nor tranquility in America until the Negro is granted his citizenship rights. The whirlwinds of revolt will continue to shake the foundations of our Nation until the bright day of justice emerges.

But there is something that I must say to my people who stand on the warm threshold which leads into the palace of justice. In the process of gaining our rightful place we must not be guilty of wrongful deeds. Let us not seek to satisfy our thirst for freedom by drinking from the cup of bitterness and hatred. We must forever conduct our struggle on the high plane of dignity and discipline. We must not allow our creative protest to degenerate into physical violence. Again and again we must rise to the majestic heights of meeting physical force with soul force. The marvelous new militancy which has engulfed the Negro community must not lead us to a distrust of all white people, for many of our white brothers, as evidenced by their presence here today, have come to realize that their destiny is tied up with our destiny and they have come to realize that their freedom is inextricably bound to our freedom. We cannot walk alone.

And as we walk, we must make the pledge that we shall march ahead. We cannot turn back. There are those who are asking the devotees of civil rights, "when will you be satisfied?" We can never be satisfied as long as the Negro is the victim of the unspeakable horrors of police brutality. We can never be satisfied as long as our bodies, heavy with the fatigue of travel, cannot gain lodging in the motels of the highways and the hotels of the cities. We cannot be satisfied as long as the Negro's basic mobility is from a smaller ghetto to a larger one. We can never be satisfied as long as our children are stripped of their selfhood and robbed of their dignity by signs stating 'For white only.' We cannot be satisfied as long as a Negro in Mississippi cannot vote and a Negro in New York believes he has nothing for which to vote. No, no we are not satisfied, and we will not be satisfied until justice rolls down like waters and righteousness like a mighty stream.

I am not unmindful that some of you have come here out of great trials and tribulations. Some of you have come fresh from narrow jail cells. Some of you have come from areas where your quest for freedom left you battered by the storms of persecution and staggered by the winds of police brutality. You have been the veterans of creative suffering. Continue to work with the faith that unearned suffering is redemptive.

Go back to Mississippi, go back to Alabama, go back to South Carolina, go back to Georgia, go back to Louisiana, go back to the slums and ghettos of our northern cities, knowing that somehow this situation can and will be changed. Let us not wallow in the valley of despair.

I say to you today, my friends, even though we face the difficulties of today and tomorrow, I still have a dream. It is a dream deeply rooted in the American dream.

I have a dream that one day this nation will rise up and live out the true meaning of its creed: "We hold these truths to be self-evident; that all men are created equal."

I have a dream that one day on the red hills of Georgia the sons of former slaves and the sons of former slaveowners will be able to sit down together at the table of brotherhood.

I have a dream that one day even the state of Mississippi, a state sweltering with the heat of injustice, sweltering with the heat of oppression, will be transformed into an oasis of freedom and justice.

I have a dream that my four little children will one day live in a nation where they will not be judged by the color of their skin but by the content of their character.

I have a dream today.

I have a dream that one day down in Alabama with its vicious racists, with its governor having his lips dripping with the words of interposition and nullification, one day right there in Alabama little black boys and black girls will be able to join hands with little white boys and white girls as sisters and brothers.

I have a dream today.

I have a dream that one day every valley shall be exalted, every hill and mountain shall be made low, the rough places will be made plains, and the crooked places will be made straight, and the glory of the Lord shall be revealed, and all flesh shall see it together.

This is our hope. This is the faith that I go back to the South with. With this faith we will be able to hew out the mountain of despair a stone of hope. With this faith we will be able to transform the jangling discords of our nation into a beautiful symphony of brotherhood. With this faith we will be able to work together, to pray together, to struggle together, to go to jail together, to stand up for freedom together, knowing that we will be free one day.

This will be the day when all of God's children will be able to sing with new meaning "My country 'tis of thee, sweet land of liberty, of thee I sing. Land where my fathers died, land of the pilgrim's pride, from every mountainside, let freedom ring."

And if America is to be a great nation this must become true. So let freedom ring from the prodigious hilltops of New Hampshire. Let freedom ring from the mighty mountains of New York. Let freedom ring from the heightening Alleghenies of Pennsylvania!

Let freedom ring from the snowcapped Rockies of Colorado!

Let freedom ring from the curvacious slopes of California!

But not only that; let freedom ring from Stone Mountain of Georgia!

Let freedom ring from Lookout Mountain of Tennessee.

Let freedom ring from every hill and mole hill of Mississippi. From every mountainside, let freedom ring, and when this happens, when we allow freedom to ring, when we let it ring from every village and every hamlet, from every state and every city, we will be able to speed up that day when all of God's children, black men and white men, Jews and Gentiles, Protestants and Catholics, will be able to join hands and sing in the words of the old Negro spiritual, "Free at last! Free at last! Thank God almighty, we are free at last!"

A Religious "Right" to Violate the Law? (1964)
WILL HERBERG

Will Herberg, a prominent writer on religion and religious pluralism, questions the legitimacy of King's doctrine of passive resistance in Christian theology.

EARLY LAST MONTH, Yale University conferred the degree LL.D. upon Martin Luther King, who had already been celebrated on the cover of *Time* magazine. True enough, nowadays the LL.D., *legum doctor,* doctor of laws (both canon and civil), no longer implies any special distinction in jurisprudence or legal learning; but it does imply a moral and social distinction which sets off its recipient as a man of intelligence, eminence, and respectability, a force in society and a leader of men—and this Dr. Martin Luther King certainly is. Dr. King is also a Christian, and sees the movement he leads as a Christian movement, grounded in Christian teachings.

It is therefore of considerable interest to inquire a little more closely into Dr. King's notions of political responsibility and social order, particularly into his central contention that Christian principles permit, perhaps even require, the violation of laws the individual conscience may hold to be "unjust." In this contention Dr. King is supported by that other influential Negro Christian leader, the Rev. Adam Clayton Powell, who is also a member of the House of Representatives. Here are their words:

Dr. Martin Luther King: "One may well ask, 'How can you advocate breaking some laws and obeying others?' The answer lies in the fact that there are two types of laws: There are *just* laws and there are *unjust* laws. . . . I submit that an individual who breaks a law that conscience tells him is unjust, and willingly accepts the penalty. . . . is in reality expressing the highest respect for law . . ." ("A Letter From the Birmingham City Jail").

Rev. Adam Clayton Powell: "People say it's against the law. What law? And who made them? There is only one great and unbreakable law, and that's the law of God" (recorded Feb. 4, 1964 by NBC-WRC News).

The two are in substantial agreement (Dr. King too derives "just" laws from "the moral law or the law of God"); and, in more or less cautious form, their position is shared by thousands of churchmen, Negro and white, throughout the country. But how does this position square with well-established Christian teaching on government, law, and civil obedience?

St. Paul's Teaching

The essential Christian teaching on government, law, and civil obedience is grounded on that celebrated Chapter XIII of Paul's Epistle to the Romans, which itself reflects earlier Jewish teaching. "Let every one be subject to the governing authorities," the Apostle enjoins. "For there is no authority except from God, and the existing authorities have been ordained by God. Therefore, he who resists the authorities resists what God has appointed, and those who resist will incur judgment. . . ." This is balanced in the New Testament by the conviction of Peter and the Apostles, "We must obey God rather than man" (Acts 5:29).

When does loyalty to God come into conflict with obedience to earthly rulers? When earthly rulers are insensate enough (as totalitarian states invariably are) to demand for themselves what is owing only to God— worship and ultimate allegiance. The classical Christian teaching emerges most profoundly perhaps in the writings of St. Augustine, whose position Professor Deane thus summarizes:

All the laws promulgated by the ruler must be obeyed by all citizens, with the sole exception of laws or commands that run contrary to God's ordinances. . . . When Augustine says that God's command overrules [human] laws and customs, it seems clear that he is referring to those commands of God that have been directly revealed to men in the Scriptures, such as the prohibition against idol worship . . . He does *not* say that if the ruler is unwise or evil, and fails to take the eternal law into account when he frames temporal laws, these laws have no validity, and the subjects have no obligation to obey them; nor does he say that the subjects have a right to determine for themselves, by reference to the natural or eternal law, whether or not such a temporal law is valid and is to be obeyed" (Herbert A. Deane, *The Political and Social Ideas of St. Augustine,* Columbia U.P., 1963, pp. 147, 89, 90; Dr. Deane is professor of government at Columbia).

This, in substance, early became the normative Christian doctrine, stated and restated by Thomas Aquinas, Martin Luther, John Calvin, and every other great moralist and theologian of the Church. It is the standard by which the position advanced by Dr. King and Rep. Powell *as Christian* must be judged; and, judged by that standard, their position permitting the violation of any law disapproved of by the individual conscience as "unjust," must be judged as not Christian at all, but seriously deviant and heretical. . . .

Strange Doctrine

Would it not be well for Dr. King, as a responsible community leader honored with a Doctor of Laws by Yale University, to consider the consequences of his strange doctrine? Every man has his conscience; and if the individual conscience is absolutized (that is, divinized), and made the final judge of laws to be obeyed or disobeyed, nothing but anarchy and the dissolution of the very fabric of government would result. Thousands and thousands of Americans, eminent, respectable, and responsible, are convinced in their conscience that the new Civil Rights Act is utterly wrong, unjust, and unconstitutional; are they therefore entitled to disobey it, and to organize civil disobedience campaigns to impede its effectuation? Grant this "right" and there would be no law at all, nothing but a clash of "consciences" that could not hope to escape becoming a clash of raw power. Strange as it may seem to Dr. King, the very purpose of government is to make us obey laws of which we do *not* approve, which indeed we may even regard as "unjust." Laws that we approve of, and regard as just, we hardly need much coercion to get us to obey.

In its essential aims, the civil rights movement led by Dr. King is not at all revolutionary: it strives not to subvert and new-model the American system, but to win for the Negro a fair and equal place within it. Its methods, however, and the political philosophy that informs these methods —the deliberate creation of "crisis-packed situations" through systematic civil disobedience—are consistent neither with Christian teaching nor with ordinary political responsibility. * Dr. King, the Christian leader, now a Yale Doctor of Laws, might do well to rethink the theological foundations of a doctrine so dubious in its social and political consequences.

* The pitch of irresponsibility this kind of thing can lead to is painfully illustrated by the words addressed by that eminently respectable citizen, Adlai E. Stevenson, to the graduating class at Colby College in Maine: "I think especially of the participation of American students in the great struggle to advance civil and human rights in America. Indeed, even a jail sentence is no longer a dishonor, but a proud achievement. Perhaps we are destined to see in this law-loving land people running for office not on their stainless record, but on their prison records."

On the Role of Martin Luther King (1965)
AUGUST MEIER

August Meier, a leading writer on black history, shrewdly analyzes the ambiguous position of Martin Luther King, Jr., who projected an image of militancy to those outside the movement while exerting a restraining influence on the more radical members of the civil rights coalition.

THE PHENOMENON that is Martin Luther King consists of a number of striking paradoxes. The Nobel Prize winner is accepted by the outside world as *the* leader of the nonviolent direct action movement, but he is criticized by many activists within the movement. He is criticized for what appears, at times, as indecisiveness, and more often denounced for a tendency to accept compromise. Yet in the eyes of most Americans, both black and white, he remains the symbol of militant direct action. So potent is this symbol of King as direct actionist, that a new myth is arising about his historic role. The real credit for developing and projecting the techniques and philosophy of nonviolent direct action in the civil rights arena must be given to the Congress of Racial Equality which was founded in 1942, more than a dozen years before the Montgomery bus boycott projected King into international fame. And the idea of mass action by Negroes themselves to secure redress of their grievances must, in large part, be ascribed to the vision of A. Philip Randolph, architect of the March on Washington Movement during World War II. Yet, as we were told in Montgomery on March 25, 1965, King and his followers now assert, apparently without serious contradiction, that a new type of civil rights strategy was born at Montgomery in 1955 under King's auspices.

In a movement in which respect is accorded in direct proportion to the number of times one has been arrested, King appears to keep the number of times he goes to jail to a minimum. In a movement in which successful leaders are those who share in the hardships of their followers, in the risks they take, in the beatings they receive, in the length of time they spend in jail, King tends to leave prison for other important engagements, rather than remaining there and suffering with his followers. In a movement in which leadership ordinarily devolves upon persons who mix democratically with their followers, King remains isolated and aloof. In a movement which prides itself on militancy and "no compromise" with racial discrimination or with the white "power structure," King maintains close relationships with, and appears to be influenced by, Democratic Presidents and their emissaries, seems amenable to compromises considered by some half a loaf or less, and often appears willing to postpone or avoid a direct confrontation in the streets.

King's career has been characterized by failures that, in the larger sense, must be accounted triumphs. The buses in Montgomery were desegregated only after lengthy judicial proceedings conducted by the NAACP Legal Defense Fund secured a favorable decision from the U.S. Supreme Court. Nevertheless, the events in Montgomery were a triumph for direct action, and gave this tactic a popularity unknown when identified solely with CORE. King's subsequent major campaigns—in Albany, Georgia; in Danville, Virginia; in Birmingham, Alabama; and in St. Augustine, Florida— ended as failures or with only token accomplishments in those cities. But each of them, chiefly because of his presence, dramatically focused national and international attention on the plight of the Southern Negro, thereby facilitating over-all progress. In Birmingham, in particular, demonstrations which fell short of their local goals were directly responsible for a major Federal Civil Rights Act. Essentially, this pattern of local failure and national victory was recently enacted in Selma, Alabama.

King is ideologically committed to disobeying unjust laws and court orders, in the Gandhian tradition, but generally he follows a policy of not disobeying Federal Court orders. In his recent Montgomery speech, he expressed a crude, neo-Marxist interpretation of history romanticizing the populist movement as a genuine union of black and white common people, ascribing race prejudice to capitalists playing white workers against black. Yet, in practice, he is amenable to compromise with the white bourgeois political and economic Establishment. More important, King enunciates a superficial and eclectic philosophy and by virtue of it he has profoundly awakened the moral conscience of America.

In short, King can be described as a "conservative militant."

In this combination of militancy with conservatism and caution, of righteousness with respectability, lies the secret of King's enormous success.

Certain important civil rights leaders have dismissed King's position as the product of publicity generated by the mass communications media. But this can be said of the success of the civil rights nonviolent action movement generally. Without publicity it is hard to conceive that much progress would have been made. In fact, contrary to the official nonviolent direct action philosophy, demonstrations have secured their results not by changing the hearts of the oppressors through a display of nonviolent love, but through the national and international pressures generated by the publicity arising from mass arrests and incidents of violence. And no one has employed this strategy of securing publicity through mass arrests and precipitating violence from white hoodlums and law enforcement officers more than King himself. King abhors violence; as at Selma, for example, he constantly retreats from situations that might result in the deaths of his followers. But he is precisely most successful when, contrary to his deepest wishes, his demonstrations precipitate violence from Southern whites against Negro and white demonstrators. We need only cite Birmingham and Selma to illustrate this point.

Publicity alone does not explain the durability of King's image, or why he remains for the rank and file, of whites and blacks alike, the symbol of the direct action movement, the nearest thing to a charismatic leader that the civil rights movement has ever had. At the heart of King's continuing influence and popularity are two facts. First, better than anyone else, he articulates the aspiration of Negroes who respond to the cadence of his addresses, his religious phraseology and manner of speaking, and the vision of his dream for them and for America. King has intuitively adopted the style of the old-fashioned Negro Baptist preacher and transformed it into a new art form; he has, indeed, restored oratory to its place among the arts. Second, he communicates Negro aspirations to white America more effectively than anyone else. His religious terminology and manipulation of the Christian symbols of love and nonresistance are partly responsible for his appeal among whites. To talk in terms of Christianity, love, nonviolence is reassuring to the mentality of white America. At the same time, the very superficialities of his philosophy—that rich and eclectic amalgam of Jesus, Hegel, Gandhi, and others as outlined in his *Stride Toward Freedom*—make him appear intellectually profound to the superficially educated middle-class white American. Actually, if he were a truly profound religious thinker, like Tillich or Niebuhr, his influence would of necessity be limited to a select audience. But by uttering moral clichés, the Christian pieties, in a magnificent display of oratory, King becomes enormously effective.

If his success with Negroes is largely due to the style of his utterance, his success with whites is a much more complicated matter. For one thing, he unerringly knows how to exploit to maximum effectiveness their growing feeling of guilt. King, of course, is not unique in attaining fame and popularity among whites through playing upon their guilt feelings. James Baldwin is the most conspicuous example of a man who has achieved success with this formula. The incredible fascination which the Black Muslims have for white people, and the posthumous near-sanctification of Malcolm X by many naïve whites (in addition to many Negroes whose motivations are, of course, very different), must in large part be attributed to the same source. But King goes beyond this. With intuitive, but extraordinary skill, he not only castigates whites for their sins but, in contrast to angry young writers like Baldwin, he explicitly states his belief in their salvation. Not only will direct action bring fulfillment of the "American Dream" to Negroes but the Negroes' use of direct action will help whites to live up to their Christian and democratic values; it will purify, cleanse, and heal the sickness in white society. Whites will benefit as well as Negroes. He has faith that the white man will redeem himself. Negroes must not hate whites, but love them. In this manner, King first arouses the guilt feelings of whites, and then relieves them—though always leaving the lingering feeling in his white listeners that they should support his nonviolent crusade. Like a Greek tragedy, King's performance provides an extraordinary catharsis for the white listener.

King thus gives white men the feeling that he is their good friend, that he poses no threat to them. It is interesting to note that this was the same feeling white men received from Booker T. Washington, the noted early twentieth-century accommodator. Both men stressed their faith in the white man; both expressed the belief that the white man could be brought to accord Negroes their rights. Both stressed the importance of whites recognizing the rights of Negroes for the moral health and well-being of white society. Like King, Washington had an extraordinary following among whites. Like King, Washington symbolized for most whites the whole program of Negro advancement. While there are important similarities in the functioning of both men vis-à-vis the community, needless to say, in most respects, their philosophies are in disagreement.

It is not surprising, therefore, to find that King is the recipient of contributions from organizations and individuals who fail to eradicate evidence of prejudice in their own backyards. For example, certain liberal trade union leaders who are philosophically committed to full racial equality, who feel the need to identify their organizations with the cause of militant civil rights, although they are unable to defeat racist elements in their unions, contribute hundreds of thousands of dollars to King's Southern Christian Leadership Conference. One might attribute this phenomenon to the fact that SCLC works in the South rather than the North, but this is true also for SNCC [Student Nonviolent Coordinating Committee] which does not benefit similarly from union treasuries. And the fact is that ever since the college students started their sit-ins in 1960, it is SNCC which has been the real spearhead of direct action in most of the South and has performed the lion's share of work in local communities, while SCLC has received most of the publicity and most of the money. However, while King provides a verbal catharsis for whites, leaving them feeling purified and comfortable, SNCC's uncompromising militancy makes whites feel less comfortable and less beneficent.

(The above is not to suggest that SNCC and SCLC are responsible for all, or nearly all, the direct action in the South. The NAACP has actively engaged in direct action, especially in Savannah under the leadership of W. W. Law, in South Carolina under I. DeQuincy Newman, and in Clarksdale, Mississippi, under Aaron Henry. The work of CORE—including most of the direct action in Louisiana, much of the nonviolent work in Florida and Mississippi, the famous Freedom Ride of 1961—has been most important. In addition, one should note the work of SCLC affiliates, such as those in Lynchburg, Virginia, led by Rev. Virgil Wood, in Birmingham led by Rev. Fred Shuttlesworth, and in Savannah, by Hosea Williams.

(There are other reasons for SNCC's lesser popularity with whites than King's. These are connected with the great changes that have occurred in SNCC since it was founded in 1960, changes reflected in the half-jocular epigram circulating in SNCC circles that the Student Nonviolent Coordinating Committee has now become the "Nonstudent Violent Noncoordinating Committee." The point is, however, that even when SNCC thrilled the nation in 1960–1961 with the student sit-ins that swept the South, it did not enjoy the popularity and financial support accorded to King.)

King's very tendencies toward compromise and caution, his willingness to negotiate and bargain with White House emissaries, his hesitancy to risk the precipitation of mass violence upon demonstrators, further endear him to whites. He appears to them a "responsible" and "moderate" man. To militant activists, King's failure to march past the state police on that famous Tuesday morning outside Selma indicated either a lack of courage, or a desire to advance himself by currying Presidential favor. But King's shrinking from a possible bloodbath, his accession to the entreaties of the political Establishment, his acceptance of face-saving compromise in this, as in other instances, are fundamental to the particular role he is playing, and essential for achieving and sustaining his image as a leader of heroic moral stature in the eyes of white men. His caution and compromise keep open the channels of communication between the activists and the majority of the white community. In brief: King makes the nonviolent direct action movement respectable.

Of course, many, if not most, activists reject the notion that the movement should be made respectable. Yet American history shows that for any reform movement to succeed, it must attain respectability. It must attract moderates, even conservatives, to its ranks. The March on Washington made direct action respectable; Selma made it fashionable. More than any other force, it is Martin Luther King who impressed the civil rights revolution on the American conscience and is attracting that great middle body of American public opinion to its support. It is this revolution of conscience that will undoubtedly lead fairly soon to the elimination of all violations of Negroes' constitutional rights, thereby creating the conditions for the economic and social changes that are necessary if we are to achieve full racial equality. This is not to deny the dangers to the civil rights movement in becoming respectable. Respectability, for example, encourages the attempts of political machines to capture civil rights organizations. Respectability can also become an end in itself, thereby dulling the cutting edge of its protest activities. Indeed, the history of the labor movement reveals how attaining respectability can produce loss of original purpose and character. These perils, however, do not contradict the importance of achieving respectability—even a degree of modishness—if racial equality is ever to be realized.

There is another side to the picture: King would be neither respected nor respectable if there were not more militant activists on his left, engaged in more radical forms of direct action. Without CORE and, especially, SNCC, King would appear "radical" and "irresponsible" rather than "moderate" and "respectable."

King occupies a position of strategic importance as the "vital center" within the civil rights movement. Though he has lieutenants who are far more militant and "radical" than he is, SCLC acts, in effect, as the most cautious, deliberate and "conservative" of the direct action groups because of King's leadership. This permits King and the SCLC to function—almost certainly unintentionally—not only as an organ of communication with the Establishment and majority white public opinion, but as something of a bridge between the activist and more traditionalist or "conservative" civil rights groups, as well. For example, it appears unlikely that the Urban League and NAACP, which supplied most of the funds, would have participated in the 1963 March on Washington if King had not done so. Because King agreed to go along with SNCC and CORE, the NAACP found it mandatory to join if it was to maintain its image as a protest organization. King's identification with the March was also essential for securing the support of large numbers of white clergymen and their moderate followers. The March was the brainchild of the civil rights movement's ablest strategist and tactician, Bayard Rustin, and the call was issued by A. Philip Randolph. But it would have been a minor episode in the history of the civil rights movement without King's support.

Yet curiously enough, despite his charisma and international reputation, King thus far has been more a symbol than a power in the civil rights movement. Indeed his strength in the movement has derived less from an organizational base than from his symbolic role. Seven or eight years ago, one might have expected King to achieve an organizationally dominant position in the civil rights movement, at least in its direct action wing. The fact is that in the period after the Montgomery bus boycott, King developed no program and, it is generally agreed, revealed himself as an ineffective administrator who failed to capitalize upon his popularity among Negroes. In 1957, he founded SCLC to coordinate the work of direct action groups that had sprung up in Southern cities. Composed of autonomous units, usually led by Baptist ministers, SCLC does not appear to have developed an overall sense of direction or a program of real breadth and scope. Although the leaders of SCLC affiliates became the race leaders in their communities—displacing the established local conservative leadership of teachers, old-line ministers, businessmen—it is hard for an observer (who admittedly has not been close to SCLC) to perceive exactly what SCLC did before the 1960's except to advance the image and personality of King. King appeared not to direct but to float with the tide of militant direct action. For example, King did not supply the initiative for the bus boycott in Montgomery, but was pushed into the leadership by others, as he himself records in *Stride Toward Freedom*. Similarly, in the late Fifties and early Sixties, he appeared to let events shape his course. In the last two years, this has changed, but until the Birmingham demonstrations of 1963, King epitomized conservative militancy.

SCLC under King's leadership called the Raleigh Conference of April 1960 which gave birth to SNCC. Incredibly, within a year, the SNCC youth had lost their faith in the man they now satirically call "De Lawd," and had struck out on their own independent path. By that time, the Spring of 1961, King's power in the Southern direct action movement had been further curtailed by CORE's stunning Freedom Ride to Alabama and Mississippi.

The limited extent of King's actual power in the civil rights movement was illustrated by the efforts made to invest King with the qualities of a Messiah during the recent ceremonies at the State Capitol in Montgomery. Reverend Abernathy's constant iteration of the theme that King is "our Leader," the Moses of the race, chosen by God, and King's claim that he originated the nonviolent direct action movement at Montgomery a decade ago, are all assertions that would have been superfluous if King's power in the movement was very substantial.

It is, of course, no easier today than it has been in the past few years to predict the course of the Negro protest movement, and it is always possible that the current state of affairs may change quite abruptly. It is conceivable that the ambitious program that SCLC is now projecting—both in Southern voter registration and in Northern urban direct action programs—may give it a position of commanding importance in civil rights. As a result of the recent demonstrations in Selma and Montgomery, King's prestige is now higher than ever. At the same time, the nature of CORE and NAACP direct action activities at the moment has created a programmatic vacuum which SCLC may be able to exploit. Given this convergence of circumstances, SCLC leaders may be able to establish an organizational base upon which to build a power commensurate with the symbolic position of their president.

It is indeed fortunate that King has not obtained a predominance of power in the movement commensurate with his prestige. For today, as in the past, a diversity of approaches is necessary. Needed in the movement are those who view the struggle chiefly as a conflict situation, in which the power of demonstrations, the power of Negroes, will force recognition of the race's humanity and citizenship rights, and the achievement of equality. Equally needed are those who see the movement's strategy to be chiefly one of capitalizing on the basic consensus of values in American society by awakening the conscience of the white man to the contradiction between his professions and the facts of discrimination. And just as necessary to the movement as both of these are those who operate skillfully, recognizing and yet exploiting the deeply held American belief that compromise among competing interest groups is the best *modus operandi* in public life.

King is unique in that he maintains a delicate balance among all three of these basic strategy assumptions. The traditional approaches of the Urban League (conciliation of the white businessmen) and of the NAACP (most pre-eminently appeals to the courts and appeals to the sense of fair play in the American public), basically attempted to exploit the consensus in American values. It would of course be a gross oversimplification to say that the Urban League and NAACP strategies are based simply on attempting to capitalize on the consensus of values, while SNCC and CORE act simply as if the situation were purely a conflict situation. Implicit in the actions of all civil rights organizations are both sets of assumptions— even where people are not conscious of the theoretical assumptions under which, in effect, they operate. The NAACP especially encompasses a broad spectrum of strategies and types of activities, ranging from time-tested court procedures to militant direct action. Sophisticated CORE activists know very well when a judicious compromise is necessary or valuable. But I hold that King is in the middle, acting in effect as if he were basing his strategy upon all three assumptions described above. He maintains a delicate balance between a purely moral appeal and a militant display of power. He talks of the power of the bodies of Negro demonstrators in the streets, but unlike CORE and SNCC activists, he accepts compromises at times that consist of token improvements, and calls them impressive victories. More than any of the other groups, King and SCLC can, up to this point at least, be described as exploiting all three tactical assumptions to an approximately equal degree. King's continued success, I suspect, will depend to a considerable degree upon the difficult feat of maintaining his position at the "vital center" of the civil rights movement.

Viewed from another angle King's failure to achieve a position of power on a level with his prestige is fortunate because rivalries between personalities and organizations remain an essential ingredient of the dynamics of the movement and a precondition for its success as each current tries to outdo the others in effectiveness and in maintaining a good public image. Without this competitive stimulus, the civil rights revolution would slow down.

I have already noted that one of King's functions is to serve as a bridge between the militant and conservative wings of the movement. In addition, by gathering support for SCLC, he generates wider support for CORE and SNCC, as well. The most striking example is the recent series of demonstrations in Selma where SNCC had been operating for nearly two years with only moderate amounts of publicity before King chose that city as his own target. As usual, it was King's presence that focused world attention on Selma. In the course of subsequent events, the rift between King and SNCC assumed the proportions of a serious conflict. Yet people who otherwise would have been hesitant to support SNCC's efforts, even people who had become disillusioned with certain aspects of SNCC's policies during the Mississippi Summer Project of 1964, were drawn to demonstrate in Selma and Montgomery. Moreover, although King received the major share of credit for the demonstrations, it seems likely that in the controversy between King and SNCC, the latter emerged with more power and influence in the civil rights movement than ever before. It is now possible that the Administration will, in the future, regard SNCC as more of a force to be reckoned with than it has heretofore.

Major dailies like *The New York Times* and the *Washington Post,* basically sympathetic to civil rights and racial equality, though more gradualist than the activist organizations, have congratulated the nation upon its good fortune in having a "responsible and moderate" leader like King at the head of the nonviolent action movement (though they overestimate his power and underestimate the symbolic nature of his role). It would be more appropriate to congratulate the civil rights movement for *its* good fortune in having as its symbolic leader a man like King. The fact that he has more prestige than power; the fact that he not only criticizes whites but explicitly believes in their redemption; his ability to arouse creative tension combined with his inclination to shrink from carrying demonstrations to the point where major bloodshed might result; the intellectual simplicity of his philosophy; his tendency to compromise and exert caution, even his seeming indecisiveness on some occasions; the sparing use he makes of going to or staying in jail himself; his friendship with the man in the White House—all are essential to the role he plays, and invaluable for the success of the movement. It is well, of course, that not all civil rights leaders are cut of the same cloth—that King is unique among them. Like Randolph, who functions very differently, King is really an institution. His most important function, I believe, is that of effectively communicating Negro aspirations to white people, of making nonviolent direct action respectable in the eyes of the white majority. In addition, he functions within the movement by occupying a vital center position between its "conservative" and "radical" wings, by symbolizing direct action and attracting people to participate in it without dominating either the civil rights movement or its activist wing. Viewed in this context, traits that many activists criticize in King actually function not as sources of weakness, but as the foundations of his strength.

RICHARD M. NIXON

&

the Great Foreign Policy Thaw

Richard M. Nixon built his career on the Cold War and the domestic emotions it aroused. Nixon used the issue of Communism to gain his first elective office, linking his opponent to Communist influences; and later he received wide recognition for his investigations of internal subversion. But in 1972 this devoted anti-Communist engineered a triumphant visit to Peking and then to Moscow for a ceremonial conclusion to the era of the Cold War.

Born in California in 1913, Nixon grew up there working for his father in a grocery store and filling station. He earned his way through both college and law school, graduating from Whittier College in 1934 and Duke University in 1937. Nixon returned to his home town, Whittier, to practice law for five years before going to Washington, D.C., in 1942 to work in the Office of Emergency Management. He served as an aviation ground officer in the South Pacific later in World War II and left the service in 1946 with the rank of lieutenant commander.

From that year on, politics became Nixon's major profession. He was elected to the House of Representatives from California's 12th District in 1946 and 1948 and then to the Senate in 1950. A member of the House Un-American Activities Committee, he had helped draft the Mundt-Nixon bill requiring registration of Communist Party members. Nixon came to national attention with his successful conviction of the alleged Communist Alger Hiss for perjury.

At the Republican convention in 1952, Nixon was named the vice-presidential nominee by acclamation. When he became Vice President, he earned a reputation for involvement in foreign affairs, making a famous trip to Latin America at President Eisenhower's behest and another, essentially on his own initiative, to Russia in 1959. In the 1960 campaign, as the Republican presidential candidate, he considered foreign affairs his strong point and domestic policy (where he had to defend the Eisenhower administration) his weak spot. Even when Nixon ran for governor of California in 1962, he spoke often of foreign issues. After this long schooling in foreign affairs, he entered the presidency in 1969 determined to devote himself to diplomacy and to allow various assistants to run things at home. The most notable events of his first term were the gradual withdrawal of American troops from Vietnam and the 1972 visits to Russia and China. In the fall of 1972 he won a second term largely because of his successes abroad, particularly in his dealings with Communist powers, and in early 1973 America's military involvement in Vietnam was formally ended with peace accords. But despite his foreign policy achievements and his overwhelming victory at the polls, the President the next year suffered possibly devastating blows to his personal reputation during the "Watergate" investigation, which began with the break-in at the Democratic national offices in the Watergate apartment complex in Washington, D.C., and spread to other related events.

That investigation revealed, among other things, Nixon's preoccupation with "national security"; his repeated use of this concept to justify his actions emphasized how much of the Cold Warrior still remained in his personality. Why this stern anti-Communist should take such obvious joy in negotiating with major Communist leaders is a puzzle. Yet it has been that way throughout his career—his favorite place has been at the summit. In 1959 he worked hard to score points against the Soviet premier, Nikita Khrushchev; in 1972 he took pleasure in seeking accommodation with the Russian and Chinese leaders. Richard Nixon has always had a hand in; he had a real, if small, role in intensifying the Cold War and a concrete and large part in its easing. One must ask whether these markedly different actions resulted from changed circumstances or from changes in Nixon himself. He is probably the only president in American history who has been compared so frequently to a chameleon. It seems that a "new Nixon" is perpetually emerging for associates and commentators to analyze afresh.

The Kitchen Debate (1962)
RICHARD M. NIXON

During his 1959 trip to Russia, Vice President Nixon met privately with Nikita Khrushchev and also played host to the Soviet premier at a preview of the American Exhibit at Sokolniki Park in Moscow. The model of an American home, meant to impress the Russians with material progress in America, sparked a debate between Nixon and Khrushchev at the very time the Four Powers were meeting at Geneva to ease international tensions. The future seemed to hold at least the possibility of peaceful competition in the production of material goods and in the achievement of better health care, greater educational opportunity, and the like. The following is an excerpt from Nixon's own account in Six Crises.

WE CAME TO THE CENTER ATTRACTION of the exhibition, a model American home, fully furnished and equipped with all our modern conveniences. The Soviet press had focused their ridicule on this model home during the past week, saying that it was no more typical of a worker's home in the United States than the Taj Mahal was typical in India or Buckingham Palace in Great Britain. Khrushchev and I walked up the center hall of the model home, looking into the exposed rooms, and we stopped at the kitchen.

And here we had our famous "kitchen conference" or, as some reporters put it, the "Sokolniki Summit." This conversation, incidentally, was not carried on television in the United States but was reported in the newspapers.

The conversation began innocently enough. We discussed the relative merits of washing machines. Then I decided that this was as good a place as any to answer the charges that had been made in the Soviet press, that only "the rich" in the United States could afford such a house as this.

I made the point that this was a typical house in the United States, costing $14,000, which could be paid over twenty-five or thirty years. Most U.S. veterans of World War II have bought houses like this, in the $10,000 to $15,000 range, I told him, adding that most any steelworker could buy one.

"We too can find steelworkers and peasants who can pay $14,000 cash for a flat," he retorted. Then he went into a harangue on how

American capitalists build houses to last only twenty years and the Soviets build for their children and grandchildren. He went on and on, obviously determined to deny the American know-how he saw so plainly in front of him:

"You think the Russians will be dumbfounded by this exhibit. But the fact is that all newly built Russian houses will have this equipment. You need dollars in the United States to get this house, but here all you need is to be born a citizen. If an American citizen does not have dollars he has the right to buy this house or sleep on the pavement at night. And you say we are slaves of Communism!"

I finally interrupted him. "In our Senate we would call you a filibusterer," I said. "You do all the talking and you do not let anyone else talk. I want to make one point. We don't think this fair will astound the Russian people, but it will interest them just as yours interested us. To us, diversity, the right to choose, the fact that we have a thousand different builders, that's the spice of life. We don't want to have a decision made at the top by one government official saying that we will have one type of house. That's the difference . . ."

"On political differences, we will never agree," Khrushchev said, again cutting in on me. "If I follow you, I will be led astray from Mikoyan. He likes spicy soups and I don't. But that doesn't mean we differ."

I tried again to point up our belief in freedom of choice, and I put in a plea for more exchanges between our two countries to bring about a better understanding. But Khrushchev did not want to debate me on my grounds. He changed the subject back to washing machines, arguing that it was better to have one model than many. I listened to his long harangue on washing machines, realizing full well that he was not switching arguments by chance or accident; he was trying to throw me off balance.

"Isn't it better to be talking about the relative merits of our washing machines than the relative strength of our rockets?" I said at the end of his long speech. "Isn't this the kind of competition you want?"

At this he gave the appearance of turning angry and, jamming his thumb into my chest, he shouted: "Yes, that's the kind of competition we want, but your generals say we must compete in rockets. Your generals say they are so powerful they can destroy us. We can also show you something so that you will know the Russian spirit. We are strong, we can beat you. But in this respect we can also show you something."

As Akalovsky translated what he was saying into my ear, I knew that now was the time to strike back. Otherwise I would leave the impression to the press and through them to the world that I, the second-highest official of the United States, and the government I represented were dealing with Khrushchev from a position of weakness—militarily, economically, and ideologically. I had to be firm without being belligerent, a most difficult posture to preserve. With this in mind, I pointed my finger at him and said:

"To me, you are strong and we are strong. In some ways, you are stronger than we are. In others, we are stronger. But to me it seems that in this day and age to argue who is the stronger completely misses the point. . . . No one should ever use his strength to put another in the position where he in effect has an ultimatum. For us to argue who is the stronger misses the point. If war comes we both lose."

Now Khrushchev changed the pace. He tried to laugh off what I had said by exclaiming: "For the fourth time I have to say I cannot recognize my friend Mr. Nixon. If all Americans agree with you, then who don't we agree with? That is what we want."

This time I was determined not to let him get off the hook. I pressed on: "I hope the Prime Minister understands all the implications of what I have just said. When you place either one of our powerful nations in such a position that it has no choice but to accept dictation or fight, then you are playing with the most destructive thing in the world. This is very important in the present world context," I went on before he could interrupt. "It is very dangerous. When we sit down at a conference table it cannot all be one way. One side cannot put an ultimatum to another. It is impossible."

Now we were going at it toe-to-toe. To some, it may have looked as though we had both lost our tempers. But exactly the opposite was true. I had full and complete control of my temper and was aware of it. I knew the value of keeping cool in a crisis, and what I said and how I said it was done with as much calm deliberation as I could muster in a running, impromptu debate with an expert. I never doubted, either, whether Khrushchev had lost control of his emotions. In situations before the kitchen debate and after it, according to my observations, Khrushchev never loses his temper—he uses it.

Now, using his temper, Khrushchev struck back. He accused me of issuing an ultimatum, he vehemently denied that the Soviet Union ever used dictation, and he warned me not to threaten him. "It sounds to me like a threat," he declared, poking his finger at me. "We, too, are giants. You want to threaten—we will answer threats with threats."

"That's not my point," I retorted. "We will never engage in threats."

"You wanted indirectly to threaten me," he shouted back. "But we have the means to threaten, too."

"Who wants to threaten?" I asked.

"You are talking about implications," he went on, apparently getting more and more excited. "I have not been. We have the means at our disposal. Ours are better than yours. It is you who want to compete. Da, da, da . . ."

"We are well aware that you have the means. To me, who is best is not material."

"You raised the point," he went on. "We want peace and friendship with all nations, especially with America."

I could sense now that he wanted to call an end to the argument. And

I certainly did not want to take the responsibility for continuing it publicly. We both had had enough. I said, "We want peace too."

He answered, "Yes, I believe that."

And so we ended our discussion on the underlying question of the whole debate—the possibility of easing Cold War tensions at the then current Four Power Conference in Geneva.

"It would be a great mistake and a blow to peace if that conference should fail," I said.

"That is our understanding as well," he said.

Then, returning to my responsibilities as his host, I put my hand on his shoulder and said with a smile, "I'm afraid I haven't been a good host." Khrushchev turned to the American guide in the model kitchen and said, "Thank the housewife for letting us use her kitchen for our argument."

As we walked away from the model house, to view the rest of the exhibition, I began to feel the effects of the tremendous tension of the past two hours. Holding back when you have something you want to say is far more wearing on the system than letting yourself go. I felt like a fighter wearing sixteen-ounce gloves and bound by Marquis of Queensberry rules, up against a bare-knuckle slugger who had gouged, kneed, and kicked. I was not sure whether I had held my own. But two widely differing sources of opinion buoyed me up on this score. Ernie Barcella, the correspondent for United Press International, came alongside and whispered in my ear, "Good going, Mr. Vice President." A moment or so later, Mikoyan took me aside and through my interpreter paid me an unexpected compliment. "I reported to Mr. Khrushchev when I came back from Washington that you were very skillful in debate and you proved it again today . . ."

Speeches in Russia and China (1972)
RICHARD M. NIXON

How does Nixon in the following toast in China and radio-television address to the Russian people shift ground from his earlier approach to world problems? Is the change one of substance or merely of tone? If of tone, what was the Cold War about?

Richard M. Nixon
Toast in China, February 21, 1972

Mr. Prime Minister and all of your distinguished guests this evening: On behalf of all of your American guests, I wish to thank you for the incomparable hospitality for which the Chinese people are justly famous throughout the world. I particularly want to pay tribute, not only to those who prepared the magnificent dinner, but also to those who have provided the splendid music. Never have I heard American music played better in a foreign land.

Mr. Prime Minister, I wish to thank you for your very gracious and eloquent remarks. At this very moment, through the wonders of telecommunications, more people are seeing and hearing what we say than on any other such occasion in the whole history of the world. Yet, what we say here will not be long remembered. What we do here can change the world.

As you said in your toast, the Chinese people are a great people, the American people are a great people. If our two people are enemies the future of this world we share together is dark indeed. But if we can find common ground to work together, the chance for world peace is immeasurably increased.

In the spirit of frankness which I hope will characterize our talks this week, let us recognize at the outset these points: We have at times in the past been enemies. We have great differences today. What brings us together is that we have common interests which transcend those differences. As we discuss our differences, neither of us will compromise our principles. But while we cannot close the gulf between us, we can try to bridge it so that we may be able to talk across it.

So, let us, in these next 5 days, start a long march together, not in lockstep, but on different roads leading to the same goal: the goal of building a world structure of peace and justice in which all may stand together with equal dignity and in which each nation, large or small, has a right to determine its own form of government, free of outside interference or domination. The world watches. The world listens. The world waits to see what we will do. What is the world? In a personal sense, I think of my eldest daughter, whose birthday is today. As I think of her, I think of all the children in the world, in Asia, in Africa, in Europe, in the Americas, most of whom were born since the date of the foundation of the People's Republic of China.

What legacy shall we leave our children? Are they destined to die for the hatreds which have plagued the old world, or are they destined to live because we had the vision to build a new world?

There is no reason for us to be enemies. Neither of us seeks the territory of the other; neither of us seeks domination over the other; neither of us seeks to stretch out our hands and rule the world.

Chairman Mao has written: "So many deeds cry out to be done, and always urgently. The world rolls on. Time passes. Ten thousand years are too long. Seize the day, seize the hour."

This is the hour. This is the day for our two peoples to rise to the heights of greatness which can build a new and a better world.

In that spirit, I ask all of you present to join me in raising your glasses to Chairman Mao, to Prime Minister Chou, and to the friendship of the Chinese and American people, which can lead to friendship and peace for all people in the world.

Radio-Television Address to the People of the Soviet Union, May 28, 1972

Dobryy vecher. [Good evening.] I deeply appreciate this opportunity your government has given me to speak directly with the people of the Soviet Union to bring you a message of friendship from all the people of the United States and to share with you some of my thoughts about the relations between our two countries and about the way to peace and progress in the world.

This is my fourth visit to the Soviet Union. On these visits I have gained a great respect for the peoples of the Soviet Union, for your strength, your generosity, your determination, for the diversity and richness of your cultural heritage, for your many achievements.

In the 3 years I have been in office, one of my principal aims has been to establish a better relationship between the United States and the Soviet Union. Our two countries have much in common. Most important of all, we have never fought one another in war. On the contrary, the memory of your soldiers and ours embracing at the Elbe as allies in 1945 remains strong in millions of hearts in both of our countries. It is my hope that the memory can serve as an inspiration of the renewal of Soviet-American cooperation in the 1970's.

As great powers, we shall sometimes be competitors, but we need never be enemies.

Thirteen years ago, when I visited your country as Vice President, I addressed the people of the Soviet Union on radio and television as I am addressing you tonight. I said then:

> Let us have peaceful competition not only in producing the best factories but in producing better lives for our people.
>
> Let us cooperate in our exploration of outer space. . . .
>
> Let our aim be not victory over other peoples but the victory of all mankind over hunger, want, misery, and disease, wherever it exists in the world.

In our meetings this week, we have begun to bring some of those hopes to fruition. Shortly after we arrived here on Monday afternoon, a brief rain fell on Moscow, of a kind that I am told is called a mushroom rain, a warm rain, with sunshine breaking through, that makes the mushrooms grow and is therefore considered a good omen. The month of May is early for mushrooms, but as our talks progressed this week what did grow was even better: a far-reaching set of agreements that can lead to a better life for both of our peoples, to a better chance for peace in the world.

We have agreed on joint ventures in space. We have agreed on ways of working together to protect the environment, to advance health, to co-operate in science and technology. We have agreed on means of preventing incidents at sea. We have established a commission to expand trade between our two nations.

Most important, we have taken an historic first step in the limitation of nuclear strategic arms. This arms control agreement is not for the purpose of giving either side an advantage over the other. Both of our nations are strong, each respects the strength of the other, each will maintain the strength necessary to defend its independence.

But in an unchecked arms race between two great nations, there would be no winners, only losers. By setting this limitation together, the people of both of our nations, and of all nations, can be winners. If we continue in the spirit of serious purpose that has marked our discussions this week, these agreements can start us on a new road of cooperation for the benefit of our people, for the benefit of all peoples.

There is an old proverb that says, "Make peace with man and quarrel with your sins." The hardships and evils that beset all men and all nations —these and these alone are what we should make war upon.

As we look at the prospects for peace, we see that we have made significant progress at reducing the possible sources of direct conflict between us. But history tells us that great nations have often been dragged into war without intending it, by conflicts between smaller nations. As great powers, we can and should use our influence to prevent this from happening. Our goal should be to discourage aggression in other parts of the world and particularly among those smaller nations that look to us for leadership and example.

With great power goes great responsibility. When a man walks with a giant tread, he must be careful where he sets his feet. There can be true peace only when the weak are as safe as the strong. The wealthier and more powerful our own nations become, the more we have to lose from war and the threat of war, anywhere in the world.

Speaking for the United States, I can say this. We covet no one else's territory, we seek no dominion over any other people, we seek the right to live in peace, not only for ourselves but for all the peoples of this earth. Our power will only be used to keep the peace, never to break it, only to defend freedom, never to destroy it. No nation that does not threaten its neighbors has anything to fear from the United States.

Soviet citizens have often asked me, "Does America truly want peace?"

I believe that our actions answer that question far better than any words could do. If we did not want peace, we would not have reduced the size of our Armed Forces by a million men, by almost one-third, during the past 3 years. If we did not want peace, we would not have worked so hard at reaching an agreement on the limitation of nuclear arms, at achieving a settlement of Berlin, at maintaining peace in the Middle East, at establishing better relations with the Soviet Union, with the People's Republic of China, with other nations of the world.

Mrs. Nixon and I feel very fortunate to have had the opportunity to visit the Soviet Union, to get to know the people of the Soviet Union, friendly and hospitable, courageous and strong. Most Americans will never have a chance to visit the Soviet Union, and most Soviet citizens will never have a chance to visit America. Most of you know our country only through what you read in your newspapers and what you hear and see on radio and television and motion pictures. This is only a part of the real America.

I would like to take this opportunity to try to convey to you something of what America is really like, not in terms of its scenic beauties, its great cities, its factories, its farms, or its highways, but in terms of its people.

In many ways, the people of our two countries are very much alike. Like the Soviet Union, ours is a large and diverse nation. Our people, like yours, are hard working. Like you, we Americans have a strong spirit of competition but we also have a great love of music and poetry, of sports, and of humor. Above all, we, like you, are an open, natural, and friendly people. We love our country. We love our children. And we want for you and for your children the same peace and abundance that we want for ourselves and for our children.

We Americans are idealists. We believe deeply in our system of government. We cherish our personal liberty. We would fight to defend it, if necessary, as we have done before. But we also believe deeply in the right of each nation to choose its own system. Therefore, however much we like our own system for ourselves, we have no desire to impose it on anyone else.

As we conclude this week of talks, there are certain fundamental premises of the American point of view which I believe deserve emphasis. In conducting these talks, it has not been our aim to divide up the world into spheres of influence, to establish a condominium, or in any way to conspire together against the interest of any other nation. Rather we have sought to construct a better framework of understanding between our two nations, to make progress in our bilateral relationships, to find ways of insuring that future frictions between us would never embroil our two nations, and therefore the world, in war.

While ours are both great and powerful nations, the world is no longer dominated by two superpowers. The world is a better and safer place because its power and resources are more widely distributed.

Beyond this, since World War I, more than 70 new nations have come into being. We cannot have true peace unless they, and all nations, can feel that they share it.

America seeks better relations not only with the Soviet Union but with all nations. The only sound basis for a peaceful and progressive international order is sovereign equality and mutual respect. We believe in the right of each nation to chart its own course, to choose its own system, to go its own way, without interference from other nations.

As we look to the longer term, peace depends also on continued progress in the developing nations. Together with other advanced industrial countries, the United States and the Soviet Union share a twofold responsibility in this regard: on the one hand, to practice restraint in those activities, such as the supply of arms, that might endanger the peace of developing nations; and second, to assist them in their orderly economic and social development, without political interference.

Some of you may have heard an old story told in Russia of a traveler who was walking to another village. He knew the way, but not the distance. Finally he came upon a woodsman chopping wood by the side of the road, and he asked the woodsman, "How long will it take to reach the village?" The woodsman replied. "I don't know." The traveler was angry, because he was sure the woodsman was from the village and therefore knew how far it was. And so he started off down the road again. After he had gone a few steps, the woodsman called out, "Stop. It will take you about 15 minutes." The traveler turned and demanded, "Why didn't you tell me that in the first place?" The woodsman replied, "Because then I didn't know the length of your stride."

In our talks this week with the leaders of the Soviet Union, both sides have had a chance to measure the length of our strides toward peace and security. I believe that those strides have been substantial and that now we have well begun the long journey which will lead us to a new age in the relations between our two countries. It is important to both of our peoples that we continue those strides.

As our two countries learn to work together, our people will be able to get to know one another better. Greater cooperation can also mean a great deal in our daily lives. As we learn to cooperate in space, in health and the environment, in science and technology, our cooperation can help sick people get well. It can help industries produce more consumer goods. It can help all of us enjoy cleaner air and water. It can increase our knowledge of the world around us.

As we expand our trade, each of our countries can buy more of the other's goods and market more of our own. As we gain experience with arms control, we can bring closer the day when further agreements can lessen the arms burden of our two nations and lessen the threat of war in the world.

Through all the pages of history, through all the centuries, the world's people have struggled to be free from fear, whether fear of the elements or fear of hunger or fear of their own rulers or fear of their neighbors in other countries. And yet, time and again, people have vanquished the source of one fear only to fall prey to another.

Let our goal now be a world free of fear—a world in which nation will no longer prey upon nation, in which human energies will be turned away from production for war and toward more production for peace, away from conquest and toward invention, development, creation; a world in which together we can establish that peace which is more than the absence of war, which enables man to pursue those higher goals that the spirit yearns for.

Yesterday, I laid a wreath at the cemetery which commemorates the brave people who died during the siege of Leningrad in World War II. At the cemetery, I saw the picture of a 12-year-old girl. She was a beautiful child. Her name was Tanya. The pages of her diary tell the terrible story of war. In the simple words of a child, she wrote of the deaths of the members of her family, Zhenya in December. Grannie in January. Leka then next. Then Uncle Vasya. Then Uncle Lyosha. Then Mama. And then the Savichevs. And then finally, these words, the last words in her diary, "All are dead. Only Tanya is left."

As we work toward a more peaceful world, let us think of Tanya and of the other Tanyas and their brothers and sisters everywhere. Let us do all that we can to insure that no other children will have to endure what Tanya did and that your children and ours, all the children of the world, can live their full lives together in friendship and in peace.

Spasibo i do svidaniye. [Thank you and goodby.]

The Week That Changed the World (1972)
FRANK VAN DER LINDEN

The week that Richard Nixon spent in Communist China, February 21–28, 1972, did not really change the world, but it did mark a final shift in the view of the world that most leaders entertained. The Vietnam war made clear that the Cold War rationale for foreign policy no longer convinced either national leaders or the public. Justification of our involvement in the war with phrases like "the need to contain China" failed to unite Americans behind the war effort and, it is now clear, did not fully persuade even some of the people voicing such arguments. Ironically, Richard Nixon, a supreme Cold Warrior, was the one to bring about a thaw in this country's relations with the

*Communist powers. In the following selection, the journalist Frank Van
Der Linden traces the steps leading to Nixon's historic trip to China.*

PRESIDENT NIXON'S "week that changed the world"—his incredible week of
summit conferences and banquets and televised spectaculars in China—had
its secret origin in a decision he made during the first two weeks of his administration.

Nixon resolved then, in early 1969, to make a revolutionary break in
United States policy towards Communist China, in an effort to end the two
decades of isolation and hostility between the two nations. He also confided
to a few close friends that, some day, he even hoped to visit China himself,
once before he died; and, if this proved impossible, he wanted his children
to see that mysterious forbidden land.

In January, 1969, there seemed little prospect that Nixon could ever do
much more than daydream about his favorite fantasy. The United States
then had more than half a million troops in Vietnam, fighting a war against
the Communists, a war officially justified by the previous administration as
necessary to stop the aggressive advance of Communism, headquartered in
Peking.

Communist China, a nation which had fought American troops in the
Korean war, was a pariah barred from the United Nations, cut off from
trade and travel and other relations with the United States. Nixon, having
built his early political career as an implacable foe of Communism, seemed
unlikely to be welcomed, as a tourist, to the homeland of Chairman Mao
Tse-tung.

In view of all these barriers to his success, I asked the President, by
letter, in early 1972, "How did you achieve the breakthrough with the
Chinese leaders?"

He had agreed to reply, in writing, to a few questions in addition to
those I had earlier asked him, face to face. He wrote to me, in April, 1972:

"The breakthrough resulted from the combined effectiveness of actions
on several levels, rather than on any reliance on a single initiative.

"We discussed our views and intentions with trusted intermediaries. We
made use of reliable diplomatic channels. When ambassadorial-level meetings with the mainland Chinese in Warsaw in 1970 revealed the handicaps
of such an approach, we acted to develop—through experimentation, exploration and testing—a reliable private means of communicating high-
policy views to the Peking authorities, and receiving theirs in return. Eventually, such a means did become available."

Understandably, the President did not feel at liberty to disclose the
identity of his reliable private link to Peking.

During his first trip to Europe, which began in late February, 1969,
Nixon shared his secret dream about China with Charles de Gaulle, con-

fiding that one of his major aims would be to seek better relations with the People's Republic. Impressed, if not surprised, the French president told his ambassador in Peking to convey this information confidentially to Premier Chou En-lai. The envoy, Etienne Manach, did so and one more step was taken in Nixon's long, elaborately camouflaged march towards his détente with China.

Contrary to reports that Henry Kissinger [the primary presidential adviser on foreign policy] led him down the primrose path to Peking, and away from his old Chinese Nationalist friends on Taiwan, Nixon himself had written in *Foreign Affairs* magazine in October, 1967, that "we simply cannot afford to leave China forever outside the family of nations, there to nurture its fantasies, cherish its hates, and threaten its neighbors."

Nixon, in his article, "Asia After Vietnam," foresaw two dangerous events in the ensuing decade which could create a crisis: (1) that the Soviets might reach nuclear parity with the United States; and (2) that China, within three to five years, might have a significant deliverable nuclear capability. In his acceptance speech at the Miami Beach convention in 1968, presidential candidate Nixon extended "the hand of friendship to all people, to the Russian people, to the Chinese people, to all the people in the world."

Nixon expressed his desire for a serious dialogue with Peking in confidential conversations with heads of state during all his overseas journeys. The leaders he met throughout Asia in 1969 welcomed his proposal as constructive and realistic, he said in his Foreign Policy Report to Congress February 18, 1970.

"In the public realm, meanwhile," the President wrote to me in April, 1972, "a carefully orchestrated series of officially announced actions showed the Chinese that we sincerely did seek a new direction in our relations. These included relaxation of various commercial and travel restrictions.

"Another signal was my deliberate public reference in October of 1970 —during the Washington visit of Romanian President Ceausescu—to 'the People's Republic of China.' That was the first official, public use of Peking's official title by an American President." It occurred during Nixon's toast to Ceausescu at a White House dinner October 26, a subtle switch from "Communist China," the term Nixon had been using for years.

Summing up his long campaign to woo the Chinese, the President informed me: "I believe we succeeded because we moved on such a number of fronts, and that any single-line attempt might not have worked."

Nixon sent his signals to the Chinese "across a broad spectrum, in a very careful and deliberate way, without asking reciprocity," Kissinger's deputy, Gen. Alexander Haig, told me in an interview. "We didn't wave a flag and expect to see them wave one back at us. Some of the communications can't be known, perhaps, until someone's memoirs are written twenty years from now."

The steady withdrawal of American combat troops from Vietnam, after the successful raid into Cambodia in 1970, evidently convinced the rulers in Peking that Nixon really meant to pull out of Southeast Asia and had no intention of using it as a base to threaten mainland China. Russia, not China, supplied most of the tanks, heavy artillery, surface-to-air missiles and other weapons with which Hanoi continued the war against its neighbors in Laos, Cambodia, and South Vietnam.

In his Foreign Policy Message of February 25, 1971, Nixon reiterated his desire for a dialogue with Peking and stressed that "the United States is prepared to see the People's Republic of China play a constructive role in the family of nations"—exactly the same phrase he had used in his 1967 magazine article. Although Peking's propaganda still cast us in the devil's role, the President said he would judge China not by its rhetoric but by its actions as he sought further contacts between the Chinese and American peoples.

Earlier, Nixon had confided to Senate Majority Leader Mike Mansfield of Montana and Minority Leader Hugh Scott of Pennsylvania that he was quietly seeking an opening to Peking. One day in early 1971, he told Scott in a telephone conversation: 'Hugh, I am going to send you and Mike to Asia sometime. I have got some things in mind that I want you to do in the Orient for me."

"Yes, sir, we accept," Scott replied for both Senate leaders.

"Well," the President added cryptically, "if China ever opens up, I'll go myself."

"Is that so, Mr. President?" Scott remarked. "If you do go, we will be with you to make sure you get back."

On Easter Sunday, the President chatted about overseas travel with his daughters, Tricia and Julie; Tricia's fiancé, Eddie Cox, and Julie's husband, David Eisenhower.

"Where do you think we ought to go on our honeymoon?" asked Tricia and Eddie, who were to be married in June.

"The place to go is Asia," the President replied. "I hope that some time in your life, sooner rather than later, you will be able to go to China to see the great cities and the people and all that is there."

"I hope they do," Nixon told a group of editors when he recounted the incident a few days later. "As a matter of fact, I hope sometime I do."

But, he added, "I am not sure that it is going to happen while I am in office."

Nixon had a big secret, and it was all he could do to keep from revealing it too soon: He had privately received word that Chairman Mao would be happy to welcome him to China.

On April 14, the United States ping-pong team had been received in China by Prime Minister Chou En-lai, who told them, "You have opened a new page in the relations of the Chinese and American people."

On the same day, Nixon decided upon several measures allowing greater trade and travel between the United States and the People's Republic of China. On May 7, he removed controls on dollar transactions with China and on June 10 he ended the twenty-one-year embargo on trade with the PRC.

Throughout April, May, and June, Nixon met privately at night with Henry Kissinger. They usually met in the Lincoln Sitting Room upstairs in the White House, making sure that no assistant might walk in and see them working on papers concerning China. Only Secretary [of State William P.] Rogers and a few senior White House staff members shared the great secret—that Kissinger would fly to Peking and prepare the way for Nixon, himself, to visit China.

In early July, Kissinger left on a world tour, amid a general presumption in Washington that he would propose some new moves to hasten an end to the Vietnam war. In Pakistan, he cancelled a formal dinner with President Yahya Khan and flew out of Rawalpindi, ostensibly headed for a mountain retreat to recover from a mysterious stomach ailment. Instead, he spent July 9–11 in Peking, conferring with Premier Chou En-lai.

For a total of twenty hours, the Chinese leader and his aides engaged in courteous, frank and businesslike discussions with Kissinger, the first United States official to visit their capital since the Communists drove Chiang Kai-shek from power in 1949.

Kissinger stopped over in Paris on his return flight for another of his secret and fruitless discussions with Hanoi's spokesman about terms for ending the Vietnam War; then he reported to Nixon at the western White House in San Clemente.

On July 15, from a Los Angeles television studio, the President made a brief broadcast that sent shock waves around the world. He revealed that he had accepted, with pleasure, Chou En-lai's invitation to visit China at an appropriate date before May, 1972.

Nixon and Kissinger (1972)
DAVID LANDAU

Henry Kissinger, appointed Secretary of State in 1973, had in fact already engineered much of Nixon's foreign policy since 1969 from his post as close presidential adviser. "I always travel with the President,"

Kissinger once remarked. Writing before the end of American involvement in Vietnam and before the Middle East conflict of 1973, David Landau has offered one of the few sustained critiques of Nixon-Kissinger foreign policy. So far, the Nixon-Kissinger policy has achieved marked success, but only the future will tell whether it is permanent détente that these architects of American policy had on their drafting boards.

THE MOST CHARACTERISTIC DEVICE in Nixon-Kissinger policy is the concept of "linkage." The rationale of linkage is that all the world's trouble spots exist on a single continuum which connects the Soviet Union and the United States. In this context, the resolution of individual issues depends not so much on the merits of the specific case as on the overall balance of power between the two sides. And the underlying assumption of linkage is that the settlement of a crisis in one area of the world can be predetermined by the strength and degree of resolution which one or both of the contending parties have shown in other areas.

Doubtless there are many international developments that are appropriate subjects of linkage. As a general rule, it would be dangerous for American decision makers to pursue each policy venture in complete disregard of the policy's general thrust and direction; indeed, any competent policy must have some such identifiable direction. And in closely connected frameworks, opposing U.S. and Soviet positions may appropriately be traded off against each other to produce a mutually beneficial settlement encompassing more than a single crisis area. It seems necessary, for example, for U.S. negotiators to make an emphatic connection between the status of intermediate-range nuclear weapons facing each other across Eastern Europe and European security agreements. More remotely, it would be justifiable under certain circumstances to draw connections between Soviet behavior in Europe and in the Mideast; to take an example offered by one of Kissinger's present assistants, the United States and the Soviet Union cannot engage in Europe-related negotiations if the two sides are also at loggerheads in a Mideast war. Yet at a certain remove, linkage becomes unjustified; it is silly to think that Soviet assistance to the Arab nations in the Mideast is in any way comparable to, or closer to a solution by virtue of, America's prosecution of a full-scale Indochina war. And it is even less reasonable to suppose that America's steadfastness in Southeast Asia measurably affects Washington's credibility in the European theater, with the Soviet Union, or even with the West European allies; from Europe's vantage point, the war is an exercise not in credibility, but in irrational and absurd theatricality. Above all else, it is mistaken to predicate the reduction of nuclear tensions on Moscow's willingness to assist Washington in the Mideast and Vietnam, because the specter of strategic nuclear warfare should transcend the other categories of international relations. Easing the threat of instant and mutual mass slaughter should not be equated with the resolution of other crises that can and must be settled without resort to intercontinental missiles.

Kissinger's tendency has been to link Europe, the Mideast, and Vietnam without much regard to political or conceptual subtleties. Seeing no viability in modified linkage, he has chosen total linkage over no linkage at all. Rather than opting for what James C. Thompson, Jr., has described as a "ripple" approach, supposing, in other words, that like ripples in a pond, events in the world arena are only as strongly interconnected as their geographic or conceptual distances are brief, Kissinger prefers to see equally firm "links" between all U.S.-Soviet intersections in every area of the globe. As Kissinger once defined linkage in an unusually bold way:

> We are trying to get a [Mideast] settlement in such a way that the moderate regimes are strengthened, and not the radical regimes. We are trying to expel the Soviet military presence, not so much the advisors, but the combat pilots and the combat personnel, before they become so firmly established . . .
>
> It is, of course, nonsense to say that we did what we did in Cambodia to impress the Russians in the Middle East. It was not as simple as that. But we certainly have to keep in mind that the Russians will judge us by the general purposefulness of our performance everywhere. What they are doing in the Middle East, whatever their intentions, poses the gravest threats in the long term for Western Europe and Japan and, therefore, for us.

There is a disturbing tendency in Nixon-Kissinger linkage theory to postulate an overall decline in U.S.-Soviet tensions before the consecration of specific agreements. The 1972 State of the World Message noted petulantly that "The Soviets sought détente in Europe without a relaxation of hostility toward the United States." Kissinger's early scenario for the progression of U.S.-Soviet accords actually *began* with the negotiation of the most important agreement, the arms treaty, with every other subsidiary issue to serve as a bargaining counter in the initial negotiation only to be settled in its wake. The success of the arms negotiation, in turn, required an improved Soviet attitude toward the West. But did it not seem strange to expect the disappearance of suspicion and animosity to precede concrete policy agreements, instead of the other way around? And was it not equally presumptuous to suppose that the most difficult and complicated negotiation with a suspicious and hostile opponent could be concluded without a prior settlement of subsidiary issues? To be sure, Kissinger would not have wished to prejudice the outcome of the most important negotiation by giving away all of his bargaining counters before the negotiation began. But if the most important settlement demanded that the Soviets first "improve their attitude," on what, other than a sensible liquidation of the subsidiary crises, was the improvement to be based? To take a paramount example, the logic of Nixon-Kissinger linkage would have demanded that the German settlement await the more fundamental agreements on nuclear arms and European security arrangements. It was only through [West German Chancellor] Willy Brandt's initiative that the German issue was settled first, and that the NATO powers were then obliged to confront the problem of Berlin. Yet ironically, it appears likely that the ratification of the treaties on Germany was an important factor in inducing Soviet willingness to host President Nixon in Moscow following the U.S. mining of North Vietnam's harbors.

What fuels Kissinger's policy is a vision of the United States and the Soviet Union reaching a unified settlement which will encompass all trouble spots and crises, a Congress of Vienna solution for each of the areas in which they confront each other throughout the globe. Such a symmetrical situation presupposes that each side will observe the same standards of restraint in international behavior that it would expect of the other. Yet there is a curious one-sidedness in Kissinger's thinking on how to reach a final accord with the Soviet Union, a trait of double vision which enables him to see restraint or legitimate self-defense in a given action if taken by the United States and yet perceive aggression in that same action if taken by the Soviet Union. This has been particularly true of Kissinger's thinking on Vietnam. America's negotiating position on the war became a good deal more moderate in the Nixon administration; rather than demanding the permanent installment of a non-Communist regime in the south, the new President and his advisers sought merely to insure that a "decent interval" would transpire between the U.S. withdrawal and the collapse of the Saigon regime. Seeing their objective as a reasonable one, despite the other side's refusal to comply with it, they did not conceive of their successive escalations—designed, they felt, only to bring about a modest settlement—as threatening and aggressive acts. North Vietnam, however, did so; and though the Soviet Union, which supports Hanoi and the NLF [National Liberation Front] only from a distance, finally chose to withstand a confrontation when the U.S. war effort reached a high pitch last May, there is a real possibility that if a settlement is not forthcoming, Washington might still draw Moscow into the conflict with another escalation of the war. Is Washington violating its own code of conduct by its behavior in Vietnam? Kissinger has described one of the principles of the Nixon Doctrine as follows:

. . . when a non-nuclear country is threatened by a nuclear country, the United States recognizes special responsibilities. It recognizes these special responsibilities because . . . there is no conceivable way non-nuclear countries can resist, unless there is some implicit backing, at least, from the nuclear countries.

Does Kissinger suppose that North Vietnam, a non-nuclear country, is being threatened by the United States, a nuclear country? Surprisingly enough, he appears to feel sincerely that Washington is not infringing on North Vietnam's sovereignty or its right to survive, that the President is simply attempting to extract a reasonable settlement. Hence, the United States can mine North Vietnam's harbors and still expect that its actions pose no "unacceptable risks" of a confrontation with Hanoi's distant ally, the Soviet Union, that Moscow must simply go ahead with the summit meeting and the signing of the arms agreement. At the same time, if the Soviets had mined Cam Ranh Bay in retaliation, there could have been no doubt that the summit would have been called off by the United States. Kissinger frequently insists that Vietnam is not nearly as dangerous a flashpoint as the Middle East, which he describes in bleak terms:

> We believe that while the war in Vietnam is our most anguishing prob-
> lem, the situation in the Middle East is our most dangerous problem.
> The danger of the Middle East situation is that you have two groups of
> countries with intense local rivalries and with an overwhelming concern
> for their grievances or their security, or both, both backed by major
> countries, but not fully under the control of the major countries con-
> fronting each other. This is the sort of situation that produced World
> War I.

Yet it does not stretch the imagination to suppose that Kissinger's depiction of the Mideast may one day be appropriate to Vietnam.

These failures of perception raise a number of ominous questions. If Nixon and Kissinger seriously believe that any U.S. action in Vietnam is justified in the pursuit of what they consider a fair settlement, what are the limits of their willingness to escalate further? And if they believe that the Soviet Union will not engage in confrontation with the United States over any development in the war, a belief doubtless encouraged in some quarter by Moscow's non-reaction to the escalation in May 1972, will they be restrained by the fear of risking a reaction from a nuclear country? The conclusion to which we are driven by the logic of events is the possible American use of tactical nuclear weapons in Vietnam. The President and Kissinger have both endorsed in principle the use of such weapons, and although Washington would probably refrain from authorizing a nuclear attack on the North for a variety of reasons, the resort to limited nuclear war is still a possibility, because the most effective use of nuclear weapons would currently be in South Vietnam. These weapons could be used to destroy the North Vietnamese armies if they should mass for ground at-tacks on South Vietnamese cities. At this stage of their efforts in the war, Nixon and Kissinger might well believe they could effectively justify the use of nuclear weapons in South Vietnam because, presumably, they would be acting with the approval of that country's President and government. And if they believe that the war policy will ultimately yield them increased credibility in other areas of the globe, then their use of tactical nuclear weapons in South Vietnam might even be conceived as a deterrent to Soviet misbehavior in Europe, where Kissinger has frequently speculated that the use of tactical nuclear weapons would first come.

But perhaps the most disturbing aspect of linkage is that it is meant to serve not as a policy of safety or surety but rather as a policy of risk. Nixon and Kissinger cannot satisfactorily demonstrate to themselves or to anyone else that a high degree of "resolution" in one area will have the desired effect in other areas. From a more detached outsider's view, it seems as plausible to say that this approach builds tension by encouraging Soviet toughness as to claim that it relaxes hostility by forcing Moscow to be more reasonable. Kissinger said after the Jordanian crisis of September 1970, "We believe that the action in Cambodia . . . did help establish the credibility of [the President's] action in Jordan. But this cannot be proved. But it is our judgment that it helped." It would be at least as reasonable to suppose that the invasion of Cambodia made the Russians even more intractable in the Mideast, caused them to violate the cease-fire in Egypt, and contributed to the atmosphere of confrontation which produced the turmoil of September 1970 in the first place.

Stated in its present terms, the linkage theory is little more than unreconstructed Cold Warriorism. It is a tired repetition of the idea that the United States must bargain from "situations of strength." For what it means in specific terms is an unwillingness to "give" in any single crisis area until general tensions begin to disappear, and linkage becomes little more than a formula for perpetuating confrontation all over the world. Ironically, the linkage approach has sometimes been prevented from doing serious damage because the Soviets, showing occasional good sense, have shied away from adopting it as well, despite the fact that they have sometimes been provoked outright into doing so. For example, Moscow offered on the day of President Nixon's Inauguration to begin arms limitation discussions immediately. But a few days later, at his first official press conference, Nixon asserted that the opening of the talks would depend on Moscow's assistance on a solution for the Mideast and Vietnam. He said:

> What I want to do is to see to it that we have strategic arms talks in a way and at a time that will promote, if possible, progress on outstanding political issues at the same time—for example, on the problem of the Mideast, and on other outstanding problems in which the United States and the Soviet Union, acting together, can serve the cause of peace.

Bluntly speaking, the White House had assumed that since the United States was strategically superior to the Soviet Union, an arms settlement would be more in Moscow's interest than in Washington's. The President was stating openly that, in exchange for arms talks, the Soviet Union must ease its stand on the Mideast. Soviet leaders subsequently answered through their own press that they would not "pay a price" for SALT [Strategic

Arms Limitation Talks]; the talks *did* open in November 1969 without abject cooperation on the Mideast—although . . . the American side had come with other bargaining counters in its position. Similarly, after the U.S. mining of North Vietnam's harbors last May [1972] the Soviets— having clearly suffered sufficient provocation to call off the summit meeting scheduled for later in the month—did not do so, instead taking the approach that an arms control agreement with the United States was a sufficiently high priority in terms of their own national interest that they were willing *momentarily* to ignore the American action.

It would be difficult to demonstrate, however, that these applications of linkage by U.S. officials contributed to improvement or conciliation in Moscow's attitude. Indeed, the opposite seems more likely. It would be surprising, after Nixon's opening statement on arms talks, if the Soviets did not privately toughen their behavior to add to their own bargaining power. And though there are doubtless many in Washington who saw signs of Moscow's weakness in the fact of the summit-cum-mining-of-North-Vietnam, it is more sensible to suppose that the response was tempered by a most unusual occasion: the imminent signing of the first meaningful agreement to limit the use of nuclear arms. After the American action against North Vietnam, the summit came about not as a result of tough, skillful U.S. diplomacy but rather as an unusual exhibition of Soviet prudence. In the face of another U.S. escalation in Vietnam, especially if it involves nuclear weapons, Moscow's reaction is not likely to be so compliant; one can only hope that Washington will not press its luck too far. And hope may be the American public's only recourse in view of the White House's reluctance to heed domestic critics in its pursuit of foreign policy.

3 4 5 6 7 8 9 10 11 12 13 14 15   88 87 86 85 84 83 82 81 80 79 78 77 76 75